USING ONLINE CATALOGS:

A Nationwide Survey

A Report of a Study Sponsored by
The Council on Library Resources

Edited by
Joseph R. Matthews,
Gary S. Lawrence,
and
Douglas K. Ferguson

Neal-Schuman Publishers, Inc.

Published by Neal-Schuman Publishers, Inc.
23 Cornelia Street
New York, NY 10014

Printed and bound in the United States of America.

Library of Congress Cataloging in Publication Data
Main entry under title:
Using online catalogs.
    Includes index.
    1. Catalogs, On-line—Use studies.   2. Library
catalogs—Use studies.   3. On-line bibliographic
searching.   4. Libraries—United States—Automation.
5. Library surveys—United States.   I. Matthews,
Joseph R.   II. Lawrence, Gary S.   III. Ferguson,
Douglas K.   IV. Council on Library Resources.
Z699.U74   1983   025.3'028'54   83-8061
ISBN 0-918212-76-6

DEDICATION

This report is dedicated to the 8,094 individuals who completed a user questionnaire and the 3,981 individuals who completed a non-user questionnaire. It is anticipated that future users of online catalogs will experience greater success and fewer frustrations than the individuals who shared their experiences and reactions with us.

TABLE OF CONTENTS

FOREWORD

THE evidence is in. For many users in many libraries, the online catalog is an exceptionally useful addition to library technology. Even in its embryonic form, it offers new ways to search for information and the prospects are great that further refinement will dramatically improve the ability of library users to search large collections with ever-improving precision.

The report that follows summarizes the results of an impressive cooperative effort to gather facts about the performance of this new tool for the library user. A substantial number of online catalogs installed in a variety of libraries are described and their features assessed on the basis of responses by users in a carefully planned survey. The results of the data gathering and subsequent analysis should encourage and give cheer to the many individuals who have assumed responsibility for designing and installing the first wave of catalogs. The analysis also provides much useful information for those who will extend past efforts into new systems and settings. A special effort has been made to make the information available promptly, for this is an arena where change comes rapidly.

If the results of the work and the quality of this summary are exceptional, the process of conducting the study also deserves special notice. A large number of individuals from several organizations and institutions took part in what became one of the most extensive and intensive research exercises in library history. From project definition through questionnaire design, from testing and training through execution, analysis, and reporting, the primary project managers acted on behalf of all parties as well as themselves. And the results show—for the first time we have a study of catalog use that successfully bridges kinds of libraries, system variations, and the full range of user needs and interests.

The project has been an important element of the Bibliographic Service Development Program of The Council on Library Resources, and the results will directly affect the quality and utility of the products of new bibliographic systems. CLR is grateful to the many people who worked so efficiently together for a useful purpose.

But before laurels come to rest too soon, we would remind all concerned that this is the beginning of a revolution, not the end. The results of the study point the way to next steps, but the process of putting recorded information to full use is a problem for society (or civilization) that has countless steps. Success requires an amplification of past effort and current wisdom that will challenge us all.

WARREN J. HAAS
President, THE COUNCIL ON LIBRARY RESOURCES

LIST OF TABLES

LIST OF FIGURES

ACKNOWLEDGMENTS

Iᴛ is imperative to acknowledge the financial support of the Council on Library Resources in funding the cooperative Public Access Online Catalog Project. Lee Jones, the Council's Program Officer, provided the highest caliber of leadership, advice and guidance throughout the course of the project.

Project staff at all participating organizations were actively involved and helpful during the course of the project. In particular, the contributions of the following must be acknowledged: Robert Zich and Rosemary Anderson of the Library of Congress Planning Office; Joan Frye Williams of J. Matthews and Associates, Inc.; Neal Kaske, Karen Markey, and Charles Hildreth of Online Computer Library Center; David Miller and Daphna Baratz of the Research Libraries Group; Edwin Brownrigg, Vicki Graham, Ray Larson, and Betsy Llosa-Sandor of the University of California. Douglas Ferguson was responsible for coordinating the development of the questionnaire and data collection procedures and Gary Lawrence managed the preparation of the data analysis reports.

Special thanks must be extended to two groups without whom the study could not have happened: the staff of the 29 participating libraries, who successfully undertook the difficult and time-consuming job of administering the questionnaires, and the 12,075 library users who willingly gave their time to answer the questions put before them. Rosemarie Reeder is to be commended for typing and revising this manuscript several times under some very short time deadlines.

We appreciate the comments and suggestions received from CLR staff and others who read drafts of the individual project reports. If, in spite of their help, errors in fact or interpretation remain, the responsibility is ours.

JOE MATTHEWS
GARY LAWRENCE
DOUGLAS FERGUSON

NOTE TO THE READER

*U*SING *Online Catalogs: A Nationwide Survey* reports on a survey of users and non-users of online catalogs in 31 libraries in the United States. It integrates and analyzes the findings of four project reports produced for the Council on Library Resources (under separate grant and contract proposals) by:

- J. Matthews and Associates, Inc. *A Study of Six Online Public Access Catalogs: A Review of Findings.* November 1982.
- Library of Congress. *Library of Congress Online Public Access Catalog Users Survey: A Report to the Council on Library Resources.* October 1982.
- Research Libraries Group, Inc. *Public Online Catalogs and Research Libraries.* September 1982.
- University of California, Division of Library Automation and Library Research and Analysis Group. *Users Look at Online Catalogs: Results of a National Survey of Users and Non-Users of Online Public Access Catalogs.* November 1982.

The findings of the nationwide survey discussed in *Using Online Catalogs* are based on data collected during April and May 1982. The final reports were submitted to the Council on Library Resources between September and November 1982. The text for this book was prepared in February and March 1983.

The *Data Collection Manual and Sampling Plan* (March 1982), produced by the Research Libraries Group and the *Data Analysis Plan* (August 1982), produced by the University of California, have been submitted to the Council as separate reports. OCLC Online Computer Library Center, which was a participant in the set of Council on Library Resources-sponsored Online Catalog Projects, will publish its own final report. All of the above mentioned reports will be available as separate documents through the ERIC information service.

All data from the questionnaires administered in this study are available in machine-readable form from the University of California at a cost of $50. The package includes User and Non-User data on magnetic tape (available in a variety of formats), and complete documentation.

Copies of the CLR User and Non-User questionnaires can be

obtained at a reasonable cost by libraries wishing to use them to evaluate their own online catalogs. Information on administering and analyzing the questionnaires will be found in the *Data Collection Manual* and *Data Analysis Plan*. Libraries wishing to compare their results to those reported here may want to acquire the data tape described previously.

Alternatively, libraries can purchase from the University of California a package of services, including questionnaires, administration materials, data conversion and statistical reporting services, including comparative analyses with groups of libraries in the CLR study. Inquiries about these services and products can be directed to any of the editors of this volume.

CHAPTER ONE

An Overview
of the Study

AUTOMATION, especially the automation of routine record-keeping or housekeeping activities, is exerting a significant force upon the delivery of library services. Examples of routine housekeeping activities that have been automated include the preparation of library catalog cards through online bibliographic utilities such as OCLC, RLIN, or WLN, the production of computer output microform (COM) catalogs, and the installation of various commercially available automated circulation systems. However, the information retrieval capabilities of the computer have not, until recently, been directly available to serve the needs of library patrons.[1]

Computer terminals, historically controlled and used solely by library staff members, are now being moved to the public catalog areas, placed in the stacks of libraries, and located in other high-use locations within the library where access to online catalogs is being provided directly to library patrons. These online catalog systems may have been developed locally by library staff, installed by a commercial circulation system vendor, or linked to a bibliographic utility.

The Council on Library Resources' (CLR) Bibliographic Service Development Program (BSDP) was organized to coordinate research and development projects sponsored by CLR in the area of bibliographic services.[2] Among the program areas of interest to BSDP is the public access online catalog. During the summer of 1980, the Council funded a joint study by the Research Libraries Group (RLG) and the Online Computer Library Center (OCLC) to assess the issues and problems in designing, developing, and operating online public access catalogs. After a survey of 35 organizations known to be operating or developing online catalogs was conducted and an issues paper prepared, a working session, known among the 25 participants as the Dartmouth Conference, identified four priorities for systematic study and cooperative effort. These priorities were:

1. Analyze user requirements and behavior at existing online catalogs.
2. Monitor existing online catalogs.
3. Develop cost management methods.
4. Develop distributed computing and system linkages.[3]

Following the Dartmouth Conference, CLR funded a set of cooperative online catalog research projects proposed by: the Online Computer Library Center (OCLC); The Research Libraries Group (RLG); J. Matthews & Associates, Inc.; University of California, Division of Library Automation; and the Library of Congress. These concurrent research project awards were based on the understanding that each of the participants would cooperate in the development of data collection instruments and data gathering procedures necessary for a detailed study of online public access catalogs. A significant element of this coordination was that standard data collection instruments and data collection procedures would be used by all of the participants in the project. Thus, one of the major limitations of card catalog use studies, which is their institutional bias or study-specific findings, was overcome through the use of standard data collection instruments. The result was a study of a larger number of online catalogs, user populations, and types of libraries than any one organization could support. Additional benefits of the cooperative effort included pooling research and organizational resources. The improved communication and cooperation which were focused on the problems and potentials of public online catalogs resulted in a study whose cumulative results were greater than the sum of its individual parts.

THE HUMAN-COMPUTER INTERACTION

Rather than a broad-based study of all aspects of online public access catalogs, the focus of the project was the interaction between the human user of the online catalog terminal and the online system which supports and responds to the user's request for information.

While it is possible to identify a number of variables that affect online catalogs, the study found it advisable to group these factors into six broad categories. These components, shown in graphic form in Figure 1, include: The user, the task, the organizational interface (the library), the online system, the database, and the human-online interface (see Figure 1, page 4).

In a typical scenario, an individual at the online catalog terminal, *the user,* is using the online catalog to answer one or more questions, *the task.* The user searches the online catalog (*the database*) using a terminal linked to the *online system.* The *human-computer interface* is the locus of the interactive communication—using a specific "language" or "protocol"—between the catalog user and the online system. The user makes known his or her information request to the catalog and it responds. Based on this response the user takes further action. The human-computer interface includes commands, displays, messages, and a means to access the online catalog database through indexes stored in the computer system. *The organizational interface,* usually a library, provides terminals, furniture and lighting, staff assistance, and printed aids for the training and orientation of the user.

Presumably, the user will be able to use an online catalog with little or no instructional or staff assistance. It is assumed that the majority of users are beginners when it comes to computer technology in general and the online catalog in particular. The majority of these first-time users probably do not seek a deep understanding of the computer system and at the same time seek to minimize the necessary learning required to gain access to information in the online catalog. Yet, because of their very limited knowledge of computer systems, the majority of first-time users are "at risk" in their use of an online catalog. If the system responds with an unfamiliar display or if an input error leads to an unusual response from the computer, the user may experience frustration and be less inclined to trust the online system in the future.

The human-computer interface has to be both a *link* with the required facilities to allow a user to accomplish a set of tasks at the online catalog and a *barrier* protecting the user from contacts with other technical (confusing) facets of the computer system.[4] An example of a computer message which has slipped through a "leaky" barrier, "ABEND at line 4376," illustrates the kind of surprise from which the naive (or even experienced) user should be protected, especially if the computer provides no suggestions on how to resolve the problem and proceed with the search. An analogy will further illustrate this point. The automobile driver need not master the intricacies of the internal combustion engine to be able to use a car safely. The attitude of the user, e.g., a rental car customer, is to say "give me the keys, a map, and make sure the gas tank is full and away I'll go."

Figure 1   Components of the Online Catalog

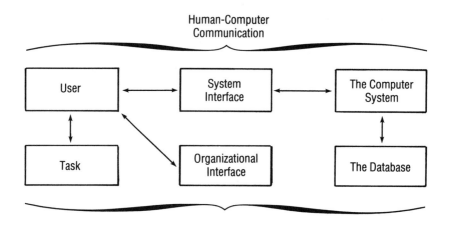

Human-Computer
Communication

| User | ←→ | System
Interface | ←→ | The Computer
System |

| Task | | Organizational
Interface | | The Database |

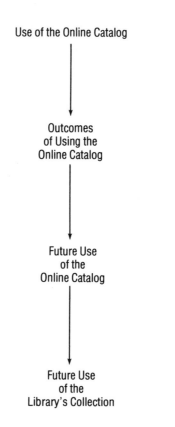

Use of the Online Catalog

Outcomes
of Using the
Online Catalog

Future Use
of the
Online Catalog

Future Use
of the
Library's Collection

A desirable objective for any online catalog is to create a human-computer interface that is "user-friendly" or "user-cordial."[5] The purpose of a user-cordial interface is to make the interaction between the user and the online system as easy and productive as possible. A user-cordial interface will reduce or compensate for common human errors.

It is anticipated that ease of use of the online catalog and accessibility of the library's database, all at the fingertips of a catalog user, will increase the user's satisfaction with the catalog as a finding tool for the collection. This increased patron satisfaction will, it is expected, lead to increased use of the catalog as reflected in the types and volumes of search activity. The success rate—number of times users find what they are looking for—might be similarly improved over that experienced by a user of a card catalog. Thus, use of an online catalog will likely be higher overall than use of a card or COM catalog. As use of the catalog increases, use of the collection may show a corresponding increase. This increased use of the library's collection may result in higher circulation and in-library use figures.

STUDY FOCUSES ON USERS AND NON-USERS OF ONLINE CATALOGS

The data collection methodology focused upon two groups of individuals. The first were library patrons who were *users* of the public access online catalog. In particular, users were asked about the problems they experience with the human-computer interface and they were encouraged to identify their preferences for improving the online catalog. The second group of individuals studied were library patrons who were *non-users* of the public access online catalog. The non-users were asked the reasons for their non-use of the online catalog and encouraged to share their perceptions of an online catalog.

Both users and non-users were asked to complete self-administered machine-scanned questionnaires. The specific goals of the questionnaire survey were:

1. to produce data for analysis that would enable designers of public online catalogs to improve online catalog system interface features. The system interface includes commands, displays, indexes, and similar software and hardware related features;
2. to gather data and prepare an analysis that would enable libraries to improve the implementation and support service for public access online catalogs; and

3. to collect additional data that would enable libraries to extend public access online catalog services to patrons who were not yet users.

This framework led to a series of questionnaire items that asked for responses from users in four areas: (1) questions and purposes users bring to the computer catalog; (2) problems with the system interface, and the organization interface; (3) preferences for improving the database, system features, and organization features; and (4) demographic characteristics of users.

Library patrons who either had or had not used the online catalog were asked to complete a self-administered questionnaire. At most participating libraries, users completed a printed six-page questionnaire. At the University of California libraries, the user questionnaire was administered online to users of UC's MELVYL online catalog system. Users were selected to complete the questionnaire immediately after using the terminal, and non-users were selected to complete the questionnaire when they entered the library.

The user questionnaire had four parts and 59 questions. Part 1 asked ten questions about the use of the computer catalog just completed, such as purpose of the search, satisfaction with search results, amount retrieved, and assistance used in searching. Part 2 asked 29 questions about problems with system features such as commands, displays, and assistance capabilities. Part 3 asked five questions about preferences for improving library capabilities, for improving services associated with the catalog (such as signs and brochures), and for improving the database. Part 4 sought demographic information.

The non-user questionnaire had two parts, and 15 questions, including a demographic part. Part 1 consisted of six questions, including the reasons for non-use, perceptions of time required to learn to use the online catalog, and difficulty expected in using the online catalog.

The two questionnaires had three substantive questions in common: overall attitude toward the online catalog, likelihood of future use, and a summary comparison of a card (and other print-form) catalog and an online catalog. In addition, the two questionnaires had several demographic items in common, including frequency of library use, frequency of catalog use, frequency of online catalog use, and the user's age, sex, and education. Academic, but not public, library users were asked about their major area of study (such as humanities or social sciences), about the focus of their academic work (such as teaching or research), and about academic level (such as freshman/sophomore or graduate student doctoral level). Copies of the questionnaires may be found in Appendixes 1 and 2.

Both questionnaires were reviewed at various stages by consultants and librarians. In the spring of 1981 they were pretested at several sites, including Evanston (Illinois) Public Library, The Library of Congress, Northwestern University, and Ohio State University. The test version provided write-in responses for many items and these were analyzed to improve question wording and response (answer) categories. In addition, the pretesting involved open-ended and follow-up interviews. After extensive revision, the entire survey was pilot-tested at almost all participating library systems in the fall of 1981. Once again, follow-up interviews were conducted and respondent write-in comments were analyzed. The pilot-test data were analyzed, and modifications were made to the questionnaires and data collection procedures. More detailed information about the data collection process may be found in the *Data Collection Manual.*[6]

Since the focus of the study was on the human-computer interface, the data collected were, of necessity, primarily from users of the online catalog. User data were collected in participating libraries during April and May 1982, in four randomly scheduled four-hour time blocks during morning, afternoon and evening sessions.[7] During each week, two four-hour time blocks were scheduled to collect non-user data. The time blocks were scheduled in such a way that terminals reflecting the greatest amount of use received proportionally more data collection activity. While a random sample from online catalog terminals located in each library was considered and used during the questionnaire pilot test conducted in October-December 1981, it was decided to concentrate data gathering at the more frequently used terminals during the final data collection period. However, some data was gathered at all terminal locations in each participating library.

The completed questionnaires were sent to the University of California where arrangements were made to have them scanned on a machine located at Stanford University. The resulting magnetic tape containing the raw data was returned to the University of California for analysis. Detailed procedures for the data analysis will be found in the *Data Analysis Plan.*[8]

The data collection instruments and overall methodology for the CLR study were carefully developed and fully tested. Within certain limits, the data reported here are reliable and valid, and provide a sound foundation for the findings and conclusions offered in later chapters.

It should, however, be understood that there are limitations to the interpretation and application of these data (as is true of any empirical study). The most important points to keep in mind when reading and analyzing this report are these:

1. Data were collected over a relatively short period of time, representing a thin "slice" of the evolving characteristics of the participating online catalogs and the changing nature of the institutions that offer them and the library patrons who use them. As a corollary, the data represent different systems at different stages of their evolution.

2. The data and analyses presented here are intended to describe user reactions, attitudes, and problems in the aggregate, and not to analyze or comment on particular online catalogs in particular libraries.

3. In evaluating the aggregate descriptive data presented here, it must be remembered that some results are influenced by factors like the unequal number of questionnaires contributed by participating libraries, the locations of terminals within various library systems (which in turn influences the characteristics of the population of online catalog users in that institution), and the wide range of differences in computer catalog systems, database characteristics, and user populations among the participating libraries. These factors must be considered when drawing any inferences from these data.

4. The chief source of information for this study was a self-completed questionnaire. For the most part, respondents' answers were not independently validated from another source. We assume that respondents understood the questions as we intended and that they answered honestly and fully, but interpretations should take into account possibilities for misunderstanding and accidental or intentional misrepresentation.

5. It should be recalled that the staffs of the participating libraries were specifically excluded from the survey sample. Data presented here are not influenced by the attitudes of library staff toward the online catalog, nor is information about staff use of the catalog included.

6. Although the CLR study included an exceptional range of online catalogs in a wide variety of libraries, it should be remembered that it did not include all known online catalogs, and did not represent a full variety of library settings (e.g., special libraries). The conclusions presented here are generally valid for the current generation of online catalogs, taken as a whole, but results may be different for a particular catalog in a particular library.

7. The chief objectives of this project were empirical and pragmatic, rather than theoretical. Our intent was to describe, through

the broadest feasible base of measurement, how library users are responding to a new bibliographic tool. Although much can be learned from this study about how online catalogs can (and must) be improved, the study was not designed to test or advance a particular theory of computer design, retrieval method, or user behavior.

NOTES

1. Joseph R. Matthews. "Online Public Access Catalogs: Assessing the Potential." *Library Journal,* 107(11), June 1, 1982, pp. 1067–1071.
2. C. Lee Jones and Nancy Gwinn. "Bibliographic Service Development: A New CLR Program." *Journal of Library Automation,* 12(2), June 1979, pp. 116–124.
3. Douglas Ferguson and Neal K. Kaske. *Online Public Access to Library Bibliographic Databases: Development Issues and Priorities* (Final Report to the Council of Library Resources, September 1980), ERIC ED 195 275.
4. T. F. M. Stewart. "Displays and the Software Interface." *Applied Ergonomics,* 7(3), 1976, pp. 137–146.
5. Charles M. Goldstein and William H. Ford. "The User-cordial Interface." *Online Review,* 2(3), 1978, pp. 269–276.
6. David C. Miller and Daphna Baratz. *Public Online Catalog Study: Data Collection Manual.* Stanford, CA: RLG, March 16, 1982.
7. The University of California used a different, but equally valid, sampling method for the MELVYL online questionnaire. The computer system was programmed to invite every twenty-fifth user of the catalog to complete a questionnaire, regardless of the time or location.
8. Gary S. Lawrence, Ray R. Larson, and Vicki Graham. *Online Catalog Evaluation Project, Data Analysis Plan, Version 2.2.* Berkeley: University of California Systemwide Administration, August 5, 1982; and Ray S. Larson. *Development and Testing of Data Collection and Analysis Tools.* Berkeley: University of California, Division of Library Automation, July 1981.

CHAPTER TWO

Participating Libraries and Their Online Catalogs

SIXTEEN online catalogs and 29 libraries were participants in the Catalog Study (see Table 1). The participating libraries include libraries from the Research Libraries Group, Online Computer Library Center, the Library of Congress, the University of California, and seven libraries participating with J. Matthews and Associates, Inc. Systems used and thus reported on include those provided by circulation turnkey vendors, systems developed by libraries or by campus computing centers following specifications provided by the library, and terminals linked to two bibliographic utilities, OCLC and RLIN.

Rather than referring to each of the participating libraries or the research organizations in alphabetical order, the libraries have been organized into logical sets, i.e., ARL libraries, academic libraries, community college libraries, public libraries, and state and federal libraries, to allow the reader the opportunity to more easily compare and contrast the results of the study by type of library.

This section presents a brief review of each library and its organizational context, and a brief history of the development of each online catalog.

ARL LIBRARIES

Dartmouth College

Dartmouth College in Hanover, New Hampshire is a private university whose population includes about 3,600 undergraduates, 900 graduate students, 500 faculty, and 1,400 staff.

TABLE 1   Participating Libraries by Study Organization

Library/Locations	Library Type	System Name
Library of Congress		
Library of Congress	State/Federal	MUMS/SCORPIO
J. Matthews and Associates, Inc. Group		
Claremont Colleges	Academic	Total Library System
Evanston Public Library	Public	CLSI
Mankato State University	Academic	Mankato OLC*
Mission/West Valley Colleges	Comm. College	ULISYS
Pikes Peak Library District	Public	Maggie's Place
Steven F. Austin State University	ARL	DataPhase Systems
OCLC, Inc. Group		
Ohio State University	ARL	LCS
Syracuse University	ARL	SULIRS
Dallas Public Library	Public	LSCAN
Iowa City Public Library	Public	CLSI
State Library of Ohio	State/Federal	OCLC
University of Akron	Academic	OCLC
University of Texas, Dallas	Academic	OCLC
Ohio University, Athens	Academic	OCLC
University of Texas, Austin	ARL	OCLC
RLG Group		
Dartmouth College	ARL	Dartmouth OLC
Northwestern University	ARL	NOTIS/LUIS
Stanford University	ARL	RLIN II
University of California (DLA) Group		
Nine campuses (Berkeley, Davis, Irvine, Los Angeles, Riverside, San Diego, San Francisco, Santa Barbara, Santa Cruz)	ARL	MELVYL

*OLC = Online Catalog

During the study period, Dartmouth had a pilot version of a system that will be in production in late 1983. The system is being designed by the Dartmouth staff jointly with Bibliographic Retrieval Services, Inc. and will be implemented on a Digital Equipment Corporation (PDP 11/70) minicomputer resident in Dartmouth's Kiewitt Computer Center.

During the study, four dial-up microcomputer terminals were available for direct patron use. One terminal was in each of the following libraries: the Baker Main Library, Dana Biomedical Library, Feldberg Business-Engineering Library and Kresge Physics-

Chemistry Library. Each terminal operated at 30 characters per second or 300 baud.

The Dartmouth database was an experimental database of books and nonbook material for the period 1977–1980, consisting of about 150,000 records. Records can be displayed in varying degrees of detail ranging from author, title, and imprint to the full MARC record.

The system offers menus or lists from which the user can choose as well as direct command entry. The following access points are provided: author, title, call number, corporate or conference name, and subject heading, as well as keyword searching of any field in the bibliographic record. Boolean searching using the logical operators AND, OR, and NOT is also provided. Figure 2 illustrates the search process experienced by a user.

Online assistance is provided by a series of menus and online explanation screens. Little printed documentation is provided but assistance is available from nearby reference staffs.

Northwestern University

Northwestern University is a private institution located in Evanston, Illinois, just north of Chicago. The Northwestern population consists of about 6,800 undergraduates, 3,200 graduate students, 2,900 faculty and 4,500 staff.

The Northwestern online catalog, known as LUIS (Library User Information Service), is based on a technical processing and circulation system that uses an in-house IBM 4331 mainframe. LUIS was made available to library patrons in mid-1980 and continues to be developed.

During the 1982 study period there were 12 terminals available in the main library, two terminals in the Science and Engineering Library and four terminals at small branch locations. The latter four terminals were not data collection sites. The terminals were directly connected to the in-house computer and operate at a speed of 4,800 baud.

Northwestern's database contains about 525,000 records including about 70,000 serial records. The book records are from 1970 to the present and the serial records represent virtually 100 percent of the library system's holdings. A separate database of all active circulation records is available on the same terminals used for the online catalog.

FIGURE 2   Sample Screens for Dartmouth College

The user starts the search by asking for help. The system provides a help screen and the user responds to a series of questions/prompts to search by author for "Commoner" and by title for "poverty of power" (B). The system then displays the one resulting record (C).

Search type? A)uthor, T)itle, S)ubject or O)ther: **H**

I'm sorry you are having trouble. I'll try to HELP. If you can tell
me what's wrong or what you don't understand, I may be able to give
you a better explanation.

To begin, let's review the procedures for telling the computer what you
want to do. To issue a command, press the RED key followed by:
S: To start searching,
P: To list search results,
X: To get special list options,
D: To display previously executed search statements,
H: To get Help!,
E: To get explanations of how the system works,
L: To logoff and reset the system for the next user,
Q: To logoff and sign off the system for the day.

Then press the RETURN key.

If you need more information about how the system works, there are lots
of topics I can EXPLAIN for you. If you'd like to see
some, please give the EXPLAIN command (RED key followed by E) and then
press the RETURN key.

Please tell the system what you want to do next by giving one of these
commands now. Press the RED key followed by S,P,X,D,H,E,L, or Q and
then press the RETURN key.

If you are still in doubt, please call X2574.

Search type? A)uthor, T)itle, S)ubject, or O)ther: **A**
Search statement: **commoner**
Checking terms. . .
Do you want to add more to your search statement?
    Y or N: **Y**
Search type? A)uthor, T)itle, S)ubject, or O)ther: **T**
Search statement: **poverty of power**
Checking terms. . .
Do you want to add more to your search statement?
    Y or N: **N**
(COMMONER).ME,AE. AND (POVERTY WITH POWER).TI.
Do you want to execute this search (Y or N)? **Y**
Searching. . .

    Result 1
    1
LO DRBU.
    GF75-C65-1974
ME Commoner, Barry, 1917–.
TI The closing circle: nature, man, & technology / Barry Commoner.
IM New York: Bantam Books c1974.
CO viii, 343 p. 19 cm.
SU Pollution.
NT Includes bibliographical references and index.

R0601 * END OF DOCUMENTS IN LIST

LUIS is a command system with no menu or list features. Author and title access was available from the beginning and subject heading access was introduced shortly before the study began. There is no keyword access and authors, titles, and subject headings are entered in a fixed order: last name then first name for authors, and word-for-word from left to right for titles and subject headings exactly as they are entered in the record except for initial articles. Truncation at any point is permissible; there are no stop words. Figure 3 provides some sample screens for the LUIS system (see Figure 3, pages 15–18).

Online assistance is provided by screens that explain the database contents, how to do different types of searches, and other helpful information. Printed handouts and command summaries are available at the terminals.

Ohio State University

Ohio State University Libraries serve about 60,000 students, faculty and staff at their Columbus, Ohio campus. The OSU Libraries are composed of one large main library, 26 departmental libraries, and two undergraduate libraries. The collection contains 3.6 million volumes.

In 1970, the OSU Libraries installed an automated circulation control system, called Library Control System (LCS), that contained minimal bibliographic information: main entry, title, LCCN, and date of publication. In June 1978, the system was expanded to store and index full MARC records. Subject heading searches became available at this time. LCS runs on an IBM 370/168 with 6 million bytes of memory.

There are a total of 210 terminals installed in the OSU Libraries and of these, about 117 are available for public access. Two dial-in ports were available for public use at the time of the survey. The patron can search by author, title, author/title combination, serial title, subject heading, series, title, exact call number, and shelf-list browse. The user enters an OCLC-like search key for author/title or any title searches. English language forms for author names, subject headings, and call numbers are accepted. Figure 4 provides sample screens for the LCS system (see Figure 4, pages 19–21). Currently there are about 1,500,000 titles in the database. Library staff members have produced a one-page handout sheet which provides basic directions on how to search using LCS. Stop word lists are posted adjacent to the terminal screen.

Stanford University

Stanford University is a private institution located in Palo Alto, California about 25 miles south of San Francisco. The library user

FIGURE 3 Sample Screens for Northwestern University

The user views the first screen and selects the introductory screen for subject searches (screen A). After reading this screen, the user wishes additional information on the Library of Congress Subject Headings (screen B). While this screen was useful the user wishes more information about LCSH (screens C and D). The user enters a subject search for "World War 1914–1918" and the system displays the appropriate subject headings and the user selects line 1 (screen E). The system then displays the first 16 records in brief form and the user selects line 2 (screen F). The system displays the bibliographic record plus holdings information (screen G).

A

```
LUIS:    LIBRARY USER INFORMATION SERVICE

        LUIS can be used to find BIBLIOGRAPHIC, CALL NUMBER and LOCATION
information for materials held by Northwestern University Libraries and by
the Garrett/Seabury Library. (Use the card catalog for materials not in the
LUIS database.) CIRCULATION information for materials charged out through
the computerized system is also available.

TYPES OF SEARCHES:                              COMMANDS:
— FOR INTRODUCTORY SCREEN FOR TITLE SEARCHES:   Type t
                        AUTHOR SEARCHES:        Type a
                        SUBJECT SEARCHES:       Type s

— FOR USERS ALREADY FAMILIAR WITH LUIS:         Type t=, a=, s=, st=, or sm=
  (To start a search from any screen)           followed by a SEARCH TERM
                                                (title, author, or subject)

— FOR CIRCULATION INFORMATION SCREEN:           Type d
  (Available for the Evanston Campus main       (call no. must be known)
  and Science-Engineering libraries only)

TO CORRECT A MISTAKE, type over the error or clear screen to start over.

TYPE COMMAND AND PRESS ENTER s
```

B

TO SEARCH BY SUBJECT: EXAMPLES:

— TYPE s=   followed by a subject term or portion   s=television   s=shakesp
    of subject.   s=symbolism in art

To determine the subject headings used in LUIS,
you may wish to consult the Library of Congress
Subject headings (LCSH) list. This two-volume
red book is available near library terminals.
EXAMPLE: LCSH indicates that materials on labor
                unions will be found under ''Trade-unions''
                but not under ''Labor-unions'', ''Unions'',
                or ''Labor, organized''.
FOR MORE INFORMATION ABOUT USING LCSH, TYPE m

NOTE: Most Transportation Library subjects must   EXAMPLES:
             be searched by st= and Medical Library   st=urban transit
             subjects by sm= ; type st or sm for details. sm=vestibular nuclei

TYPE t FOR INTRODUCTION TO TITLE SEARCHES, OR a FOR AUTHOR.
TYPE e TO START OVER.
TYPE COMMAND AND PRESS ENTER **m**

C

USING THE LIBRARY OF CONGRESS SUBJECT HEADINGS LIST

The Library of Congress Subject Headings (LCSH) list is an alphabetic guide
to the forms of subject headings to be used when searching for materials by
subject in LUIS or in the subject card catalog. When you consult LCSH you
will find:

— Exact form of subject headings (in bold face type), which may be used to
    search in LUIS

— Subdivisions of those headings (preceded by a dash ——), which will display
    automatically in LUIS under the term you enter if materials on those topics
    are in the database

— Related subject terms (preceded by sa for narrower or related terms or
    xx for broader terms), which may also be used to search in LUIS

— Terms which should NOT be used to search in LUIS (preceded by x)

TYPE m FOR LCSH EXAMPLES.

TYPE e TO START OVER.
TYPE COMMAND AND PRESS ENTER **m**

D

LIBRARY OF CONGRESS SUBJECT HEADINGS LIST: EXAMPLES

LCSH EXAMPLES:	USE IN LUIS:
Costume	s=costume
sa Arms and armor	s=arms and armor (all ''sa'' terms are related terms)
Clothing and dress	s=clothing and d
x Costume, Theatrical	Do not use s=costume, theatrical; use s=costume
Fancy dress	Do not use s=fancy dress; use s=costume
xx Art	s=art (all ''xx'' terms are broader related terms)
Fashion	s=fashion
— History	For a broad search, use s=costume (all
——15th century	subdivisions will display). To narrow your
	search, use s=costume——hist NOTE: In LUIS,
	subdivisions display in alphabetic and then
	numeric order, not in chronologic order.
Costume, Theatrical	Do not use s=costume, theatrical (not in bold face);
See Costume	use s=costume

IF YOU NEED ASSISTANCE, ask a library staff member.

TO RESTORE PREVIOUS LIBRARY OF CONGRESS SUBJECT HEADINGS SCREEN, press ENTER.
TYPE s= (AND SEARCH TERM) TO START A SUBJECT SEARCH. TYPE e TO START OVER.
TYPE COMMAND AND PRESS ENTER **S=WORLD WAR 1914–1918**

E

LUIS SEARCH REQUEST: S=WORLD WAR 1914–1918
  SUBJECT HEADING GUIDE —— 243 HEADINGS FOUND, 1 — 18 DISPLAYED

1	WORLD WAR 1914–1918
2	—ADDRESSES ESSAYS LECTURES
3	—ADDRESSES SERMONS ETC.
4	—AERIAL OPERATIONS
5	—AERIAL OPERATIONS —BIBLIOGRAPHY
6	—AERIAL OPERATIONS —CHRONOLOGY
7	—AERIAL OPERATIONS BRITISH
8	—AERIAL OPERATIONS CANADIAN
9	—AERIAL OPERATIONS FRENCH
10	—AERIAL OPERATIONS GERMAN
11	—AERIAL OPERATIONS ITALIAN
12	—AFRICA
13	—AFRICA EAST
14	—AFRICA FRENCH—SPEAKING WEST
15	—AFRICA NORTH
16	—ALGERIA
17	—ARABIA
18	—ARMISTICES

TYPE m FOR MORE SUBJECT HEADINGS. TYPE LINE NO. FOR TITLES UNDER A HEADING.
TYPE e TO START OVER. TYPE h FOR HELP.
TYPE COMMAND AND PRESS ENTER **1**

F

LUIS SEARCH REQUEST: S=WORLD WAR 1914–1918
 SUBJECT/TITLE INDEX —— 65 TITLES FOUND, 1 — 16 DISPLAYED

WORLD WAR 1914–1918

1	transactions of the grotius soci	NU main:341.06;G881
2	short history of world war i	(1981)NU main:940.3;S874s
3	great war	(1980)NU main:L940.3;B261g
4	no mans land: 1918 the last year	(1980)NU core:940.3;T647n
5	no mans land: 1918 the last year	(1980)NU main:940.3;T647n
6	no mans land: 1918 the last year	(1980)NU schf:940.3;T647n
7	world war i: an illustrated hist	(1980)NU main:L940.3;E93w
8	zweite internationale und der kr	(1979)NU main:324.1;B632z
9	italia unita e la prima guerra m	(1978)NU main:945.09;R7631i
10	lenin e mussolini: protagonisti	(1978)NU main:320.945;B793l
11	ocherki vneshnei politiki rossii	(1977)NU main:327.0947;E532o
12	congres socialistes internationa	(1976)NU main:335.00904;C749
13	istoriia pervoi mirovoi voiny: 1	(1975)NU main:940.347;I875
14	history of world war i	(1974)NU main:L940.4;T238h
15	great war 1914–1918	(1973)NU main:940.3;F395gX
16	world war i a compact history	(1973)NU main:940.4;H417w

TYPE LINE NO. FOR BIBLIOGRAPHIC RECORD WITH HOLDINGS.
TYPE m FOR MORE TITLES. TYPE d FOR CIRCULATION STATUS (WRITE DOWN CALL NO.)
TYPE g TO RETURN TO GUIDE. TYPE e TO START OVER. TYPE h FOR HELP.
TYPE COMMAND AND PRESS ENTER **2**

G

LUIS SEARCH REQUEST: S=WORLD WAR 1914–1918
 BIBLIOGRAPHIC RECORD —— NO. 2 OF 65 ENTRIES FOUND

Stokesbury, James L.
 A short history of World War I / by James L. Stokesbury. —— 1st ed. ——New
York : Morrow, 1981.
 348 p. : maps ; 24 cm.
 Bibliography: p. 325–336.
 Includes index.
 SUBJECT HEADINGS (Library of Congress; use s=):
  World War, 1914–1918.

HOLDINGS IN NORTHWESTERN UNIVERSITY LIBRARY:
LOCATION: main
CALL NUMBER: 940.3;S874s

TYPE m FOR NEXT RECORD, d FOR CIRCULATION STATUS (FIRST WRITE DOWN CALL NO.)
TYPE i TO RETURN TO INDEX, g TO RETURN TO GUIDE, e TO START OVER, h FOR HELP.
TYPE COMMAND AND PRESS ENTER

Figure 4   Sample Screens for the Ohio State University

The user enters an author/title search for "Lillian Hellman's *Little Foxes.*" Note the user must enter a OCLC-like search key (screen A). The system responds with a brief record display and the user selects line 3 for display of bibliographic, location and status information (screen B). The user then enters an author search for "Benson Edw." The system displays a brief record display of the matching records (screen C) and the user asks for a display of record number 8 (shown in screen D). The user then enters a subject search for "Communication in Management" and the system provides a display of subject headings (screen E). The user asks for a short list of titles for line number 11 (screen F). The user enters a command to display record number 1 (screen G) and subsequently a full bibliographic display (screen H).

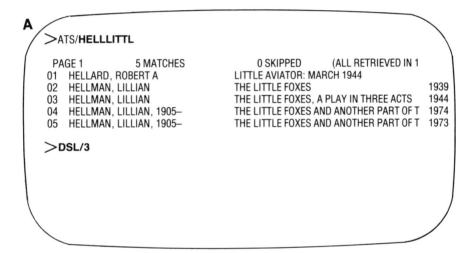

A

>ATS/**HELLLITTL**

```
   PAGE 1              5 MATCHES              0 SKIPPED        (ALL RETRIEVED IN 1
   01   HELLARD, ROBERT A              LITTLE AVIATOR: MARCH 1944
   02   HELLMAN, LILLIAN               THE LITTLE FOXES                        1939
   03   HELLMAN, LILLIAN               THE LITTLE FOXES, A PLAY IN THREE ACTS  1944
   04   HELLMAN, LILLIAN, 1905–        THE LITTLE FOXES AND ANOTHER PART OF T  1974
   05   HELLMAN, LILLIAN, 1905–        THE LITTLE FOXES AND ANOTHER PART OF T  1973
```

>**DSL/3**

B

```
   PS3515F355L51944       HELLMAN, LILLIAN     THE LITTLE FOXES, A PLAY IN THREE ACTS
   39-27320          621133       1944        1
   01         pp1 WTHON MAI
   PAGE 1 END
```

>**AUT/BENSONEDW**

C

```
PAGE 1                    83 MATCHES           0 SKIPPED      (NOT ALL RETRIEVED)
01   BENSON, EDWARD FREDERIC. 1867–19    THE RELENTLESS CITY              1903
02   BENSON, EDWARD FREDERIC. 1867–       LUCIA IN LONDON                 1928
03   BENSON, EDWARD FREDERIC              OUR RAMILY AFFAIRS              1921
04   BENSON, EDWARD FREDERIC              FERDINAND MAGELLAN             1930
05   BENSON, EDWARD FREDERIC              KING EDWARD VII, AN APPRECIATION 1934
06   BENSON, EDWARD FREDERIC, 1867–19    THE BLOTTING BOOK /            1976
07   BENSON, EDWARD FREDERIC, 1867–19    DODD'S DAUGHTER                1914
08   BENSON, EDWARD FREDERIC              OLD LONDON                     1937
09   BENSON, EDWARD FREDERICD1867–194    REX                  1925
10   BENSON, EDWARD FREDERIC              DAILY TRAINING                  1903

>DSL/8
```

D

```
EL80B47501        BENSON, EDWARD FREDERIC      OLD LONDON      37-21955
            823514      1937       4
01   001   001        MAI
02   002   001        MAI
03   003   001        MAI
04   004   001        MAI

>SIS/COMMUNICATION IN MANAGEMENT
```

E

```
11     3 COMMUNICATION IN MANAGEMENT
12     1 COMMUNICATION IN MEDICINE
13     1 COMMUNICATION IN NURSING
14     1 COMMUNICATION IN ORGANIZATIONS
15     1 COMMUNICATION IN POLITICS—UNITED STATES
16     1 COMMUNICATION IN RURAL DEVELOPMENT—CASE STUDIES
17     3 COMMUNICATION IN SCIENCE
18     1 COMMUNICATION IN SCIENCE—UNITED STATES—STATISTICS
19     1 COMMUNICATION IN WATER RESOURCES DEVELOPMENT
20     1 COMMUNICATION OF TECHNICAL INFORMATION—UNITED STATES—STATISTICS
   INPUT:  COMMUNICATION IN MANAGEMENT
   PAGE 2 OF 3      FOR OTHER PAGES ENTER PS AND PAGE NUMBER

>SBL/11
```

F

PAGE 1 OF 1   3 MATCHES.   FIRST   0 SKIPPED.
01   HF5736K87 / KUTTNER, M / MANAGING THE PAPERWORK PIPELINE :/1978
02   HF5718P3751978 / PARKINSON, / COMMUNICATE :/1978
03   HF5549.5C6I48 / INTERNATIO / WITHOUT BIAS:/1977
COMMUNICATION IN MANAGEMENT   ALL RETRIEVED

>DSL/1

G

HF5786K87   KUTTNER, MONROE S , 1929–   MANAGING THE PAPERWORK PIPELINE :
77–15041   2222111   1978   1   ADDED: 780603   FBR
01   001   COM CF528241   0   CHGD   780906/781206
PAGE 1 END

>FBL/1

H

HF5736K87
KUTTNER, MONROE S , 1929
   MANAGING THE PAPERWORK PIPELINE : ACHIEVING COST-EFFECTIVE PAPERWORK AND
INFORMATION PROCESSING / MONROE S. KUTTNER. NEW YORK : WILEY, C1978. XXI,
244 P. ; 24 CM.
   INCLUDES INDEX. "A RONALD PRESS PUBLICATION." BIBLIOGRAPHY: P. 237–240.
SUB: 1. BUSINESS RECORDS 2. OFFICE MANAGEMENT 3. COMMUNICATION IN MANAGEMENT
LC CARD :77-15041 TITLE :2222111 OCLC :3327400 &9Q780620
PAGE 1 END

population consists of about 6,600 undergraduates, 5,200 graduate students, 1,200 faculty, and 6,500 staff.

For the study, Stanford made a trial use of the Research Libraries Information Network (RLIN II) system. RLIN is implemented on an IBM mainframe, a 3033 during the study period, and search-only access was provided on the public terminals during the study.

During the study period, four terminals were available: two in the Green Main Library, one in the Meyer Undergraduate Library, and one in the Engineering Library. All terminals were directly connected to the RLIN mainframe, located on the Stanford campus, and operated at speeds in excess of 120 characters per second or 1,200 baud.

Stanford's RLIN database, at the time of the study, consisted of about 490,000 book records and about 160,000 serial records. The database is searchable by author, title, call number, corporate name, subject heading, and other index points. Authors names may be entered using last or first name first and titles and corporate entries are keyword searchable but subject headings must be entered in exact order left-to-right. Access points or indexes and keywords may be combined using Boolean operators. Figure 5 illustrates the search process using the RLIN system (see Figure 5, pages 23–26).

Four screens of information are available for online assistance. They describe system changes, summarize the indexes, summarize search and display commands, and show current news about the system. The Stanford staff prepared a one-page explanation and a more detailed booklet that was placed at each terminal.

Syracuse University

The Syracuse University Libraries, located in Syracuse, New York, serve about 17,000 students and faculty. The Libraries have developed their own in-house library system which provides support for circulation, acquisitions, and an online catalog. Library administration developed the specifications for the system which was programmed by the University's computing staff. The command driven system uses two-letter field labeled mnemonics for the entry of access points. Two display formats are available. The brief display is the default display and details author, title, edition, publisher, place and dates of publication, call number, library and floor and circulation information.

During the study period, 36 terminals in the Libraries were connected to the libraries' computer system which is called SULIRS—

FIGURE 5   Sample Screens for the RLIN II System

The user wishes information about general news (screen A), search and display capabilities (screen B), and what indexes are included in what files (screen C). The user then conducts a search by subject phrase for "Hughes, Howard#" and title phrase "Empire#" and the system retrieves and displays three records (screen D). The user selects the first record and a partial display is provided by the system (screen E). The user then asks for a long display of the same record (screen F).

A

```
:? show news
PROD                         Search                          CRLG-JRB
News display — last updated 11/1/82 at 3:51pm pacific time

CONSPECTUS — The RLG ON-LINE CONSPECTUS is now in production. CONSPECTUS
users please SHO CHANGES for important documentary information. (11/1/82)

TABLES — The Country of Publication and Language tables (CP and L) have been
rebuilt. The codes now agree with the LC codes. Also, cross references are
now available in the on-line system. (11/1/82)

MARC TAPES — We have loaded MARC tapes for the FILMS, MAPS and SERIALS
formats for 9/16/82–10/13/82 on October 31.
We have loaded the MARC Books tape for 9/21/82–9/27/82 on October 31. (11/1/82)

****Statistics as of November 1, 1982****
  BKS          SER          SCO            REC         FLM          MAP
  6,666,461    978,015      58,174         23,017      65,474       79,686
```

B

:? **show information**
PROD   Search   CRLG-JRB
Information display

Searching
  FINd <index> <value> — initiates search
  AND, &   — restricts search   AND NOT, &~,~— restricts search
  OR, :   — expands search   RESume — continues search in next file

  SELect FILes <file> , . . . — Determines which files are to be searched

Display
  MUL — Multiple record display   FUL — Fully tagged display
  LON — Long, card-like display   CAT — Cataloged holdings display
  PAR — Partial record display   PRI — Primary cluster member display

  SET DISplay <display name> — sets default local-version record display

Information
  SHO NEWs — RLIN system news
  SHO CHAnges — Subsystem-specific news
  SHO INFormation — [this display]
  SHO SETtings — User status information
  SHO INDexes — Index information

C

:? **show indexes**
PROD   Search   CRLG-JRB
Index display

General Indexes		BKS	FLM	MAP	REC	SCO	SER
PN, PE	— Personal name & exact personal name	x	x	x	x	x	x
TP, TW	— Title phrase & title word	x	x	x	x	x	x
RT	— Related title phrase						x
CP, CW	— Corp. name phrase & corp. name word	x	x	x	x	x	x
SP, SD	— Subject phrase & subdivision	x	x	x	x	x	x
LCCN	— LC Card number	x	x	x	x	x	x
CLS	— LC and Dewey classification	x	x	x	x	x	x
GC	— Geographic class code	x	x	x	x	x	x
DOC	— U.S. Government document number	x	x	x	x	x	x
ISBN	— International standard book number	x	x	x	x	x	
ISSN	— International standard serial number	x		x		x	x
CODEN	— Coden						x
PUB	— Publisher or issuing agency				x	x	
NUM	— Publisher/issue number				x	x	
QD	— Queuing date	x	x	x	x	x	x

Local Indexes
  CAL — Call number   ST — Record Status
  LDN — Library Data Number UST — Unit Status
  ID — Record ID   ADD — Added records   SAV — Today's saved records
  UID — Unit ID   UPD — Updated records USV — Today's saved units
:? **FIND SP HUGHES, HOWARD# AND TP EMPIRE#**

D

FIN SP HUGHES, HOWARD# AND TP EMPIRE# — 3 clusters in BKS

1)   Bartlett, Donald L. EMPIRE : [Book club ed.] (New York : W. W. Norton
     [c1979])
AZFG (c-9116 AzF)

2)   Bartlett, Donald L. EMPIRE : (New York : Norton, c1979.)
NYPG (c-1665 NN)   AZFG (c-9610 AzF)   AZPG (c-9610 AzTPC)   CFCG (c-9610 CF)
CMCG-1 (c-9616 COMC)   CMCG-2 (c-9610 COMC)   CNBG (c-9610 CStrNB)
CPAG (c-9610 CPa)   CRPG (c-9610 CRic)   CSCG (c-9666 CSjCL)   CSFX (c-9610 CSf)
CSUG (c-9610 CSt)   CSUU (c-9610 CSt)   CUBG (c-9610 CU)   CUBU (c-9610 CU-BANC)
CUDG (c-9610 CU-A)   DCLC (c-9110 DLC)   ILEG (c-9610 IE)   MIUG (c-9610 MiU)
NJRG (c-9610 NjR)   NVRG (c-9610 NvU)   UTBG (c-9610 UPB)

3)   Davenport, Joe. THE EMPIRE OF HOWARD HUGHES / 1st ed. (San Francisco : Peace
    and Pieces Foundation, 1975.)
DCLC (c-9110 DLC)   CCSG (c-9110 C)   CSCG (c-9660 CSjCL)   CSUG (c-9660 CSt)
NVRG (c-9610 NvU)
:? **PAR 1**

E

+B
Barlett, Donald.L.
   Empire : the life, legend, and madness of Howard Hughes / by Donald L. Barlett
and James B. Steele. —— 1st ed. —— New York : Norton, c1979.
   687 p. : ill., facsims., genealogical tables, ports. ; 24 cm.

   ISBN 0393075133
   LCCN: 791331
   050: CT275.H6678 B37 1979
   ID: CSUG10713948–B   CC: 9610   DCF: i

CT275.H6678.B37 1979

STK
   c.1   (CAT 05/16/79)
:? **LONG**

F

Syracuse University Library Information Retrieval System. The user can search by author, title, author/title keyword, subject keyword, series title, call number and any combination thereof through an explicit or implicit Boolean "AND" operation. SULIRS uses a subject keyword approach; that is, every significant word in title or subject heading in an item is indexed and searchable. The user may enter any combination of types of searches using the Boolean operator "AND." As yet, there is no "OR" or "NOT" in SULIRS. The Syracuse University database, at the time of the study, consisted of about 535,000 records. Figure 6 provides some sample screens using the SULIRS system. Library staff prepared a handout describing use of the system (see Figure 6, pages 28–33).

University of California

The University of California consists of nine campuses and total University enrollment exceeds 127,000. There are about 69,000 employees, including 20,000 academic staff. As of June 1982, the UC libraries held about 19 million bound volumes and maintained about 312,000 serials subscriptions.

The University of California online catalog, known as MELVYL,[1] provides access to recently acquired books. Currently, the catalog is offered in a prototype version containing approximately 733,000 records, representing 1.3 million books in the combined collection of all the campuses. This is only a small fraction of the total number of books in the entire university, and represents only items cataloged between 1976 and December 1980. The production version of MELVYL, with new capabilities and a regularly-updated database, is scheduled to be available in the summer of 1983. There are no records for journals, music scores, phonograph records, maps, audiovisual materials, or other types of materials, although these formats will be added in the future.

In the prototype version, MELVYL supports about 100 dedicated terminals in the libraries of all nine campuses. By the mid-1980s, it is expected that MELVYL will expand to something on the order of 1,000–2,000 terminals and the database will grow to about 6 million records.

MELVYL is supported on four Magnuson M80/43 (IBM plug-compatible) computers, each having 8 megabytes of memory. MELVYL features two search modes: Lookup Mode and Command Mode. In Lookup Mode, MELVYL gives complete instructions and asks the user to make choices or supply information. This is useful to users

FIGURE 6   Sample Screens for Syracuse University

To start the search, the user requests help from the system (screen A) and then reviews the appropriate search commands by reviewing a series of help screens. The user then enters a Subject search for "Energy Policy United States" (screen B). The system responds with a display of the first five, out of 122 retrieved records (screen C). The user then asks for a full record display of records 4 and 2 (screens D and E). The user then conducts a new word search for "Einstein" and "Relativity." The system responds with a display of the first five records (screen F). The user then asks for a full display of record number 5 (screen G).

A

```
ENTER SEARCH: )HELP

        "FORMAT ERROR" INDICATES AN INVALID COMBINATION
             OF CHARACTERS IN A CALL NUMBER.

        "MISSING OR BAD SEARCH CODE" MEANS THAT THE SEARCH
             WAS NOT STARTED WITH A VALID SEARCH CODE. TRY )HELP SEARCH

        "PREVIOUS SEARCH COMPLETE" MEANS THERE IS NO PREVIOUS
             INCOMPLETE SEARCH TO BE CONTINUED.

                  TO LIST THE SEARCH TYPES AND PREFIXES TRY ")HELP SEARCH"
ENTER SEARCH: )HELP SEARCH

        ENTER "AU;"  FOR AUTHOR,            "TI;"   FOR TITLE
              "SB;"  FOR SUBJECT,           "CN;"   FOR CALL NUMBER
              "ST;"  FOR SERIES TITLE,      "WD;"   FOR TITLE OR SUBJECT
              "LC;"  FOR LC CARD NUM.,      "OC;"   FOR OCLC NUMBER
              "IB;"  FOR ISBN NUMBER,       "IS;"   FOR ISSN NUM.
              "AN;"  FOR ACCESSION NUMBER.
        ENTER ONE OR MORE WORDS OF THE TYPE SELECTED.
        PRESS ENTER. YOUR WORDS WILL BE SEARCHED FOR.

        ALSO TRY )HELP AND ONE OF THE ABOVE CODES.

ENTER SEARCH: )HELP SB
```

B

ENTER THE SUBJECT SEARCH CODE "SB;" AND WORD OR
PHRASE DESCRIBING THE SUBJECT YOU ARE INTERESTED IN.

THE ORDER OF THE WORDS IS NOT IMPORTANT BUT TRY NOT
TO USE TOO COMMON A WORD FIRST.

ENTER SEARCH: **)HELP AU**

ENTER THE AUTHOR SEARCH PREFIX "AU;", THE AUTHOR'S
LAST NAME, AND FULL FIRST NAME. THEN PRESS
RETURN.

NOTE: INITIALS ARE NOT SEARCHED FOR.
IF THE AUTHOR IS THE SAME AS THE TITLE THEN ONLY
THE TITLE MAY BE SEARCHED FOR.

ENTER SEARCH: **)HELP TI**

ENTER THE TITLE SEARCH CODE "TI;". ENTER THE MOST
IMPORTANT WORDS FROM THE TITLE. THEY MAY BE IN ANY ORDER
AND PUNCTUATION DOESN'T MATTER. ENTER THE LEAST COMMON
WORD FIRST FOR THE BEST RESULT.

ENTER SEARCH: **)HELP CN**

ENTER THE CALL NUMBER SEARCH PREFIX 'CN;'. TYPE AS MUCH
OF THE CALL NUMBER AS YOU KNOW. INCLUDE ALL PERIODS.
YOU MUST ENTER AT LEAST UP TO THE FIRST PERIOD.

NOTE: VOLUME, COPY, DATE, ETC. INFO. FROM THE END OF CALL
NUMBERS CANNOT BE SEARCHED.

ENTER SEARCH **)HELP WD**

ENTER THE WORD SEARCH PREFIX 'WD;'. THEN ENTER THE WORD(S)
YOU ARE INTERESTED IN. THOSE ITEMS WILL BE FOUND THAT
HAVE THESE WORDS IN EITHER THEIR TITLE OR SUBJECT INFORMATION.

ENTER SEARCH: **SB;ENERGY POLICY + UNITED STATES**

C

SEARCHING "ENERGY"
SEARCHING "POLICY"
SEARCHING "UNITED"
SEARCHING "STATES"
122 ITEMS. PRESS RETURN FOR DISPLAY, OR S AND RETURN FOR NEW SEARCH:

   1. ENERGY COMMUNICATIONS ; NEW YORK, M. DEKKER
      HD9502.A1E534 ; SCI & TECH LIB

   2. UNITED STATES. DEPT. OF ENERGY. OFFICE OF CONSUMER AFFAIRS
      THE ENERGY CONSUMER *
WASHINGTON, D.C, DEPT. OF ENERGY, OFFICE OF CONSUMER AFFAIRS
      UNCAT ; 1ST FLOOR-BIRD

   3. MONITOR (WASHINGTON, D.C.) *
      MONITOR ; WASHINGTON, D.C.?, FEDERAL ENERGY COMMISSION
      UNCAT ; 1ST FLOOR-BIRD

   4. WILSON, KENNETH D
      PROSPECTS FOR GROWTH : CHANGING EXPECTATIONS FOR THE FUTURE
NEW YORK, PRAEGER, 1977
      HD82.P74 C.3 ;

   5. WILSON, KENNETH D
      PROSPECTS FOR GROWTH : CHANGING EXPECTATIONS FOR THE FUTURE
NEW YORK, PRAEGER, 1977
      HD82.P74 C.2 ;

122 ITEMS. PRESS RETURN FOR DISPLAY, OR S AND RETURN FOR NEW SEARCH: **D4**

D

   4. A 015019105 015019105 000000009 LD,MOA 9Z9Z C+I 0 1 0   0 79/267
    1
C HD82.P74 C.3
M.1 WILSON, KENNETH D
T.1 PROSPECTS FOR GROWTH : CHANGING EXPECTATIONS FOR THE FUTURE
I /NEW YORK/PRAEGER/1977
S.1 (PRAEGER SPECIAL STUDIES IN U.S. ECONOMIC, SOCIAL, AND POLITICAL ISSUES)
B ENG
L 77-14567
O 3273803
R DISCHARGED - ON 4/26/82
Y.1 ECONOMIC DEVELOPMENT—SOCIAL ASPECTS—ADDRESSES, ESSAYS, LECTURES
Y.2 NATURAL RESOURCES—ADDRESSES, ESSAYS, LECTURES
Y.3 ENERGY POLICY—SOCIAL ASPECTS—UNITED STATES—ADDRESSES, ESSAYS, LECTURES

122 ITEMS. PRESS RETURN FOR DISPLAY, OR S AND RETURN FOR NEW SEARCH: **D2**

E

2. A 006035724 006035724 000000000 PH,PKA 1G1Q CNI 0   0   1   11879   81/302
      1
C UNCAT
M.1 UNITED STATES. DEPT. OF ENERGY. OFFICE OF CONSUMER AFFAIRS
T.1 THE ENERGY CONSUMER
T.2 CONSUMER BRIEFING SUMMARY
I   /WASHINGTON, D.C./DEPT. OF ENERGY, OFFICE OF CONSUMER AFFAIRS
V.1 APR. 1979-
B ENG
E 000011879   IRV
0 4860055
W ITEM #429-T-5
X.1 SUPERSEDES: CONSUMER BRIEFING SUMMARY
Y.1 ENERGY POLICY—UNITED STATES—PERIODICALS
Y.2 ENERGY CONSUMPTION—UNITED STATES—PERIODICALS
Y.3 ENERGY CONSERVATION—UNITED STATES—PERIODICALS
Y.4 POWER RESOURCES—UNITED STATES—PERIODICALS
Z 0

  122 ITEMS. PRESS RETURN FOR DISPLAY, OR S AND RETURN FOR NEW SEARCH: **S**

F

ENTER SEARCH: **WD; EINSTEIN+ RELATIVITY**
SEARCHING "EINSTEIN"
SEARCHING "RELATIVITY"
  23 ITEMS. PRESS RETURN FOR DISPLAY, OR S AND RETURN FOR NEW SEARCH: **D1**

   1. A 010647212 010647212 008321800 LD,MOA 7P7P WDW D   0   0   0   74/182
         1
C 530.1.L716EA
M.1 LIEBER
T.1 EINSTEIN THEORY OF RELATIVITY
I *S1945
W CC;C.1,2.   WDN

  23 ITEMS. PRESS RETURN FOR DISPLAY, OR S AND RETURN FOR NEW SEARCH:

  2. NITSCHKE, IAN
   INTEGRAL FORMULATION OF EINSTEIN'S EQUATIONS AND MACH'S PRINCIPLE
  SYRACUSE, N.Y, SYRACUSE UNIVERSITY, 1977, C1978
      FILM 300 ; SCI & TECH LIB

  3. NORDMANN, CHARLES *
   THE TYRANNY OF TIME, EINSTEIN OR BERGSON? *
  NEW YORK, INTERNATIONAL PUB, 1925
      115.N83T ; 3RD FLOOR-BIRD

  4. CASSIRER, ERNST, 1874-1945 *
   SUBSTANCE AND FUNCTION, AND EINSTEIN'S THEORY OF RELATIVITY *
  CHICAGO, THE OPEN COURT PUBLISHING COMPANY, 1923
      BD221.C285 C.2 ; 3RD FLOOR-BIRD

  5. MEDRA, JAGDISH
   EINSTEIN, HILBERT, AND THE THEORY OF GRAVITATION
  HISTORICAL ORIGINS OF GENERAL RELATIVITY THEORY ; DORDRECHT, REIDEL, 1974
      QC178.M4 ; PHYSICS

G

23 ITEMS. PRESS RETURN FOR DISPLAY, OR S AND RETURN FOR NEW SEARCH: **D5**
   5. A 032112761 032112761 032112761 TD,MBA 7P7P CNI   0   0   40132 75/182
      1
C   QC178.M4
M.1 MEDRA, JAGDISH
T.1 EINSTEIN, HILBERT, AND THE THEORY OF GRAVITATION
    HISTORICAL ORIGINS OF GENERAL RELATIVITY THEORY
I /DORDRECHT/REIDEL/1974
N 9027704406
P 90-277-0440-6

23 ITEMS. PRESS RETURN FOR DISPLAY, OR S AND RETURN FOR NEW SEARCH:

who are unfamiliar with the catalog and who do not want to learn the command language (see Figure 7, pages 35–41, for sample MELVYL screens).

In Command Mode, the user can take full advantage of MELVYL's capabilities. A search, based on commands entered by the user, may be conducted using an author name (personal or corporate), a title, a series name, or a subject. Exact entries are not required. MELVYL will respond to all keywords that are entered regardless of their order. Searches may be limited or expanded in a variety of ways. Truncation, Boolean searches, and limiting by date are all available. Library staff prepared a brochure explaining use of the online catalog and MELVYL provides an extensive set of HELP screens.

University of Texas, Austin

The University of Texas, Austin Libraries serve about 66,000 students, faculty, and staff. The UT, Austin Libraries hold about 4,700,000 bound volumes and maintain some 60,000 periodical subscriptions.

The library is in the process of developing its own in-house automated library system. During the study, the library made a total of three OCLC terminals available for public use in two university libraries. The library has about 750,000 records in machine-readable form in the OCLC database. Sample screens illustrating the search process using the OCLC system may be found in Figure 8 (see Figure 8, pages 42–45). The patron must enter the appropriate search-key when conducting a search by author, title, author/title combination, etc. Name authority information is available but a separate file must be accessed. Subject searching is not available.

OTHER ACADEMIC LIBRARIES

Claremont Colleges Libraries

The Claremont Colleges Libraries serve about 12,000 registered borrowers from the independent Claremont Colleges, located in Southern California. The Claremont Online Public Access Catalog is a part of an automated library system called the Total Library System, which was developed by the Claremont Colleges library staff, now being marketed in a modified form by OCLC. The Total Library System runs on a Hewlett Packard 3000 Series II minicomputer. The

FIGURE 7   Sample Screens for the University of California

In response to the initial screen the user selects the Command Mode or asks for help (screen A); after reading the help screen the user then enters a subject for "online" (screen B); the user then modifies the search request by adding another subject "catalog #" (the # is an explicit Truncation Symbol) and requests to see only records at the Berkeley campus (screen C); the request is again modified by date and then a record is displayed (screen D). The user then requests a full MARC display which is shown in screens E and F. Returning to the initial screen the user selects the Lookup Mode (screen G); selects records from all northern campuses (screen H); wants to search by subject (screen I); enters "online catalog," retrieves 2 records and requests a longer display of a record (screen J); which is shown in screen K and L.

A

```
                       WELCOME TO MELVYL

             The University of California's Prototype On-Line Catalog

   MELVYL contains 733,412 records representing approximately 1.3 million books
   in the University of California libraries.

        * * * * * * * * * * * * * * * * * * * * * * * * * * * * * * * * * * * * * * * * * * * *
        *       This is NOT a complete record of books in the UC libraries.      *
        *CHECK your local catalog if you don't find what you need in MELVYL.*
        * * * * * * * * * * * * * * * * * * * * * * * * * * * * * * * * * * * * * * * * * * * *



   _____
   * *Type the number of the search mode you want, then press RETURN.
     Or, for more information, type HELP and press RETURN.

     1. LOOKUP mode     (for new or occasional users)
     2. COMMAND mode  (for users familiar with COMMAND language)

  ─>2

     Welcome to Command Mode. You may now begin typing commands.
     For a brief review of the commands, type HELP and press RETURN.

  ─>help
```

B

To search for books in the catalog, type FIND, followed by the index you wish
to search, followed by the keywords you want to search in that index. To
search more than one index, continue your search request with a conjunction
(AND, OR, or AND NOT), another index name, and more keywords. The index names
you may use are:

PA (personal author)   UT (uniform title)
CA (corporate author)   SE (series name)
TI (title)   SU (subject)

After you have retrieved some records, you may display them by typing DISPLAY,
followed by the record numbers you want to see, followed by the format in
which you want to see them.

The following are all valid search and display commands:

FIND PA JAMES BALDWIN AND TI DEVIL   DISPLAY
FIND PA WILLIAM SHAKESPEARE   DISPLAY ALL BRIEF
FIND SU ATOMIC ENERGY   DISPLAY 1-14 REVIEW

For more detailed instructions, type:
HELP HELP   HELP FIND   HELP DISPLAY

⇒ **find su online**

C

Search request: FIND SU ONLINE
Search result: 114 records at UC libraries

⇒ **and su catalog#**

LONG SEARCH: type YES and press RETURN to continue search [7]
                  type NO and press RETURN to cancel search
                  or type a new search command

⇒ **yes**

.....[6] more cycles until completion. To cancel search, press BREAK.

.....[5] more cycles until completion. To cancel search, press BREAK.

.....[4] more cycles until completion. To cancel search, press BREAK.

.....[3] more cycles until completion. To cancel search, press BREAK.

.....[2] more cycles until completion. To cancel search, press BREAK.

.....[1] more cycle until completion. To cancel search, press BREAK.

Search request: FIND SU ONLINE AND SU CATALOG#
Search result: 9 records at UC libraries

⇒ **at ucb**

D

Search request: FIND SU ONLINE AND SU CATALOG#
Search result: 5 records at Berkeley
                 9 records at UC libraries

⟶ and date 1980-

Search request: FIND SU ONLINE AND SU CATALOG# AND DATE 1980-
Search result: 1 record at Berkeley
                 1 record at UC libraries

1. Juergens, Bonnie.
     Self-instructional introduction to the OCLC Models 100 and 105 terminals
     / by Bonnie Juergens ; revised by Michelle Duffy. Rev. ed..
     Dallas, Tex. : AMIGOS Bibliographic Council, inc., c1980.
        UCB LibSchLib Z699.4.042 J83 1980

⟶ display marc

E

Search request: FIND SU ONLINE AND SU CATALOG# AND DATE 1980-
Search result: 1 record at Berkeley
                 1 record at UC libraries

1. U01621159	STA c	REC am	ENC	DCF i	CSC d	ENT	
INT	INX 0	GOV	FSC 0	BIO	CTY txu	CON	ILS
REP	MEI 1	CNF 0	FIC 0	MOD	LAN eng	PD s1980	

035      $# 0001 $a BER $e RL18253440 $q 65043157 $z 810411<BER-G>
040   IaU $c IaU<BER-G>
090      $# 0001 $a Z699.4.042 $b J83 1980 $e BER $f CU-LSL $g LibSchLib $z LSL
         <BER-G>
100 10   Juergens, Bonnie.<BER-G>
245 10   Self-instructional introduction to the OCLC Models 100 and 105
         terminals / $c by Bonnie Juergens ; revised by Michelle Duffy.<BER-G>
250   __Rev. ed.__.<BER-G>
260 0   Dallas, Tex. : $b AMIGOS Bibliographic Council, inc., $c c1980.
         <BER-G>
300   iv, 40 p. ; $c 28 cm.<BER-G>
490 1   Amigos training series ; no. 1<BER-G>
610 20   OCLC, inc.<BER-G>
650 0   Cataloging $x Data processing.<BER-G>
                              (Record 1 continues on the next screen.)

Press RETURN (or type NS) to see the next screen.
⟶ ns

F

Search request: FIND SU ONLINE AND SU CATALOG# AND DATE 1980-
Search result: 1 record at Berkeley
                 1 record at UC libraries

1. (continued)
650 0   Computer input-output equipment.<BER-G>
650 0   On-line data processing.<BER-G>
700 10   Duffy, Michelle.<BER-G>
810 2   Amigos Bibliographic Council. $t Amigos training series ; $v no. 1.
                <BER-G>
910             $# 0001 $a 09/08/80 $d 09/15/80<BER-G>
952   cam i<BER-G>

There are no more records to display. Type PS to see the previous screen.

⟶**end**

G

WELCOME TO MELVYL

The University of California's Prototype On-Line Catalog

MELVYL contains 733,412 records representing approximately 1.3 million books
in the University of California libraries.

```
************************************************************
*      This is NOT a complete record of books in the UC libraries.      *
*CHECK your local catalog if you don't find what you need in MELVYL.*
************************************************************
```

_____

**Type the number of the search mode you want, then press RETURN.
  Or, for more information, type HELP and press RETURN.

  1. LOOKUP mode   (for new or occasional users)
  2. COMMAND mode   (for users familiar with COMMAND language)

⟶**1**

H

Welcome to Lookup Mode.

You can search for books at any one of the following campuses or groups of libraries. Select one of the following, and type its code.

UCD	(Davis)	UCSF	(San Francisco)	UCLA	(Los Angeles)
UCI	(Irvine)	UCB	(Berkeley)	UCSD	(San Diego)
UCR	(Riverside)	UCSC	(Santa Cruz)	UCSB	(Santa Barbara)

UC	(all UC libraries)
HAS	(Hastings law library)
CLU	(San Diego Cluster library)
LBL	(Lawrence Berkeley Laboratory)
LAW	(all UC law libraries)
MED	(all UC medical libraries)
NOR	(all northern campuses: UCB,UCD,UCSF,UCSC,HASTINGS)
SOU	(all southern campuses: UCLA, UCSB, UCI, UCR, UCSD)

_____

Type the code for the libraries you want to search, or type HELP, then
press RETURN:

—>**nor**

I

You may search for books in one of two ways:

    by AUTHOR and/or TITLE
    or by SUBJECT.

_____

Type the number you want below or type HELP, then press RETURN.
    1. AUTHOR/TITLE search.
    2. SUBJECT search.

—>**2**

J

Type SUBJECT words below or type HELP, then press RETURN.

⟶**online catalog**

Your search for: subject words ONLINE CATALOG
        retrieved: 2 books from Northern campuses.

1. Griffith, Jeffrey C. THE USE OF A MICROFICHE CATALOG FOR PUBLIC. . . 1976
2. University of California (System). Division of Library Automation.
        UNIVERSITY OF CALIFORNIA PROTOTYPE ON-LINE CATALOG : A PROSPECTUS. 1980

_____

Type the number you want below or type HELP, then press RETURN.
1. See some of these records in a BRIEF display. 4. Begin new subject search.
2. See some of these records in a LONG display. 5. End the session.
3. Begin new author/title search.
⟶**2**

K

Type the numbers of the records you want to see in LONG format, or type HELP,
then press RETURN. To see current REVIEW screen again, simply press RETURN.
⟶**1**

Your search for: subject words ONLINE CATALOG
        retrieved: 2 books from Northern campuses.

1.
Author: Griffith, Jeffrey C.
Title: The use of a microfiche catalog for public sevice and on-line
                           retrieval of bibliographic data / J. C. Griffith, R. M. Hayes.
                       [Los Angeles] : Graduate School of Library and Information
                           Science, UCLA ; Arlington, Va. : Prepared by ERIC Document
                           Reproduction Service, 1976.
                       74 leaves ; 28 cm.
Series: ERIC reports

Notes: Author's name in ''document resume'': Griffith, C. C.
                       Bibliography: leaves 24-35.
                                        (Record 1 continues on the next screen.)
_____

Type the number you want below or type HELP, then press RETURN.
1. See next screen of this display.   4. Begin new author/title search.
2. See other records in LONG format.   5. Begin new subject search.
3. See the review display again.   6. End the session.
⟶**1**

L

Your search for: subject words ONLINE CATALOG
      retrieved: 2 books from Northern campuses.

1. (continued)
Subjects: California. University. Libraries.
                         Library catalogs on microfilm.
                         Catalogs, Union — California.
                         On-line data processing.
                         CARD (Microfiche reader)

Other entries: Hayes, Robert Mayo, 1926–, joint author.

Call numbers: UCB LibSchLib Z699.3.G75 (CU-LSL)

—————————————————————————————————————

Type the number you want below or type HELP, then press RETURN.
1. See next screen of this display.
2. See previous screen of this display.
3. See different records in LONG format.
4. See the review display again.
   —>**end**

5. Begin new author/title search.
6. Begin new subject search.
7. End the session.

FIGURE 8   Sample Screens for OCLC Online Computer Library Center

The user enters the appropriate search key for name/title search. The user was looking for a work by "Bell" with "Dictionary" in the title. The system displays ten matching records and the user selects number 1 (screen A). The system displays a brief record for two matching records and the user selects number 2 (screen B). The system then displays the full MARC record. The user now conducts a new search for works by "Robert E. Bell" — note the search key entered by the user. The system displays ten matching records and the user selects number 3 (screen D). The system then displays a brief record for nine records and the user selects number 2 (screen E). The system then displays a full MARC record (screen F).

A

> **bell,dict**
To see title for a COLLECTIVE ENTRY, type line#, DEPRESS DISPLAY RECD, SEND.

```
  1   BELL   (2)
  2   Bell, Sydney Smith, Sir,    Dictionary of the decisions of the Court of
Session, from November 1808, to November 1833.    Edinburgh,    1842
  3   BELL WILLIAM    (2)
  4   BELLAMY JOYCE M    DICTIONARY OF LABOUR BIOGRAPHY (3)
  5   BELLEISLE J G GERALD    DICTIONNAIRE TECHNIQUE GENERAL ANGLAISFRANCAIS (3)
  6   BELLEN (2)
  7   BELLEW HENRY WALTER    DICTIONARY OF THE PUKKHTO OR PUKSHTO LANGUAGE IN
WHICH THE WORDS ARE TRACED TO THEIR SOURCES IN THE INDIAN AND PERSIAN LANGUAGES
(2)
  8   BELLIER DE LA CHAVIGNERIE EMILE    DICTIONNAIRE GENERAL DES ARTISTES DE
LECOLE FRANCAISE DEPUIS LORIGINE DES ARTS DU DESSIN JUSQU (4)
  9   Bellour, Raymond,     Dictionnaire du cinbema.    1966
 10   BELLOWS   (18)
```

> 1

B

    1   Bell, G. J.   A dictionary and digest of the law of Scotland /
Edinburgh,
    2   Bell, Robert E.   Dictionary of classical mythology, symbols, attributes,
& associations / Oxford, England ; Santa Barbara, CA :   1982 DLC

   > 2

C

NO HOLDINGS IN CUV — FOR HOLDINGS ENTER dh DEPRESS   DISPLAY RECD SEND
OCLC: 7977116   Rec stat: p Entrd: 811030   Used: 830318
Type: a Bib lvl: m Govt pub: Lang: eng   Source: Illus:
Repr: Enc lvl: Conf pub: 0 Ctry: enk Dat tp: s M/F/B: 10

Indx: 1 Mod rec: Festschr: 0 Cont: d

Desc: a Int lvl: Dates: 1982,

    1 010   81-19141
    2 040   DLC c DLC
    3 020   0874363055 : c $29.95
    4 020   0874360234 (pbk.)
    5 039 0   2 b 3 c 3 d 3 e 3
    6 043   e— — — — — — a ff— — — — — a aw— — — — —
    7 050 0   BL715 b .B44 1982
    8 082 0   292/.13/0321 2 19
    9 049   CUVA
  10 100 10   Bell, Robert E.
  11 245 10   Dictionary of classical mythology, symbols, attributes, &
associations / c by Robert E. Bell ; illustrations by John Schlesinger.
  12 260 0   Oxford, England ; a Santa Barbara, CA : b ABC-Clio, c c1982.
  13 300   xi, 390 p. ; c 26 cm.
  14 500   Includes index.

Screen 2 of 2
  15   650 0   Mythology, Classical x Dictionaries.

D

bell,rob,e
To see title for a COLLECTIVE ENTRY, type line#, DEPRESS DISPLAY RECD, SEND.

  1   BELL ROBERT E   B (2)
  2   Bell, Robert E.   Dictionary of classical mythology, symbols, attributes,
& associations / Oxford, England ; Santa Barbara, CA :   1982 DLC
  3   Bell, Robert E.,   Education in Great Britain and Ireland; a source book,
London, Boston,   1973 DLC
  4   Bell, Robert E.,   A mythology of British education   St. Albans,   1974
DLC
  5   Bell, Robert E.,   Patterns of education in the British Isles / London
; Boston :   1977 DLC
  6   Bell, Robert E.   The role of predispositions in newswriters' reports; a
re-examination of the "Gatekeeper" process.   1959
  7   Bell, Robert E.   Safety factors in highway design.   [Salt Lake City]
1947
  8   BELL ROBERT EUGENE   (16)
  9   Bellamy, Robert E.   Pulmonary infiltrates with eosinophilia [syndrome]
1975 [Videorecording]
  10   Bellet, Robert E.   Clinical trials : design and analysis / New York :
1981

> 8

E

  1   Bell, Robert Eugene.   Career education and its implications for
industrial arts. [Chico, Calif.] 1973
  2   Bell, Robert Eugene,   Chronology in the middle Mississippi Valley /
Chicago :   1947 [Microform]
  3   Bell, Robert Eugene,   The first[-second] annual report[s] of Caddoan
archaeology, Spiro focus research.   Norman,   1964
  4   Bell, Robert Eugene,   Guide to the identification of certain American
Indian projectile points.   [Norman]   1958
  5   Bell, Robert Eugene,   The Harlan site, Ck-6, a prehistoric mound center
in Cherokee County, Eastern Oklahoma   [Norman?]   1972 DLC
  6   Bell, Robert Eugene,   History of the Grabhorn Press /   [s.1. :   1974
  7   Bell, Robert Eugene.   Investigaciones arqueolbogicas en el sitio de El
Inga, Ecuador,   Quito   1965 DLC
  8   Bell, Robert Eugene,   Lithic analysis as a method in archaelogy /
1976
  9   Bell, Robert Eugene,   Oklahoma archaeology; an annotated bibliography,
Norman,   1969 DLC

> 2

F

OCLC: 3299176   Rec stat: n Entrd: 770927   Used: 800911

Type: h Bib lvl: m Govt pub: Lang: eng Source: d Illus:

Repr: Enc lvl: I Conf pub: 0 Ctry: ilu Dat tp: s M/F/B: 10

Indx: 0 Mod rec: Festschr: 0 Cont:

Desc: i Int lvl: Dates: 1947,

1	010	
2	040	IQU c IQU
3	090	E78.M75 b B4x
4	049	CUVA
5	100 10	Bell, Robert Eugene, d 1914–
6	245 10	Chronology in the middle Mississippi Valley / c by Robert E. Bell.
7	260 0	Chicago : b University of Chicago, c 1947.
8	300	112 leaves : b ill., maps
9	502	Thesis—University of Chicago.
10	504	Bibliography: leaves 111–112.
11	500	Microfilm. Chicago : University of Chicago Library, [1947?] —1 reel ; 35 mm.
12	651 0	Mississippi Valley x Antiquities.
13	650 0	Dendrochronology z Mississippi Valley.

application programming languages are COBOL and SPL. Currently only the science libraries at Claremont have online public access catalog terminals. There are a total of eight terminals, three of which are in the Joint Science Library and one each in five branch science libraries.

The Total Library System allows the patron to gain access to both the online catalog and circulation system. At present, the online catalog does not provide access to the acquisitions database. Author, title, series, subject heading, and call number searches are possible. Figure 9 provides sample screens of the Claremont system (see Figure 9, pages 47–50). Currently there are about 69,000 records reflecting science library holdings in the Total Library System database.

Minnesota State University
Online Union Catalog

The Mankato State University Library is located about 60 miles south of Minneapolis, Minnesota. Mankato State University has about 15,000 registered library patrons and 311,000 items in its total collection, housed in a four-floor library facility. Of these, approximately 232,000 titles, including almost all of the monographs, have been converted to machine-readable form and thus are available in the online catalog.

The Minnesota State Universities Systems Project for Automation of Library Systems (MSUS/PALS) began in 1978 with plans to develop a Minnesota State University System-wide Online Union Catalog. The online catalog was developed at Mankato State University by library staff and in 1980 the online catalog capabilities were demonstrated in a prototype system. By September 1980, a full database composed of OCLC records from participating member libraries was loaded into the computer system and made available for use by library patrons. In the spring of 1982, a total of 93 terminals in six state university libraries were operational and 22 terminals were available to library patrons at Mankato State.

The online catalog software runs on a UNIVAC 1100 model 80A, a mainframe computer shared with other academic applications (e.g., programs submitted by students and faculty). Currently the bibliographic database contains approximately 640,000 unique titles reflecting 1,226,000 "location holding symbols." The 232,000 records of Mankato State are included in this larger database. The system is available 105 hours per week and the online catalog backup is a microfiche catalog produced once a year. The online catalog can be

Figure 9   Sample Screens for the Claremont Colleges System

In response to the initial screen the user enters "H" for help (screen A); the user then enters "S" for a subject search and searches using the word "Geology" (screen B)—note that the "@" character will display the bibliographic record and a "c" will retrieve the circultation status of the item; the user then conducts a call number search (screen C); an author search (screen D); and a "/" will clear the screen and display the original screen (screen E).

A

```
                    O N L I N E  C A T A L O G  S E A R C H
          ENTER CODE LETTER;D FOR CODE LIST; H FOR HELP;E TO END:
                  [USER ENTERS "D" REQUESTING A CODE LIST.]

          CODE—BASIC WAYS TO SEARCH
             C      LOOKUP BY CALL NUMBER
             A      LOOKUP BY AUTHOR, ADDED ENTRY (EDITOR, ETC.)
             T      LOOKUP BY TITLE
             S      LOOKUP BY SUBJECT
             Y      LOOKUP BY SERIES (PUT "(" BEFORE ENTRY WORD)
                    ADDED WAYS TO SEARCH
             P      PARTIAL CALL NUMBER (5 CHAR.CODE & AS MUCH OF CALL AS KNOWN)
             L      COMPLETE CALL NUMBER SEARCH (NEED 5 CHARACTER LOCATION CODE)
             R      SUBJECT SEARCH RESTRICTED BY DATE OF ACQUISITION
                    (POSSIBLE USE: LISTING NEW BOOKS IN A GIVEN SUBJECT AREA)
             E      SUBJECT SEARCH USED IN COMBINATION WITH AUTHOR AND/OR TITLE
                    WORDS OR PHRASES (LEADING OR EMBEDDED). SEE HELP #5

      NOTE:    *USE "/" (SLASH) TO STOP CURRENT SEARCH MODE SO THAT A NEW
                OPTION MAY BE ENTERED.
               *USE "@" TO OBTAIN A FULL DISPLAY OF THE RECORD LAST SHOWN.
               *USE "J" FOLLOWED BY ONE NUMERAL TO JUMP FORWARD IN TH FILE
                BY 1 TO 9 ENTRIES.
               *USE "K" FOLLOWED BY ONE NUMBERAL TO JUMP BACKWARD IN THE FILE
                BY 1 TO 9 ENTRIES.
               *USE "C" TO DISPLAY CIRCULATION DATA ABOUT THE ENTRY JUST
                DISPLAYED ABOVE.
               *USE "SPACE BAR" TO SEE NEXT ITEM.
            ***FOR "FAST SCANNING" RECORDS COLLECTED WITH THE "C,A,T,Y,OR S
                CODES, INSERT "F" (FAST FORWARD) OR "R" (FAST REVERSE) IN 2ND
                CHARACTER POSITION. EXAMPLE: "TF" FOR TITLE SEARCH(SEE HELP7)
              **USE "X" TO EXIT "FAST SCAN" AT END OF GROUP DISPLAY
```

B

/
ENTER CODE LETTER;D FOR CODE LIST;H FOR HELP:**S**
ENTER SUBJECT (3 CHARACTERS OR MORE OF THE ENTRY) :

_____

GEOLOGY
GEOLOGY
      GEOLOGY   550   A37
AGER , DEREK VICTOR.
INTRODUCING GEOLOGY :/THE EARTH'S CRUST CONSIDERED AS

GEOLOGY
      GEOLOGY   557.94   AN23S
ANDERSON , FRANK MARION.
A STRATIGRAPHIC STUDY IN THE MOUNT DIABLO RANGE OF CALI

@
ANDERSON , FRANK MARION./A STRATIGRAPHIC STUDY IN THE MOUNT DIABLO RAN
GE OF CALIFORNIA . . ./ <SAN FRANCISCO, CALIF., ACADEMY OF SCIENCES, 1905
. > 155–247 P. 35 PLATES (PART. COL.) 26 CM./# GEOLOGY./# GEOLOGY— CAL
IFORNIA./# MT. DIABLO RANGE (CALIFORNIA)—GEOLOGY./

C
*** CIRCULATION DATA ***

####	VOL/COPY	BARCODE	HANDLING	BORROWER DUE	DATE & TIME	HOLDS
0001		0611853				

GEOLOGY
      GEOLOGY   550.09   AU19
AUBUISSON DE VOISINS , JEAN FR
TRAITE DE GEOGNOSIE,OU EXPOSE DES CONNAISSANCES ACTU

C

/
ENTER CODE LETTER;D FOR CODE LIST;H FOR HELP:**C**
ENTER SHORT CLASS NUMBER BELOW PATTERN
MUST HAVE AT LEAST 1 CHARACTER IN 3RD TO 6TH SPACES
EXAMPLES: (Q   1) OR (575   )
SS++++.++ C9
QA   5
MATHEM.   QA   5   A54   A: T: A/T:
AMERICAN MATHEMATICAL SOCIETY.
RUSSIAN-ENGLISH VOCABULARY,/WITH A GRAMMATICAL SKETCH

SPRAGUE   QA   5   B921   A: T: A/T:
BURLAK , J
RUSSIAN-ENGLISH MATHEMATICAL VOCABULARY,/BY J. BURLAK

@
BURLAK , J/RUSSIAN-ENGLISH MATHEMATICAL VOCABULARY,/BY J. BURLAK. WIT
H A SHORT GRAMMATICAL SKETCH BY K. BROOKE. ＜EDINBURGH, OLIVER AND BOYD
; NEW YORK INTERSCIENCE PUBLISHERS, 1963.＞305 P. 19 CM./(UNIVERSITY M
ATHEMATICAL TEXTS)/& BROOKE , KENNETH/#   MATHEMATICS—DICTIONARIES—RUS
SIAN/#   RUSSIAN LANGUAGE—DICTIONARIES—ENGLISH/

C
*** CIRCULATION DATA ***
VOL/COPY   BARCODE   HANDLING   BORROWER DUE   DATE & TIME   HOLDS
0001   0636107

D

/
ENTER CODE LETTER;D FOR CODE LIST;H FOR HELP:**A**
ENTER AUTHOR (AS MUCH AS KNOWN) AT LEAST 3 CHARACTERS.
INCLUDE COMMAS, SPACES, PERIODS ONLY IF PRESENT IN THE
RECORD; LAST NAME FIRST (EXAMPLE: HENLE, JAMES M)

DARWIN

| | PHYSICS | QC 171 | D259 | / |

DARWIN , CHARLES GALTON, 1887–
THE NEW CONCEPTIONS OF MATTER,/BY C. G. DARWIN.<LONDON,

| ` SPRAGUE | QC 171 | D259 |
DARWIN , CHARLES GALTON, SIR,
THE NEW CONCEPTIONS OF MATTER,/BY CHARLES G. DARWIN.<LO

| | GEOLOGY | 575.009 | D259 |
DARWIN , CHARLES R.
DARWIN AND HENSLOW, THE GROWTH OF AN IDEA. LETTERS 18

@
DARWIN , CHARLES R./DARWIN AND HENSLOW, THE GROWTH OF AN IDEA. LETTERS
1831–1860./ED. BY NORA BARLOW FOR THE BENTHAM-MOXON TRUST. BERKELEY,
UNIV. OF CALIF. PR., 1967. 251 P./HENSLOW , JOHN S. /& BARLOW , NORA (
D.) ED./& BENTHAM-MOXOM TRUST./# NATURALISTS—CORRESPONDENCE, REMINISC
ENCES, ETC./# BEAGLE EXPEDITION, 1831–1836./

C
*** CIRCULATION DATA ***

####	VOL/COPY	BARCODE	HANDLING	BORROWER DUE	DATE & TIME	HOLDS
0001		0612693				

| | GEOLOGY | 570.8 | D259 D4 |
DARWIN , CHARLES R.
THE DESCENT OF MAN, AND SELECTION IN RELATION TO SEX./WI

E

/
ENTER CODE LETTER;D FOR CODE LIST;H FOR HELP:

searched using author, title, combined author and title, subject headings, and descriptive terms or keywords from either the title, corporate author, or subject headings. A mnemonic command language is used by the library patron for searching. Search results can be modified or limited by publication date, by language, by type of material, and by library location. The system also allows the library patron to broaden or narrow a search using explicit or implied Boolean operators. Figure 10 illustrates the search and display capabilities of the Minnesota State University system (see Figure 10, pages 52–54).

Mankato State library staff members have produced a one-page handout sheet which provides basic directions to the library catalog access system as well as a multiple-page booklet explaining how to use the online catalog. A summary command guide is affixed to the front of the terminal next to the CRT screen.

Ohio University, Athens

The Vernon R. Alden Library at Ohio University, located in Athens, Ohio, serves about 20,000 students and 1,000 faculty and staff. Library patrons may use one OCLC terminal which is available for public use. The patron must enter the appropriate OCLC search key when conducting a search by author, title, author/title combination, etc. Subject searching is not available. Name authority information is available but a separate file must be accessed. Figure 8 illustrates the search process with some sample screens using the OCLC system.

Stephen F. Austin State University Library

The Steen Library at the Stephen F. Austin State University in Nacogdoches, Texas is an open stack library housed in a four-floor building containing approximately 750,000 volumes in all formats. The library serves a community of about 11,000 students and 450 faculty members and the general public in the surrounding community. The library contracted with DataPhase Systems Inc. to install a turnkey automated circulation system. The library decided to use the existing inquiry function of the automated circulation system, without modification, to place terminals in the library and allow patrons to gain access to the library's machine-readable database. Thus users were not using a true online catalog in terms of a system that was designed with a user-cordial interface. The Stephen F. Austin State University began to use the DataPhase Systems Inc. circulation system as a public access catalog in January 1980.

FIGURE 10   Sample Screens for the Minnesota State University
Online Union Catalog

The user enters an author search for "Haley, Alex" (screen A); the retrieved records are
displayed (screen B); the user asks for a full display of record number "9" (screen C); and
a full MARC display of the same record (screen D); the user then enters and saves two
separate term or keyword searches. These two saved sets are then combined using a
Boolean logic "AND" (screen E); and the resulting 17 records are then displayed (screen F).

A

>**AU HALEY ALEX**
  11 RECORDS MATCHED THE SEARCH
TYPE DI 1-11 TO DISPLAY THE RECORDS
>**DI**

B

Screen 001 of 001

NMBR	DATE	—————————TITLE—————————	—AUTHOR——
0001	1966	The autobiography of Malcolm X.	X, Malcolm,
0002	1965	The autobiography of Malcolm X.	Malcolm X,
0003	1966	The autobiography of Malcolm X.	Malcolm X,
0004	1966	The autobiography of Malcolm X.	Malcolm X,
0005	1980	The autobiography of Malcolm X /	Malcolm X,
0006	1965	The autobiography of Malcolm X /	Malcolm X,
0007	1978	The inside story of TV's "Roots" /	Wolper, David L.
0008	1977	Public education: more than survival.	National Education A
0009	1976	Roots /	Haley, Alex.
0010	1975	Roots in Africa.	
0011	1977	Roots /	Haley, Alex.

——— Type DI NMBR(s) to display specific records
>**DI MSU 9**

C

```
LOCTN:  E185.97.H24   A33
AUTHR:  Haley, Alex.
TITLE:  Roots / Alex Haley.
EDITN:  1st ed.
PUBLR:  Garden City, N.Y. : Doubleday, 1976.
DESCR:  viii, 688 p. ; 22 cm.
NOTES:  ''A condensed version of a portion of this work first appeared in
            Reader's digest''
SUBJT:  Kinte family.
SUBJT:  Haley family.
SUBJT:  Haley, Alex.
SUBJT:  Blacks—history
OCLC#   02188350
>DI MSU 9 T
```

D

```
IDL 02188350 MNM 810724 MST 0639
LDR          00639cam  2200145  i  45  0
001          oc172188350
008          760420s1976      nyu             00010ceng
010          72076164
020          0385037872 : #c $12.50
040          DLC  #c  DLC  #d  GXM  #d  MNM
043          n — us — — — #a f — gm — — —
049          MNMA
050     0    E185.97.H24   #b   A33
082          929/.2/0973
096          E   185.97   H168r   1976
100    10    Haley, Alex.
245    10    Roots / #c   Alex Haley.
250          1st ed.
260     0    Garden City, N.Y.  :  #b  Doubleday,  #c  1976.
300          viii,  688  p.  ;  #c  22  cm.
500          ''A condensed version of a portion of this work first appeared in
                Reader's digest.''
600    30    Kinte family.
600    30    Haley family.
600    10    Haley, Alex.
>NS
```

```
650     2 Blacks  #x   history
```

E

```
>TE SENIOR AND CITIZEN OR AGED OR ELDERLY
   147 RECORD MATCHES AFTER TERM SENIOR
     5 RECORD MATCHES AFTER TERM CITIZEN
   633 RECORD MATCHES AFTER TERM AGED
   658 RECORDS MATCHED THE SEARCH
TYPE DI 1-20 TO DISPLAY FIRST 20 RECORDS          (or)
Use AND command with additional WORD(s) or LIMITING command to reduce results
>SA
WORK AREA SAVED IN SET 1
>TE FOOD AND HABIT? OR NUTRITION??
  1500 RECORD MATCHES AFTER TERM FOOD
    55 RECORD MATCHES AFTER TERM HABIT?
   695 RECORDS MATCHED THE SEARCH
TYPE DI 1-20 TO DISPLAY FIRST 20 RECORDS          (or)
Use AND command with additional WORD(s) or LIMITING command to reduce results
>SA
WORK AREA SAVED IN SET 2
>BO 1 AND 2
   658 RECORD MATCHES AFTER SET   1
    17 RECORDS MATCHED THE SEARCH
TYPE DI 1-17 TO DISPLAY THE RECORDS
>DI
```

F

```
    Screen 001 of 001
   NMBR    DATE    —————————TITLE—————————— AUTHOR——
   0001    1979    Back to basics : food and shelter for the el   Southern Conference
   0002    1978    Caloric selected nutrient values of persons a
   0003    1975    The cookbook that tells you how : the retire   Zaccarelli, Herman E
   0004    1967    A cookbook for the leisure years, with divid   MacDonald, Phyllis.
   0005    1977    Establishing a national meals-on-wheels progr  United States. Cong
   0006    1974    Food guide for older folks.                    United States. Agri
   0007    1961    The golden age cookbook.                       MacDonald, Phyllis
   0008    1976    Help yourself to better health.
   0009    1980    Leisure preferences of the elderly in Bowling  Prochazka, Lawrence
   0010    1980    Minnesota Valley Action Council's Senior Dinn  Chompaisal, Chananet
   0011    1976    Nutrition, longevity, and aging :   proceeding Symposium on Nutriti
   0012    1978    Nutrition and the later years /                Weg, Ruth B.
   0013    1979    Nutrition and the elderly : policy developme   Posner, Barbara Mill
   0014    1979    Nutrition and aging : a bibliographic survey   Metress, Seamus P.
   0015    1981    Nutrition and the elderly : January 1977 thr   Kenton, Charlotte.
   0016    1981    Nutrition problems of the elderly : hearing    United States. Cong
   0017    1980    A process model for developing educational pr  Richie, Mary L.
   ————— Type DI (NMBR(s) to display specific records
```

The DataPhase system utilizes a Data General Eclipse S/130 minicomputer with a programming language called MIIS, a proprietary version of ANSI standard MUMPS. A total of 19 terminals are attached directly to the computer system of which 10 are public access online catalog terminals. The system is a combination online catalog and circulation system.

The user has access to approximately 100,000 records in the database using author, title, subject headings, and call number searches. Figure 11 illustrates the search process with some sample screens (see Figure 11, pages 56–58). Library staff developed a one-page handout explaining how to use the online catalog terminals.

University of Akron

The Bierce Library at the University of Akron, a private institution, is located in Akron, Ohio. The Library serves about 30,000 students, faculty, and staff.

The Library provided a total of three OCLC terminals for direct patron use in two university libraries. These terminals complement the library's existing card catalog. The library has about 500,000 records in the OCLC database. The user can search by author, title, author/title combination, etc., entering the appropriate OCLC search-key. Name authority information is available but a separate file must be accessed. Figure 8 provides sample OCLC search screens.

University of Texas, Dallas

The University of Texas at Dallas serves some 8,500 faculty and students. The library provided two OCLC terminals for public use in the university library. Figure 8 illustrates the search process using the OCLC system. The user must enter the OCLC search-key to search the database by author, title, author/title combination, etc. Name authority information is available but a separate file must be accessed. The OCLC terminals complement the library's existing catalog.

COMMUNITY COLLEGE LIBRARIES

West Valley Joint Community College District

The West Valley Joint Community College District is located in Santa Clara County, California and is composed of two community

FIGURE 11   Sample Screens for the Stephen F. Austin State University System

The Inquiry screen is normally displayed at the beginning of a search and the user enters "S" for a subject search and the phrase "Library Automation" (screen A); the search has retrieved 4 subject headings and the user selects number "1" (screen B); there are five records with this subject heading and brief records for the first two are displayed. The user presses the ESCAPE key to continue (screen C); the user selects record number "3" (screen D); Brief bibliographic data and circulation status information is displayed (screen E) and the user requests more bibliographic information; and the full bibliographic information is displayed (screen F).

A

```
                            INQUIRY

ENTER INQUIRY REQUEST: ?

TO DO AN INQUIRY, TYPE A SEARCH CODE FOLLOWED BY THE TEXT YOU WANT TO
SEARCH FOR
     CODE   TYPE                        CODE   TYPE
      A     AUTHOR                        L     LC CARD #
      T     TITLE                         I     ISBN
      S     SUBJECT                       V     VENDOR #
      C     CALL #                        P     PATRON NAME
  NO CODE ITEM-ID (OCR)#                  P     PATRON-ID (OCR) #


  EXAMPLES:   ASANDBURG CARL   L743829
              TLIGHT IN AUGUST  I3282938491
              SFARM LIFE        PSMITH, JAMES


ENTER INQUIRY REQUEST: SLIBRARY AUTOMATION
```

B

```
                        SUBJECT INQUIRY
   1   LIBRARIES—AUTOMATION
   2   LIBRARIES—AUTOMATION—COLLECTIONS
   3   LIBRARIES—AUTOMATION—CONGRESSES
   4   LIBRARIES—AUTOMATION—PERIODICALS

CHOOSE ONE, ADD * FOR OTHER LIBRARIES, Q TO QUIT, H TO HALT : 1
```

C

5 MATCHES FOR ALL SYSTEMS. YOUR SYSTEM OWNS:

1) Henley, John Patrick.   76101223
Computer-based library and information systems by J. P. Henley.
  Macdonald; 1970.   MONOGRAPH

2) Mathies, Lorraine.   73009967
Computer-based reference service by M. Lorraine Mathies and
  American Library Association, 1973.   MONOGRAPH

CHOOSE ONE, ADD * FOR OTHER LIBRARIES, ESC TO CONTINUE, Q TO QUIT, H TO HALT:___

D

5 MATCHES FOR ALL SYSTEMS. YOUR LIBRARY OWNS:

3) Matthews, Joseph R.   80-17882
Choosing an automated library system: A planning guide / by
  American Library Association, 1980.   MONOGRAPH

4)   80-11636
The Professional librarian's reader in library automation and
  Knowledge Industry Publication c1980.   MONOGRAPH

CHOOSE ONE, ADD * FOR OTHER LIBRARIES, ESC TO CONTINUE, Q TO QUIT, H TO HALT: **3**

E

ITEM STATUS

AUTHOR: Matthews, Joseph R.
TITLE: Choosing an automated library system : a planning guide / by
ED: PUB: American Libra   YEAR: 1980.   TOTAL COPIES: 1

COPY STATUS FOR: STEEN

	LOC	STATUS	DATE	ITEM ID	HO	MEDIA	CALL NUMBER
1	HU	CHARGED	05/20/81	R0000829349	0	101	Z678.9 .M37

ENTER 1 FOR CIRCULATION INFORMATION   ESC TO SEE MORE
    2 FOR BIBLIOGRAPHIC INFORMATION   Q TO QUIT
    3 FOR OTHER BRANCH HOLDINGS   H TO HALT INQUIRY
      CHOICE: **2**

F

BIBLIOGRAPHIC INFORMATION FOR RECORD 35839

AUTH: Matthews, Joseph R.
TITL: Choosing an automated library system : a planning guide / by
       Joseph R. Matthews.
IMPR: Chicago: American Library Association, 1980.
COLL: viii, 119 p. : ill. : 23 cm.
NOTE: Bibliography: p. 115–116.
SUBJ: Libraries Automation.
LCCN: 80-17882
LCCL: Z678.9 .M37
VEND: OCL76521661
ISBN: 083890310X

Q TO QUIT, H TO HALT : ___

colleges—Mission College and West Valley College. These two community colleges serve approximately 19,000 students. In 1979 they contracted with Universal Library Systems, a turnkey vendor, to deliver an automated circulation system and to develop an online public access catalog for the two college libraries.

Universal Library Systems (ULISYS) utilizes a Digital Equipment Corporation PDP 11/70 minicomputer with application software written in BASIC PLUS. There are a total of 33 terminals linked to the computer system and, of these, five terminals at Mission College and five at West Valley College are public access catalog terminals. The computer system is located at Mission College and is linked via telephone lines to West Valley College, located about 15 miles away. There are about 79,000 records in the computer database and the library patron may search by author, title, combination of author and any title word, subject headings, call number, and by course and instructor for items located in the reserve book room. The holdings of both campus libraries are displayed for the user. Figure 12 provides some sample screens (see Figure 12, pages 60–63). Explicit Boolean searching and keyword or term searching capabilities are not currently available on the ULISYS system.

A one-page handout explaining the basic system capabilities and attractive brochures were designed by library staff members to aid in the introduction of the online catalog to library patrons.

PUBLIC LIBRARIES

Dallas Public Library

The Dallas (Texas) Public Library, with its central and 18 branch (community) libraries, serves approximately 163,000 patrons. The Dallas Public Library's automated circulation system was developed in 1973 by the Library and the City's Data Processing Department and the online catalog, called LSCAN, runs on an IBM-compatible mainframe computer. In 1979, subject search became available and a full record bibliographic conversion project (460,000 titles) was completed in January 1982. Each community library has at least one CRT terminal for public use and there are numerous terminals for the public in the Library's new Central building. In all there are 74 terminals for public use. The user moves the cursor to the appropriate screen location and fills in the blanks to initiate a search. Access points include author, title, author/title combination, subject headings and

FIGURE 12   Sample Screens for the System at the West Valley Joint Community
             College District

The user views the initial display (screen A) and enters a subject search for "information;"
the system displays the matching subject headings (screens B and C); the user asks for a
display of those titles with the subject heading of "Information services—United States"
which is displayed (screen D); the user asks for a display of the circulation status for the
first title (screen E); a display of the bibliographic information for the first title (screen F);
and a display of the circulation status and bibliographic information for the second title
(screens G and H).

A

```
————————————————————————————————————————————————

             Mission / West Valley College — Library Catalog

  Hi, when you need information assistance please type the word
  HELP then press the RETURN key.

  PLEASE NOTE  :-  The RETURN key must be pressed after you type each message

  You can search for material by SUBJECT or AUTHOR or TITLE

  Please enter your search


  ?S=INFORMATION
```

B

```
  ?                                                    S=INFORMATION
  Line #     Subject Heading or Terms

  1          Information display systems
  2          Information networks
  3          Information science—Dictionaries
  4          Information services
  5          Information services—California—Directories
  6          Information services—Directories
  7          Information services—United States
  8          Information services—United States—Directories
  9          Information services—User education
  10         Information storage and retrieval systems
  11         Information storage and retrieval systems—Accounting
  12         Information storage and retrieval systems—Addresses, essays, lectures



  For more type NS and RETURN
  To see those titles in the catalog under the subject heading you've chosen
  type   DT=    followed by the line number. Example: DT=4 and RETURN


  ?NS
```

C

13	Information storage and retrieval systems—Directories
14	Information storage and retrieval systems—Hospitals—Congresses
15	Information storage and retrieval systems—Medicine
16	Information storage and retrieval systems—Medicine—Code numbers—Colle
17	Information storage and retrieval systems—Museums
18	Information storage and retrieval systems—Music
19	Information theory
20	Information theory—Collected works
21	Information theory in Psychology
22	Information theory in psychology—Addresses, essays, lectures

To repeat previous screen type PS and RETURN
To see those titles in the catalog under the subject heading you've chosen
type   DT=   followed by the line number. Example: DT=4 and RETURN

?**DT=7**

D

?

                 DT=7

Line#	Call #	Author	Title
1	Z731 .K56	Knight, Douglas M.,	Libraries at large: tradition, innovati
2	Ref*Z663.379	U.S. Library of Con	A directory of information resources in
3	Z674.5.U5 W3	Warnken, Kelly	The information brokers : how to start

To repeat previous screen type PS and RETURN
To determine the location and availability of a specific title, type ST=
followed by the line number. EXAMPLE: ST=2 and RETURN
For more detailed information on a specific title, type   BI=   followed by the
line number. EXAMPLE: BI=5 and RETURN

?**ST=1**

E

```
?                                                                    ST=1
Z            Knight, Douglas M., 1921–
731
.K56         Libraries at large: tradition, innovation, and the national interest;
             the resource book based on the materials on the National Advisory
             Commission on Libraries.

             New York, Bowker, 1969


LOCATION              VOL      MED      AVAILABILITY        DATE—DUE—TIME

W VALLEY WV LRC                         ON SHELF
MISSION MIS LRC                         ON SHELF



To repeat previous screen type PS and RETURN
For more detailed information on a specific title, type   BI=   followed by the
line number. EXAMPLE:   BI=5 and RETURN


?BI=1
```

F

```
?                                                                    BI=1
Z            Knight, Douglas M., 1921–
731
.K56         Libraries at large: tradition, innovation, and the national interest;
             the resource book based on the materials of the National Advisory
             Commission on Libraries.

             New York, Bowker, 1969

             xxiv, 664 p. illus. 26 cm

             1. Libraries—United States
             2. Information services—United States
             I. Nourse, E. Shepley, joint comp
             II. United States. National Advisory Commission on Libraries



For more type NS and RETURN      To repeat previous screen type PS and RETURN
To determine the location and availability of a specific title, type   ST=
followed by the line number. EXAMPLE:   ST=2 and RETURN


?ST=2
```

G

? ST=2
Ref U.S. Library of Congress. National Referral Center for Science and
Z Technology
663.379
.D53 A directory of information resources in the United States : social
sciences.

Washington : For sale by the Superintendent of Documents, U. S. Govt.
Print. Off., 1965

LOCATION   VOL MED   AVAILABILITY   DATE—DUE—TIME

W VALLEY WV LRC   ON SHELF

To repeat previous screen type PS and RETURN
For more detailed information on a specific title, type   BI=   followed by the
line number. EXAMPLE: BI=5 and RETURN

?**BI=2**

H

? BI=2
Ref U.S. Library of Congress. National Referral Center for Science and
Z Technology
663.379
.D53 A directory of information resources in the United States : social
sciences.

Washington : For sale by the Superintendent of Documents, U. S. Govt.
Print. Off., 1965

v., 218 p. ; 27 cm.

1. United States—Learned institutions and societies—Directories
2. Information services—United States
L.C.CARD NUMBER   65—62583

To repeat previous screen type PS and RETURN
To determine the location and availability of a specific title, type   ST=
followed by the line number. EXAMPLE: ST=2 and RETURN

?

call numbers. Sample screens are shown in Figure 13 (see Figure 13, pages 65–66). The patron is not provided with a handout explaining use of the online catalog.

Evanston Public Library

The Evanston Public Library, located just north of Chicago, has approximately 48,000 registered borrowers. The Evanston Public Library uses the CL Systems, Inc. (CLSI) turnkey automated circulation system—the LIBS 100 system. In October 1980, the system was expanded and patrons have been locating library materials through a Public Access Catalog (PAC). The CLSI Public Access Catalog uses a touch-sensitive online terminal in lieu of a standard CRT keyboard terminal.

The CLSI system runs on a Digital Equipment Corporation PDP 11/34 minicomputer with software written in MACRO 11 and assembly-level programming language. Fifteen touch-screen public access catalog terminals are linked to the computer system. Twelve of these touch-screen terminals are located in the main library and three are located in branches.

The Evanston Public Library's computer database has records for about 219,000 unique titles and approximately 324,000 copies. During the data collection period for this study, approximately 60 percent of the records contained subject headings and a retrospective conversion project was underway to provide full MARC records for the total collection. The library patron, using a touch-screen terminal, can gain access to the database using author, title, and subject heading searches. The computer system displays on the screen a series of choices and patrons indicate their choice by touching the screen in the appropriate location. The computer accepts this input and in turn displays another series of choices for the library patron. Up to seven touches to the screen are required to gain access to a specific individual record. Figure 14 illustrates a typical search (see Figure 14, pages 67–71). The library's staff developed a one-page public access catalog instruction sheet as an aid to assist patrons in using the online catalog.

Iowa City Public Library

The Iowa City Public Library, located about 20 miles south of Cedar Rapids, Iowa, has approximately 45,000 patrons. The library uses the CL Systems, Inc. LIBS 100 touch-screen public access online catalog, like that at the Evanston Public Library. The library has nine touch-screen terminals available for public use to search their

FIGURE 13   Sample Screens for the Dallas Public Library

The user enters subject search using a fill-in-the-blanks screen. Note the user can not enter more than the first 5 characters of the first word and the first 4 characters of the second word (screen A). The system responses with a brief display of matching records and the user selects line 2 (screen B). The system displays the bibliographic record and holdings and status information for the two copies owned by the Library (screen C).

A

SUBJECT **PEOPL TEMP** ___ ___   AUTHOR _____ ___ ___ ___
TITLE _____ ___ ___ ___   CALL NUMBER _____ ____ ____

B

                      MASTER BIBLIOGRAPHIC DATA BASE
SUBJECT SEARCH PEOPLTEMP

	SUBJECT	TITLE	CALL NUMBER
01	PEOPLES TEMPLE	AWAKE IN A NIGHTMARE JONESTOW	289.9 F299A
02	PEOPLES TEMPLE	BROKEN GOD	289.9 T376B
03	PEOPLES TEMPLE	CHILDREN OF JONESTOWN —1st MC	362.7044 W886C
04	PEOPLES TEMPLE	CULT THAT DIED	289.9 J77YK
05	PEOPLES TEMPLE	IN MY FATHERS HOUSE	973.92092 Y421
06	PEOPLES TEMPLE	JESUS AND JIM JONES	B J77434R
07	PEOPLES TEMPLE	JOURNEY TO NOWHERE	289.9 N157B
08	PEOPLES TEMPLE	SIX YEARS WITH GOD	289.9 M657S
09	PEOPLES TEMPLE	STRONGEST POISON	988.11 L266S
10	PEOPLES TEMPLE—BIO	WHITE NIGHT	B J77434N
11	PEOPLES TEMPLE—HIS	HOLD HANDS AND DIE	289.9 M213H

LINE# **2**
SUBJECT ____ ___ ___ ___   AUTHOR _____ ___ ___ ___
TITLE _____ ___ ___ ___   CALL NUMBER _____ ____ ____

C

The user sees an initial display and selects a subject search by touching the word
"Subject" (screen A); the user is interested in the topic "jewelry" and thus touches
"Gabo, Naum, 1980" on the next display (screen B); to the next display the user touches
"Jazz Music-Bibl." (screen C); the user then selects "Jerusalem—History." in order to
see all entries for jewelry (screen D); the user responds to the next display by touching "Jet
Planes—Flight Testing." (screen E); to the next display the user touches "Jewelry."
(screen F); the user then selects a specific record and touches "Coate, Sharr." (screen G);
and receives the full bibliographic information and circulation status information (screen H).

A

Hello,

Welcome to Evanston Public Library's Public Access Catalog (PAC)

This is a touch sensitive terminal which provides up-to-date
listings of the library's holdings by author, title and subject.

Librarians will be happy to assist you.

Author

Title

Subject

Community

START
OVER   HELP

B

101 Ranch, Oklahoma.

Choral Music-Bibliography.

Gabo, Naum, 1890.

Malamud, Bernard-Bibliography.

Provence-Description And Travel-Guide-Books.

United States-Description And Travel-1960.

START

OVER   HELP

C

Gabo, Naum, 1890.

Glass Manufacture-Maine-Portland.

Greek Poetry-(Collections)

Hearst Corporation.

Horticulture-Italy-Pompeii.

Inclined Planes-Juvenile Literature.

Interior Decoration-England-History-17th Century.

Jazz Music-Bibl.

Keller,Helen Adams, 1880-.

Latin America-Politics And Government-Addresses, Essays, Lecture.

Lions-Behavior.

START

OVER   HELP

D

Jazz Music-Bibl.

Jerusalem-History.

Jewelry, French-Exhibitions.

Jews-History.

Jews In Spain.

Jiu-Jitsu

Johnson, Sir William, Bart., 1715–1774-Fiction.

Journalism-California.

Judaism-Dictionaries.

Jury-United States-Addresses, Essays, Lectures.

Kangaroos.

START
OVER   HELP

E

Jerusalem-History.

Jerusalem. Temple.

Jesuits-North America.

Jesus Christ-Biography.

Jesus Christ-Childhood.

Jesus Christ-Friends And Associates.

Jesus Christ-Miracles.

Jesus Christ-Passion-Sermons.

Jesus Christ-Royal Office.

Jet Planes-Flight Testing.

Jewelry-Catologs.

START
OVER   HELP

F

FROM: Jet Planes Testing.

Jet Stream.

Jet Transports.

Jet Transports-Juvenile Literature.

Jet Transports-Piloting.

Jetta Automobile.

Jewelers.

Jewelry.

Jewelry, American.

Jewelry, American-Catologs.

TO: Jewelry, Ancient.

START

OVER   HELP

G

* THERE ARE 34 SATISFIERS FOR THIS SELECTION. *

Baerwald, Marcus.
The story of jewelry;
739.27 B14s

Baxter, William Thomas.
Jewelry, gem cutting, and metal craft.
736 B337, 1950

Baxter, William Thomas.
Jewelry, gem cutting, and metal craft, by William T. Baxter.
736 B337;

Coate, Sharr.
Creative casting: jewelry, silverware, sculpture.

START   BACK   SCROLL

OVER   UP   UP   HELP

H

```
CALL::        739 C451 c
AUTHOR::      Choate, Sharr
TITLE::       Creative casting: jewelry, silverware, sculpture.
SUBTITLE::    Drawings by the author; photos. by the author except where otherwise
IMPRINT::     New York, Crown Publishers (1966)
DESC::        x, 213p. illus. (part. col.) 27 cm.
NOTES1::      Bibliography: p. 209–210.
SUBJ1::       Founding—Amatures' manuals.
SUBJ2::       Jewelry.
SUBJ3::       Silverwork.
SUBJ4::       Sculpture—Technique.
OCLC::        307852
```

PUB	PUBYR	COST	MC	ED	L.A.D.
	1966	$6.95	b		2/24/82

* COPY INFORMATION FOLLOWS *

EVK 3 1192 00359 2233 ON SHELF

BACK   PAGE   PAGE

UP   BACK   NEXT   HELP

124,000 titles. Use of the touch-screen terminals began in October 1980 and when the library moved to its new building in June 1981 and discarded the card catalog. All the library's materials are available in the online catalog and are accessible by author, title, subject headings and call number. Use of the catalog and use of the library's collection has increased substantially since the switch to the online catalog. Figure 14 illustrates the search process using the touch-screen terminals. A single sheet of step-by-step directions is posted at every terminal in the library.

Pikes Peak Library District

The Pikes Peak Library District, located in Colorado Springs, Colorado, has about 100,000 registered borrowers. The Pikes Peak Library developed its own automated library system, called Maggie's Place, and uses a Digital Equipment Corporation PDP 11/70 and a second PDP 11/44 minicomputer. The application software is written in BASIC PLUS/II. Maggie's Place provides the patron with access to the online catalog and to the circulation system database. In addition, the system provides acquisitions and acquisitions accounting, access to community databases, decision support system, budget system, carpools, furniture and equipment inventory, payroll, and an electronic mail system. The system has a total of 88 terminals linked to the computer and of these, 13 terminals at the main library are for online patron access catalog use. In addition, six dial-in ports are available for approximately 450 home users who use their own personal microcomputer or a terminal with a modem.

The computer database contains information about approximately 240,000 unique titles and approximately 356,000 copies. The computer system provides the user of the online catalog with access to author, title, subject headings, and call number searching capabilities. Explicit Boolean and keyword or term searching capability are not available. Figure 15 provides some sample screens for the Pikes Peak system (see Figure 15, pages 73–74). The online catalog became available for public use in June 1981.

STATE AND FEDERAL LIBRARIES

Library of Congress

The Library of Congress' SCORPIO system (Subject-Content-Oriented Retriever for Processing Information Online) dates from the

FIGURE 15   Sample Screens for the Pikes Peak Library

In response to the first display the user selects "Inventory" and asks for "help." The user then enters a command for a subject search for "photography" (screen A). The system provides a display of the record in brief form and enters the command to move forward twice to see other matching entries (screen B). The user then enters a subject search for "Solar Heating" and views three records (screen C).

A

```
                          Public Dial-Up Access
                                ]Menu[
                        For HELP enter "?selection"


         AGENCIES        COURSES       CALENDAR      GOODBYE

         INFO            INVENTORY     TERMINAL      CLUBS

         WELCOME
Program: INVENTORY

"__PPLINV V7.1 (100,155) RSTS V7.1-11 Maggie's Place


PPL>HELP

Command choices:
   A/data        = author search
   B/data        = Barcode search
   C/data        = Call number search
   E/            = Expand this record
   F/            = Forward
   L/data        = LCCN search
   N/            = Next author/title
   S/data        = Subject search
   T/data        = Title search
   X/            = Exit program

PPL>S/PHOTOGRAPHY
```

B

Barcode:101667087   Patron:000000000   DueDate:None
     SNELLING,H   LastUse:17-Jan-83
771.   HISTORY AND PRACTICE OF THE ART OF PHOTOGRA(1970)
S671H   LCCN:73-119993
East Branch   InvDate:01-Jan-78
Subjects: Daguerreotype.   TotCirc:9
     Photography.
PPL>**F/**

Barcode:100363225   Patron:000000000   DueDate:None
J   ZARCHY,HAR   LastUse:20-Mar-82
770.   PHOTOGRAPHY
Z36P   LCCN:66-010892
Palmer Lake Br.   InvDate:01-Jan-78
Subjects: Photography.   TotCirc:0
PPL>**F/**

Barcode:102567930   Patron:000000000   DueDate:None
     HILLSON,P.   LastUse:26-Nov-82
770.   PHOTOGRAPHY
H655P   LCCN:76-077920
Old Colo City   InvDate:15-Jan-80
Subjects: Photography.   TotCirc:14

C

PPL>**S/SOLAR HEATING**
Barcode:101384303   Patron:000000000   DueDate:None
0   WING,CHARL   LastUse:18-Feb-83
643.7   FROM THE WALLS IN
W769F   LCCN:78-026354
Processing B   InvDate:28-Sep-79
Subjects: Dwellings — Energy conservation.   TotCirc:10
     Solar heating.
     Dwellings — Remodeling — Amateurs' manuals.
PPL>**F/**
Barcode:100586296   Patron:000000000   DueDate:None
     LUCAS,TED   LastUse:03-Mar-83
697.78   HOW TO BUILD A SOLAR HEATER
L933H   LCCN:75-018097
Penrose (Main)   InvDate:01-Jan-78
Subjects: Solar heating.   TotCirc:20
PPL>**F/**
Barcode:102510146   Patron:000000000   DueDate:None
0   SHURCLIFF,   LastUse:16-Dec-82
721.   SOLAR HEATED BUILDINGS OF NORTH AMERICA: 120 OUTST
S562SO   LCCN:78-057234
Basement   InvDate:10-Oct-79
Subjects: Solar houses — North America.   TotCirc:1
     Solar heating.
PPL>

late 1960s, when the Library's Congressional Research Service (CRS) began developing an online information retrieval system furnishing legislative and bibliographic data. The structure of the SCORPIO/ LOCIS Library System is based on work which originated in the middle 1960s, sponsored by the National Aeronautics and Space Administration, under the names "Dialog" and "Recon" at Lockheed. SCORPIO programs were in use in a few Congressional offices by 1974. In April 1975, the first computer terminal for public use was installed in the Science Reading Room. Without any special announcements or training, the system was set up to test software, hardware, and public acceptance.

SCORPIO evolved based on feedback from this successful experiment and from LC and Congressional staff, and in May 1977, the Computer Catalog Center (CCC) was opened adjacent to the Main Reading Room giving Library of Congress readers online access to all MARC records (i.e., the online catalog) and certain other files. There are currently a total of 24 terminals and 16 printers for public use in the Main Reading Room area, and many other public terminals scattered throughout other reading rooms. The Library's computer systems support over 2,000 terminals for reference, processing, and administrative use (including terminals in Congressional offices).

"SCORPIO" refers to a retrieval language with consistent command and display techniques across the different files of the Library of Congress Information System (LOCIS). Access points include authors, other personal names, titles, corporate names, subject terms, and identifying numbers such as LC card number or other accession number. Searchers may browse through dictionary indexes of these access points, and then create as many stored sets as desired. Sets may be manipulated with Boolean logic, or may be limited by various elements in the record such as language or date. Entries may be displayed in full or abbreviated formats. Figure 16 illustrates a sample search using the SCORPIO system (see Figure 16, pages 76–78). Patrons use the system directly, without a librarian as intermediary, except for initial instruction or when responding to specific questions. While offline prints cannot be generated for public users of SCORPIO, they may print at no charge on local terminal printers.

MUMS (Multiple Use MARC System) had its origin in the need for the Library's Processing Department to develop online access to records for "known items," that is, a book in hand, with the idea of developing expanded services later. At the same time that CRS was beginning to use SCORPIO, the Processing Department was beginning to use MUMS. The system employed truncated search keys that,

FIGURE 16   Sample Screens for the Library of Congress

The user views the first screen provided by SCORPIO and enters a request to browse "libraries—history" (screen A). The system provides a display and the user selects line six (screen B); the system creates a set and the user asks for a display (screen C); the first five records of the set are displayed in short form (screen D).

A

TUESDAY, 03/15/83   08:48 P.M.
***LCCC— THE LIBRARY OF CONGRESS COMPUTERIZED CATALOG
          is now available for your search.
          The Term Index was updated on 03/09/83.

          To learn about the contents of this file, type
          SHOW FILE and transmit.
          For a description of available commands, type
          SHOW COMMANDS and transmit.

LCCC lists books cataloged at LC beginning with language and date indicated:
    ENGLISH 1968   GERMAN PORTUGUESE SPANISH 1975
    FRENCH 1973   OTHER EUROPEAN 1976–1977   NON-EUROPEAN 1978–1979
        New items are added every two weeks. Some books listed are not
    actually in the Library. You may search by author, subject heading,
    title, card number and partial call number.
READY FOR NEW COMMAND: **b libraries—history**

B

BRWS TERM FILE:LCCC; ENTRY TERM: LIBRARIES—HISTORY—
B01   LIBRARIES—HAWAII—AUTOMATION//(INDX=2)
B02   LIBRARIES—HAWAII—DIRECTORIES//(INDX=1)
B03   LIBRARIES—HAWAII—HISTORY//(INDX=1)
B04   LIBRARIES—HISTORIOGRAPHY//(INDX=1)
B05   LIBRARIES—HISTORIOGRAPHY—CONGRESSES//(INDX=1)
B06+ LIBRARIES—HISTORY//(INDX=66)
B07   LIBRARIES—HISTORY—ADDRESSES, ESSAYS, LE//(INDX=5)
B08   LIBRARIES—HISTORY—ANECDOTES—FACETIAE,//(INDX=1)
B09   LIBRARIES—HISTORY—BIBLIOGRAPHY//(INDX=3)
B10   LIBRARIES—HISTORY—CONGRESSES//(INDX=2)
B11   LIBRARIES—HISTORY—OUTLINES, SYLLABI, ET//(INDX=1)
B12   LIBRARIES—HISTORY—TO 400//(INDX=5)
B13   LIBRARIES—HISTORY—1400–1600//(INDX=2)
B14   LIBRARIES—HISTORY—17TH–18TH CENTURY//(INDX=1)
B15   LIBRARIES—HISTORY—19TH CENTURY//(INDX=1)
B16   LIBRARIES—HISTORY—20TH CENTURY//(INDX=1)
B17   LIBRARIES—HISTORY—20TH CENTURY—CONGRE//(INDX=1)
B18   LIBRARIES—HISTORY—400–1400//(INDX=13)
B19   LIBRARIES—HONGKONG//(INDX=1)
B20   LIBRARIES—HONGKONG—DIRECTORIES//(INDX=1)
READY FOR NEW COMMAND (FOR NEXT PAGE, XMIT ONLY): **s b12**

C

SET 1   5: SLCT INDX/LIBRARIES —HISTORY —TO 400
READY FOR NEW COMMAND: **d 1**

D

1. 67-4900:Lipsius, Justus. A brief outline of the history of libraries.
      Chicago, A. C. McClurg, 1907. 121 p, 18 cm.
      LC CALL NUMBER: Z674 .L552 no. 5
2. 75-536193:Wendel, Carl Theodor Eduard. Kleine Schriften zum antiken Buch-
      und Bibliothekswesen /. Koln, Greven, 1974. 240 p, ill., 25 cm.
      LC CALL NUMBER: Z722 .W45 1974
3. 76-486317:Tnsberg, Jeppe. Offentlige biblioteker i Romerriget i det 2.
      arhundrede e. Chr. /. Kbenhavn, Danmarks Biblioteksskole, 1976. 151 p
      , ill., 26 cm.
      LC CALL NUMBER: Z722 .T63
4. 77-73645:Wright, Herbert Curtis. The oral antecedents of Greek
      librarianship /. Provo, Utah, Brigham Young University Press, c1977.
      xxvi, 237 p., 24 cm.
      LC CALL NUMBER: Z722 .W74
5. 79-306120:Makowiecka, Elzbieta. The origin and evolution of architectural
      form of Roman library /. Warszawa, : Wydaw-a UW, 1978 (Pozn UAM). 108,
      4 p, 25 ill., 24 cm.
      LC CALL NUMBER: Z679 .M16
READY FOR NEW COMMAND: **ends**

initially, permitted access by title, author/title, and LC card number. In the mid-seventies it became possible to search MUMS by author, in truncated or full form, and in the late-seventies to do free-text searching (called component word searching in MUMS) of author, title, note, and tracing fields in the MARC records.

Until 1978, when component word searching became possible, reference staff did not routinely instruct the public in the use of MUMS. The MARC tagged display, and certain complexities in syntax and subcommands, kept them from doing so, as did the need to sign off a SCORPIO file and sign into MUMS when making the switch. The advent of component-word searching made public use of MUMS far more attractive—indeed essential for some searches.

In searching the online catalog, Library of Congress users have free access to the following files: 1) Library of Congress Computerized Catalog (LCCC), the most heavily used file, representing 80 percent of the use on public terminals and 40 percent of overall SCORPIO use, and allowing searches by author, title, LC subject heading, class number, and card number of the entire MARC monographs database; 2) the entire MARC file (books, serials, maps) through the MUMS system.

State Library of Ohio

The State Library of Ohio located in Columbus, Ohio, serves about 10,000 patrons. Holdings include approximately 1,600,000 bound volumes and the Library maintains some 700 periodical subscriptions. The Library provides three OCLC terminals for public use. The patron must enter the appropriate OCLC search-key when searching by author, title, author/title combination, etc. Name authority information is available but a separate file must be accessed. Subject searching is not available. Figure 8 provides some sample OCLC screens.

SUMMARY INFORMATION

Table 2 on pages 80–82, provides summary comparative information for each of the libraries that participated in the CLR Online Catalog Study. The variety of online catalogs is demonstrated by a brief review of only a few factors, e.g., number of online catalog terminals, status information provided, single vs. multiple library catalog, percent of collection in machine-readable form, etc.

TABLE 2   Computer System and Online Catalog Characteristics

ARL LIBRARIES

	Dartmouth College[1]	Northwestern University	Ohio State University	Stanford University	Syracuse University	University of California	University of Texas, Austin
Computer System Characteristics:							
Type of computer	Mainframe	Mainframe	Mainframe	Mainframe	Mainframe	Mainframe	Mainframe
Size of CPU	2	2,048K	8MB	3	2,048K	4x 8,192 K	4
Number of online catalog terminals	4	18	117	4	36	100	—
Command language or menus	Com./Menu	Command	Command	Command	Command	Com./Menu	Command
Printer available	No	No	Yes	No	No	No	Yes
Online Catalog Characteristics:							
Status information provided	No	Yes	Yes	No	Yes	No	No
Single vs multiple library catalog	Single	Single	Multiple	Multiple	Single	Multiple	Multiple
Number of access points (indexes) available to user[5]	14	7	10	14	7	14	8
Keyword or term searching	Yes	No	No	Yes	Yes	Yes	No
Boolean searching	Yes	No	No	Yes	Yes	Yes	No
Expand or limit results by date, language, publisher	Yes	No	Yes	No	No	Yes	No
Sort search results	Yes	No	No	No	No	Yes	No
Database Characteristics:							
Size of collection (titles)	1,435,000	1,280,000	1,800,000	4,750,000	1,172,000	10,850,000[6]	1,700,000
Total number of records in online catalog	150,000	525,000	1,800,000	669,000	535,000	733,000	750,000
Percent of collection in online catalog	10%	36%	100%	14%	46%	7%	44%
Number of registered borrowers	17,000	18,000	10,000	20,000	21,000	196,000	66,000

	Claremont Colleges	Mankato State University	Ohio University, Athens	Stephen F. Austin State University	University of Akron	University of Texas, Dallas
Computer System Characteristics:						
Type of computer	Mini	Mainframe	[4]	Mini	[4]	[4]
Size of CPU	768K	—	—	192K	—	—
Number of online catalog terminals	8	22	1	19	3	2
Command language or menus	Menus	Command	Command	Menus	Command	Command
Printer available	No	No	No	No	No	No
Online Catalog Characteristics:						
Status information provided	Yes	No	No	Yes	No	No
Single vs multiple library catalog	Single	Multiple	Multiple	Single	Multiple	Multiple
Number of access points (indexes) available to user[5]	6	11	8	10	8	8
Keyword or term searching	No	Yes	No	No	No	No
Boolean searching	No	Yes	No	No	No	No
Expand or limit results by date, language, publisher	No[7]	Yes	No	No	No	No
Sort search results	No	Yes	No	No	No	No
Database Characteristics:						
Size of collection (titles)	136,000	311,000	800,000	239,000	500,000	188,000
Total number of records in online catalog	69,000	232,000	450,000	87,000	500,000	166,000
Percent of collection in online catalog	51%[8]	75%	56%	36%	100%	88%
Number of registered borrowers	12,252	15,000	20,000	16,875	30,000	8,500

[1] Represents configuration during study.
[2] Shared system using BRS computers.
[3] RLIN shared a CPU with Stanford University.
[4] Uses the OCLC system.
[5] A maximum of 14 access points under the direct control of the user was considered for the purposes of this comparison: author, title, author/title combination, subject headings, series, corporate author term or keyword, title term, subject term, call number, ISBN, ISSN, LCCN, document number, and local system number.
[6] Unofficial estimates of unique title holdings for UC as a whole; includes only bound volumes.
[7] Subject search only (limit by date).
[8] Science libraries only.

TABLE 2 Computer System and Online Catalog Characteristics (continued)

	COMMUNITY COLLEGE LIBRARIES	PUBLIC LIBRARIES				STATE AND FEDERAL LIBRARIES	
	Mission/ West Valley College	Dallas Public	Evanston Public	Iowa City Public	Pikes Peak	Library of Congress	State Library of Ohio
Computer System Characteristics:							
Type of computer	Mini	Mainframe	Mini	Mini	Mini	Mainframe	4
Size of CPU	384 K	3,072 K	128 K	128 K	2,048 K	16 MB	—
Number of online catalog terminals	10	74	16	9	13	24	3
Command language or menus	Command	Form Filing	Menus	Menus	Command	Command	Command
Printer available	Yes	No	No	No	Yes	Yes	No
Online Catalog Characteristics:							
Status information provided	Yes	Yes	Yes	Yes	Yes	No	No
Single vs multiple library catalog	Multiple	Single	Single	Single	Single	Single	Multiple
Number of access points (indexes) available to user[5]	10	6	3	3	8	14	8
Keyword or term searching	No	No	No	No	No	Yes	No
Boolean searching	No	No	No	No	No	Yes	No
Expand or limit results by date, language, publisher	No	No	No	No	No	Yes	No
Sort search results	No	No	No	No	No	No	No
Database Characteristics:							
Size of collection (titles)	85,000	529,000	219,000	118,000	240,000	19,000,000[9]	1,200,000[10]
Total number of records in online catalog	79,000	529,000	219,000	118,000	240,000	2,000,000	178,340
Percent of collection in online catalog	93%	100%	100%	100%	100%	11%	15%
Number of registered borrowers	19,205	163,000	48,061	37,000	100,000	?	10,000

[9]Includes bound volumes and pamphlets.
[10]Includes government documents.

NOTES

1. A detailed discussion of MELVYL will be found in a series of related articles in the December 1982 and March 1983 issues of *Information Technology and Libraries.*

CHAPTER THREE

Users and Non-Users of Online Catalogs

O<small>F</small> all the components of the online catalog—hardware, software, databases—arguably the most important and least understood is the user. The user's approach to solving a problem or filling an information need is, or should be, the very foundation of online catalog design. Hardware can be upgraded, software rewritten, and databases improved, but the user cannot be redesigned to match the "needs" of the system. Most users do not want to take an introductory computer science course (especially from the library staff) before they can begin to look up books with the online catalog. System behavior must conform to and complement user behavior. Failure in this matter can exact a heavy penalty—a major capital investment in a resource that goes unused by the library's clientele.

UNDERSTANDING THE USERS' CHARACTERISTICS

The importance of understanding more about user behavior was highlighted at the Dartmouth Conference, and is the chief motivation for the series of CLR studies discussed here. In this chapter, we will recount our discoveries about the users themselves and their characteristics, as well as analyze library patrons who do not use the online catalog. In subsequent chapters, we will see how users approached the online catalog, how successful they were, what problems they had, and how their attitudes were affected by these experiences.

Users of the Online Catalog Are Frequent
Library Users

Based on the results of the survey, users of the online catalog are frequent library users. Overall, slightly more than two-thirds of online catalog users (68%) use their libraries at least once a week (see Table 3, page 86). Use is more frequent in academic libraries of all types; between 77 percent and 84 percent of academic library respondents use the library once a week. Use in public, state, and federal libraries is less frequent.

Online Catalog Users Are Only Modest Users
of Other Catalogs

Online catalog users make only modest use of the library's book, card, or COM catalog. About one-third of the respondents use the non-online catalog "occasionally" and about one-half (55%) either occasionally or on "most visits" (see Table 3). Prior card catalog use studies suggest that users are likely to use the catalog about half the time they enter a library.[1] Use of the library's non-online catalog is considerably higher in the state and federal library environment.

Users of the Online Catalog
Consult It Frequently

Almost two-thirds of the respondents (64%) use the online catalog either "most visits" or "occasionally" (see Table 3). An additional 21 percent of the users find themselves at an online catalog terminal "every visit" to the library. This distribution is characteristic of all types of libraries. Almost one-fourth of the users at the state and federal libraries (principally Library of Congress respondents) were first-time users, however.

Online Catalog Users Are Not
Necessarily Users of Other Computers

There are a number of possible explanations for this high frequency of use of the online catalog. The majority of users of the online catalog might be devotees of computers in general. Yet, interestingly, slightly more than one-third of the users of the online catalog (36%) for all types of libraries indicate that they never use another computer system. And so, for a fair number of users, familiarity with and

TABLE 3 Frequency of Library and Catalog Use for Users of the Online Catalog

	ARL Libraries %	Other Academic Libraries %	Community College Libraries %	Public Libraries %	State and Federal Libraries %	Aggregate Sample %
I come to this library:						
Weekly	43	53	47	42	28	42
Daily	37	31	30	4	11	26
Monthly	12	11	18	34	22	18
4 times a year	5	5	3	12	17	7
I use the library's Book, Card, or COM Catalog:						
Occasionally	38	38	33	29	21	34
Rarely	22	27	29	18	15	21
Most visits	21	19	8	24	24	21
Every visit	11	9	3	16	26	12
Not before today	9	8	27	13	15	11
I use this online catalog:						
Most visits	40	36	35	32	31	37
Occasionally	31	36	40	17	14	27
Every visit	17	11	18	32	27	21
Not before today	6	9	5	15	23	10
I use another computer system:						
Never	34	40	46	40	36	36
Weekly	19	15	14	14	16	17
Daily	12	9	17	17	12	13
Monthly	14	12	13	12	12	13
4 times a year	13	12	5	10	14	12
Once a year	9	11	4	8	10	9

prior use of computer technology are not prerequisites for using the online catalog. Of equal interest, the library and its online catalog represent the first exposure to computer technology for this group of library users. Another one-third of the users, however, are fairly active users of other online systems (see Table 3).

Playing with the Online Catalog

The novelty of the online catalog may also attract people to "play with the new toy in the library." While not as exciting as the majority of the video games in an arcade, an interactive online catalog is perhaps a bit more entertaining than the card catalog. And the library's online catalog does not require quarters to "play." Dale Carrison, Dean of the Library at Mankato State University, has noted that when a library first goes "online" to the Minnesota State University Online Union Catalog system, the number of transactions is highest during the first few months of use and then drops off slightly. This suggests that novelty is initially a factor in the use of an online catalog.

Online Catalog User Is a Young Adult

The typical user of the online catalog is male (60% of the users surveyed were male). Almost 40 percent of the respondents are between the ages of 20–24 years; an additional 25 percent are between the ages of 25–34 years; and only two percent are 55 years or older (see Table 4, pages 88–89). Thus, the majority of online catalog users are young adults. The youngest and oldest age groups are likely to be found in public libraries. The greatest concentration of the 20–24 age group are found among the academic library respondents.

Online Catalog Users Are Highly Educated

The educational level of users of the online catalog is quite high— 90 percent have completed some college education or are college graduates. This distribution varies significantly by type of library, with public library respondents having lower average educational levels.

The Majority of Academic Online Catalog
Users Are Undergraduates

Within academic libraries, slightly more than one-third of all users are in the junior-senior class and less than two-thirds (60%) of

TABLE 4   Characteristics of Users of the Online Catalog

	ARL Libraries %	Other Academic Libraries %	Community College Libraries %	Public Libraries %	State and Federal Libraries %	Aggregate Sample %
Male	61	57	66	57	65	60
Female	39	43	34	43	35	40
Age group:						
20–24 years	45	52	45	19	32	38
25–34 years	25	19	16	30	39	27
15–19 years	20	19	33	22	7	20
35–44 years	7	6	4	15	14	9
45–54 years	2	4	1	5	5	3
14 and under	1	0	1	5	1	2
55–64 years	1	1	1	3	2	1
65+ years	1	0	0	2	1	1
Current or highest grade completed:						
High school	3	1	17	26	4	9
Some college	53	68	77	28	22	46
College graduate	44	31	6	44	73	44

Class level:						
Freshman-Sophomore	23	32	83	NA	NA	26
Junior-Senior	34	41	7	NA	NA	34
Graduate-Master level	14	15	1	NA	NA	13
Graduate-Doctoral level	11	3	0	NA	NA	10
All Other	18	9	9	NA	NA	17
Academic area:						
Arts and Humanities	28	20	11	NA	NA	26
Social Sciences	18	15	4	NA	NA	18
Business Management	12	20	26	NA	NA	13
Engineering	12	9	20	NA	NA	12
Physical-Biological Sciences	12	12	6	NA	NA	12
All Other	18	24	33	NA	NA	19
Main focus of academic work:*						
Course work	74	75	88	NA	NA	74
Research	38	38	26	NA	NA	38
Teaching	10	10	3	NA	NA	10

*Multiple responses possible; therefore totals may be larger than 100%

NA = Not Applicable.

the users are undergraduates. Faculty and non-library staff together accounted for less than seven percent of users.[2] This distribution did not vary significantly among the three types of academic libraries.

Most Academic Use of the Online Catalog
Is Course-Related

An overwhelming number of users in academic libraries are engaged primarily in course-related work (74%). Similar results were reported in prior card catalog use studies.[3] Research is the primary focus of the academic work of more than one-third (38%) of the users of the online catalog (see Table 4). These distributions are essentially the same for all three types of academic libraries.

Academic Users Are From All Disciplines

Analysis of the academic areas of users suggests that the online catalog is used by all academic disciplines. There is no evidence of an a priori bias against use of the online catalog by any disciplinary group. Users from the Arts and Humanities, Social Sciences, and Business and Management represent 57 percent of all respondents (see Table 4). This user pattern may be influenced by factors such as terminal distribution in branch libraries, length of exposure to an online catalog, and relative use of the book literature among disciplines.

THE USER'S TASK

The user comes to the online catalog for different purposes and often with incomplete or inaccurate information. Personal characteristics of the user affecting the successful use of the catalog include the amount of training and experience in using the catalog and, perhaps more importantly, the perseverance and skill of the searcher. While some of the individual characteristics of the user can be influenced to some degree through training and online assistance, e.g., help screens and prompts, a considerable amount of what the user brings to the online catalog experience is unchangeable from the perspective of system designers and librarians. Understanding more about the information-seeking behavior of users and non-users is crucial in order to design online catalogs that truly complement the search strategies of information seekers. More will be said about how people learn to use the online catalog in Chapter 4.

Most Users Come with
Subject-Related Information

Slightly more than half (53%) of the online catalog users are trying to "find books, journals or magazines on a topic or subject" (see Table 5, page 92). This would seem to suggest that users are arriving at the online catalog with an expectation to do more subject searches than has been possible with "alphabetical" forms of the catalog. Prior card catalog studies have suggested that known item searches and subject searches occur about equally, although the proportion of known item searches is considerably higher in academic libraries.

In addition, half of the searches reported by users were for a specific book—most likely a known item search. An additional 24 percent of the users conduct searches for an author's multiple works and 17 percent of the users were seeking book availability information.

Class Assignments Are Primary Purpose
for Using Online Catalogs

As found in prior card catalog use studies, the user's primary purpose for using the catalog was to complete a course paper or report—a class assignment (39% of the users). Class or course reading was the reason given for use of the online catalog by an additional 29 percent of the respondents. Clearly the type of library influences this result. The online catalogs in academic libraries are used by students primarily for course-related activities. In public libraries the vast majority of users (82%) want the information contained in the catalog primarily for personal interest or recreational uses as shown in Table 5.

Users Report Bringing Complete
Information to the Catalog

According to prior card catalog use studies, few people ever remember complete bibliographic data. And if people arrive at the catalog with written information it is only slightly more likely to be correct than if the information was memorized. In sum, the bibliographic information brought to the catalog is likely to be partially complete and/or incorrect.[4] Yet a large number of users of the online catalog report that they know a complete subject heading (44%), a complete author (42%), and a complete title (39%) as shown in Table 5. Because the study design called for a self-administered question-

TABLE 5 Information Search Task

	ARL Libraries %	Other Academic Libraries %	Community College Libraries %	Public Libraries %	State and Federal Libraries %	Aggregate Sample %
I was trying to find:*						
Books on a topic	51	54	64	54	69	53
Specific book	52	49	43	49	37	50
Books by a specific author	25	21	20	24	21	24
If book is available	18	14	18	19	4	17
I need this information for:*						
Course paper or report	45	51	57	21	29	39
Personal interest	23	23	25	51	20	30
Class or course reading	33	38	57	17	16	29
Work or job	15	14	5	17	42	17
Recreational uses	13	10	14	31	7	17
Thesis-dissertation	12	9	7	4	16	10
I came with:*						
Subject heading	42	40	67	48	54	44
Complete author	45	38	32	39	37	42
Complete title	41	42	34	39	31	39
Topic word or words	28	36	24	25	42	29
Part of an author's name	14	12	11	10	12	13
Part of a title	12	11	10	10	9	11

*Legitimate multiple responses possible; therefore totals may be larger than 100%.

naire, it was not possible to ascertain the accuracy of the patron's perception of bringing complete information to the catalog.

UNDERSTANDING THE NON-USERS' CHARACTERISTICS

Online Catalog Non-Users Are Less Frequent Users of the Library

Compared to users of the online catalog, non-users visit the library only slightly less frequently. A bit less than one-third (32%) come weekly, and an additional one-fourth arrive daily, as shown in Table 6 (see Table 6, page 94). In general, online catalog non-users at public and state and federal libraries visit the library less frequently than do their academic library counterparts.

Non-Users Use the Library's Other Catalog Less Frequently

Non-users of the online catalog, in general, consult the library's existing card, book, or COM catalog slightly less often than users of the online catalog. And non-users of the online catalog in public and state and federal libraries tend also not to use the library's non-online catalog while academic library non-users will more likely consult the non-online catalog.

Non-Users Have Less Experience with Computers

Non-users of the online catalog may have had little prior contact with computer technology in general and thus may be disinclined to use the online catalog in the library. As shown in Table 6, 50 percent of non-users have never used a computer system. This distribution is uniform across types of libraries with the exception of community college libraries, where 76 percent of non-users have never used another computer system. Non-users have had much less experience with other computer systems when compared to users of the online catalog.

Uniform Non-User Sample Population

Unlike users, the non-user sample population was almost evenly split between male (52%) and female (48%), as documented in

TABLE 6 Frequency of Library and Catalog Use for Non-Users

	ARL Libraries %	Other Academic Libraries %	Community College Libraries %	Public Libraries %	State and Federal Libraries %	Aggregate Sample %
I come to this library:						
Weekly	36	38	40	29	12	32
Daily	38	39	46	4	6	27
Monthly	12	11	8	30	17	17
4 times a year	8	6	1	19	16	11
Not before today	4	4	4	13	33	9
I use the library's Book, Card or COM Catalog:						
Occasionally	34	40	13	31	12	32
Rarely	30	28	36	17	9	25
Not before today	12	11	49	19	41	18
Most visits	16	16	1	18	13	15
Every visit	7	4	1	15	25	10
I use another computer system:						
Never	43	50	76	58	46	50
Weekly	16	13	9	9	12	13
Monthly	13	11	4	8	13	11
4 times a year	11	9	5	7	12	9
Once a year	11	10	1	7	9	9
Daily	9	8	6	11	8	8

Table 7 (see Table 7, pages 96–97). Women are more likely to be non-users of online catalogs than men. Although women make up only 40 percent of the user population, they comprise 48% of the non-user group. Among the community college libraries, the population of non-users was evenly split between males and females.

Non-Users Are Slightly Older Than Users

The majority of non-users are between the ages of 20–34, which is similar to the composition of the user sample. In general, however, non-users are slightly older than users of the online catalog. Non-users have greater senior citizen representation, especially from the public and state and federal libraries (see Table 7).

Academic Non-Users Similar to Academic Users

Academic library non-users of the online catalog have about the same distributions as users in terms of grade level, e.g., freshman-sophomore, and the primary focus of academic work, that is, course work. However, as shown in Table 7, more non-users of the online catalog come from the following disciplines: Business-Management, Arts and Humanities, and Engineering.

Most Non-Users Have Not Had Time
to Obtain Training for Online Catalog Use

Non-users of the online catalog report that the reasons for non-use include: 1) have not taken the training (45%); 2) no time to learn the online catalog (40%); and 3) no need to use any library catalog (41%). Further, 30 percent reported they did not know there was an online catalog and another 29 percent reported they were a visitor or an infrequent user of the library. Some 18 percent claimed they did not know where the online catalog was located and 16 percent felt that the card catalog was easier to use (see Table 8, pages 98–99). "Fear of computers" was not an important reason for non-use: only nine percent gave "I do not like to use computers" as a reason for their non-use of the online catalog. The distributions of responses by type of library were fairly similar.

Most Non-Users Think the Online Catalog
Will Be Easy to Learn to Use

Despite the fairly widespread belief that training was required to learn to use the online catalog, 82 percent anticipated that it would be

TABLE 7 Characteristics of Non-Users

	ARL Libraries %	Other Academic Libraries %	Community College Libraries %	Public Libraries %	State and Federal Libraries %	Aggregate Sample %
Male	58	53	50	42	55	52
Female	42	47	50	58	45	48
Age group:						
20–24 years	50	53	52	19	30	40
25–34 years	21	18	15	29	28	23
15–19 years	23	21	21	11	7	18
35–44 years	4	5	6	16	18	9
45–54 years	2	2	4	10	8	5
55–64 years	1	0	1	8	7	3
65+ years	1	1	0	7	3	3
Current or highest grade completed:						
High school	3	4	7	18	10	8
Some college	59	70	82	36	30	53
College graduate	37	26	11	45	60	38

Class level:						
Freshman-Sophomore	29	33	78	NA	NA	35
Junior-Senior	36	47	5	NA	NA	36
Graduate-Master level	11	9	1	NA	NA	9
Graduate-Doctoral level	7	3	0	NA	NA	5
All Others	8	2	2	NA	NA	5
Academic area:						
Business-Management	16	32	26	NA	NA	22
Arts and Humanities	19	11	7	NA	NA	15
Engineering	16	11	23	NA	NA	15
Social Sciences	15	10	5	NA	NA	13
Physical-Biological Sciences	11	14	6	NA	NA	12
Medical-Health	9	6	12	NA	NA	8
All Other	13	16	21	NA	NA	15
Main focus of academic work:*						
Course work	83	84	90	NA	NA	84
Research	23	21	20	NA	NA	22
Teaching	5	7	0	NA	NA	5

*Multiple responses possible; therefore totals may be larger than 100%

NA = Not Applicable

TABLE 8 Non-User Attitudes About the Online Catalog

	ARL Libraries %	Other Academic Libraries %	Community College Libraries %	Public Libraries %	State and Federal Libraries %	Aggregate Sample %
Haven't used the online catalog:*						
Have not taken training	45	52	38	42	40	45
No time to learn how to use	41	42	31	44	35	41
No need to use any library catalog	42	43	62	36	25	40
Did not know there was an online catalog	28	29	16	34	36	30
Visitor, infrequent user of library	24	20	14	37	51	29
Did not know where it is	19	21	9	15	23	18
Card catalog easier	17	17	11	17	8	16
Ease of learning to use the online catalog:						
Somewhat easy	47	51	44	41	52	46
Very easy	38	27	30	42	33	36
Somewhat difficult	15	20	18	15	15	16
Very difficult	1	2	7	2	1	2
Time needed to learn to use online catalog:						
0–15 minutes	38	28	32	49	32	38
15–30 minutes	27	27	34	23	25	26
30 minutes–1 hour	21	25	20	16	20	20
1 hour – half day	9	11	7	5	10	8
Half day – a day	3	5	3	3	9	4
Day or more	2	5	5	5	4	4

How likely to use online catalog in future:

Somewhat likely	42	44	45	37	35	41
Very likely	29	32	27	40	46	34
Somewhat unlikely	19	16	19	14	12	16
Very unlikely	10	8	9	9	6	9

General attitude toward online catalog:

Very favorable	43	42	50	47	59	46
Somewhat favorable	48	47	33	40	32	43
Somewhat unfavorable	7	9	11	10	7	8
Very unfavorable	2	2	6	3	2	2

Compared to the card, book, or microfiche catalog, this online catalog is:

Better	29	37	53	32	40	34
Equal	16	19	20	16	7	16
Worse	3	3	7	5	3	4
Can't decide	52	41	20	47	50	46

*Multiple responses possible; therefore totals may be larger than 100%.

somewhat or very easy to learn to use the online catalog. Most notable, only two percent of responding non-users believe that it would be very difficult to learn to use the catalog. This belief in an "easy to learn" online catalog is demonstrated by the expectation of 64 percent of the non-users that the time needed to learn to use the online catalog is 30 minutes or less. Non-users at state and federal libraries (principally the Library of Congress) anticipate a training period slightly longer than average.

Non-Users Are Likely to Use
the Online Catalog in the Future

While non-users have yet to use the online catalog, three-fourths expect to become users in the future, as shown in Table 8. This expectation is consistent across all types of libraries.

Non-Users Have Favorable Attitudes
Towards the Online Catalog

To say that non-users have strong positive attitudes about the online catalog is perhaps an understatement. Of the non-users surveyed, 89 percent said their attitude toward the online catalog was very or somewhat favorable. Only two percent of the responding non-users felt very unfavorable towards the online catalog. Non-users have strong positive feelings about the online catalog and more than one-third rate the online catalog as better than the card, book, or COM catalog. However, almost one-half of the non-users (46%) cannot decide what form of the catalog they do prefer (see Table 8).

Further Analysis of the Non-User

Upon closer inspection, the image of the non-user contains some curious inconsistencies. For example, of those respondents who said that they had no time to learn to use the online catalog, 29 percent believed it would take 15 minutes or less to learn, and 55 percent thought the task required 30 minutes or less. Enhanced publicity or online catalog training may have little chance to succeed with patrons who are unable or unwilling to expend as little as 15 minutes in learning to use the online catalog. Further analysis of the responses to this question suggests that the chief reasons for non-use are that respondents simply do not use library catalogs or the library itself very often.[5] From this it may follow that strategies to increase acceptance of the online catalog should not focus on the catalog itself, but rather on use and users of the library as a whole.

This emphasis may explain what otherwise might remain a curious paradox: that "typical" non-users, characterized as people who use neither libraries nor catalogs with any frequency, nonetheless tend to characterize the online catalog as quick and easy to learn, and claim to be likely to use it in the future. The implication here is that, if one can promote use of the library and its bibliographic tools, the online catalog may well be able to promote itself. There is another potentially interesting interpretation of this paradox: that the non-user, unsure of how to use an online catalog and perhaps even a bit fearful of it, nonetheless is reluctant to admit the fact.

SUMMARY AND OBSERVATIONS

The typical online catalog user is a young, well-educated adult who frequents the library on a fairly regular basis. Familiarity with and prior use of computer technology is not a dominant characteristic of the online catalog user. Within academic libraries, the user of the online catalog is attempting to meet the needs of course-related work. Slightly over three-fourths of the public library users are at the online catalog for personal interest or recreational uses. A similar profile of the library catalog user emerged from prior card catalog use studies.

Users of the online catalog expect to do more subject searches than they have performed in the past with card, book, or COM catalogs. Users also feel that they bring complete information about subject headings, titles, or author's names. Yet based on prior card catalog use studies, few people arrive at the catalog with complete or accurate bibliographic information. Given that almost half the users arrive at the online catalog with a subject heading and over one-third of the users with a topic word or words, the provision of term or keyword searching may be a mandatory requirement for a "successful" computer catalog.

Until a great deal more research is completed about users of interactive computer-based systems, and the problem-solving skills of most people are better understood, designers of online catalogs must recognize the unchangeableness of the user and provide several ways or methods for easily using and interacting with online catalogs.

Any online catalog marketing campaign should take advantage of the perceptions of non-users by emphasizing: 1) the location of online catalog terminals; 2) the short period of time necessary to learn basic skills; 3) that no formal training is necessary to learn to use the online catalog; and 4) the improved information retrieval capabilities of the online catalog. Given that the non-user of the online catalog is an infrequent visitor to the library, the challenge may well be to attract the individual back to the library on a more frequent basis.

NOTES

1. H. MacLean. "Using the Library Catalog." *New Zealand Libraries,* 35, 1972, pp. 165–172 and A. Maltby. *U.K. Catalogue Use Study: A Report.* London: Library Association, 1973.
2. Library staff did not participate in the survey.
3. Richard P. Palmer. *Computerizing the Card Catalog in the University Library.* Littleton, CO: Libraries Unlimited Inc., 1972 and Ben-Ami Lipetz. *User Requirements in Identifying Desired Works in a Large Library.* New Haven, Conn.: Yale University Library, 1970.
4. American Library Association. *Catalog Use Study.* V. Mostecky (Ed). Chicago: American Library Association, 1958 and Renta Tagliacozzo, Lawrence Rosenberg, and Manfred Kochen. "Access and Recognition: From Users' Data to Catalogue Entries." *Journal of Documentation,* 26, September 1970, pp. 230–249.
5. See *Users Look at Online Catalogs.* Berkeley, CA: University of California, Division of Library Automation and Library Research and Analysis Group, November 16, 1982 (available through ERIC), pp. 34–39 for an elaboration of the analysis.

CHAPTER FOUR

The Organizational Setting

T<small>HE</small> online catalog user typically comes to the library (although this is not a requirement with an online catalog) and is provided direct access to the online catalog. In addition to an online catalog terminal, the library provides a complement of online catalog support. This includes: 1) assistance services, e.g., staff assistance, printed aids, classes or videotape instructions, 2) the physical setting, furniture, lighting, and 3) possibly a printer or printers attached to the terminal. These support services are collectively identified as the "organizational interface" since these services, provided by the library, do have an effect on the ultimate success of the online catalog and influence the satisfaction experienced by the online catalog user. The organizational interface has been described as everything from the edge of the terminal screen outward.[1] Everything from the edge of the screen inward is called the system interface or human-computer communications.

THE USER-ORGANIZATION INTERFACE

Users Discover the Online Catalog by Seeing Terminal in the Library

The majority of users (64%) first discover that the library has an online catalog by simply observing the terminal in the library (see Table 9, page 104). Given the "developmental" nature of these online catalogs, most libraries may have adopted a low "public relations" profile when introducing their online catalogs. About ten percent of the users hear about the online catalog either through a library

TABLE 9 Learning to Use the Online Catalog

	ARL Libraries %	Other Academic Libraries %	Community College Libraries %	Public Libraries %	State and Federal Libraries %	Aggregate Sample %
Heard about the online catalog:						
Noticed terminal in library	66	44	62	70	47	64
Library course or orientation	13	18	13	3	7	10
Friend or family member	8	10	8	9	22	9
Library staff	6	17	6	10	18	9
Instructor	5	10	9	1	5	4
Learned how to use online catalog:*						
By printed instructions	56	48	46	46	71	53
By library staff	20	43	40	38	53	30
By instructions on terminal	32	30	44	22	22	29
By myself	21	15	22	21	12	20
From a friend	15	18	14	16	14	16
From a library course	7	15	16	1	4	6
I got help from:*						
Printed matter, signs	41	36	32	36	62	41
Terminal screen instructions	33	34	52	27	34	32
Did not get help	35	30	24	27	16	31
Library staff member	12	33	31	34	50	22
Person nearby	4	4	7	8	7	6

*Multiple responses possible; therefore total may exceed 100%.

course or orientation program (10%), from a friend or family member (9%), or from a library staff member (9%). The Evanston Public Library has found that children who learned about the library's online catalog from a library orientation program during the week bring their parents to the library on Saturday to show them how to use it. A school instructor was a source of the news about the online catalog for about four percent of the users. Non-ARL academic libraries and state and federal libraries seem to have placed their online catalog terminals in locations somewhat remote from the general flow of traffic.

Users Learn to Use the Online Catalog
by Themselves

Almost one-third (30%) of the users learn with the assistance of library staff members. The vast majority of users learn to use the online catalog by themselves (consulting either the printed instructions provided by the library via brochures or signs (53%) or the instructions displayed on the online catalog terminal screen (29%)—see Table 9). An additional 20 percent report that they learned to use the system "by myself." The extent to which the user relied on printed instructions or instructions provided by the online catalog in learning to use the online catalog "by myself" is not known, but in all likelihood these resources were probably tapped by the beginning user.

Almost One-Third of Users Said
They Required No Assistance at All

Interestingly, about one-third of the users (31%) required no help during their search—an encouraging sign. When the user did need help or assistance during the course of a search, the user turned most frequently to the instructions found on printed materials—brochures or signs—or to the online catalog terminal itself (32%) as indicated in Table 9. Users in state and federal libraries (principally the Library of Congress) responded about half as often (16%) to "I did not get help." This suggests that these systems may be less "user-friendly" and thus are a bit more difficult to master.

First-Time Users Get Help from Library Staff

As a group, first-time users of the online catalog are more likely to get some kind of help. Only 10 percent said they did not get help during their first session, as compared to 31 percent overall. For new users, library staff are apparently the most important form of assistance. Over half (51%) of first-time users mentioned staff as a source of aid, compared to 22 percent of users with some prior experience.

What Happens When Online Aids Are Provided?

"Instructions on the terminal screen," one source of help for first-time users, is, however, not directly associated with library support services. Also, not all systems offer explicit online instruction, making it difficult to interpret the importance of this response. To correct for this bias, the catalog systems were defined as having one of three levels of online assistance:[2]

1. None at all.
2. One form of online assistance (either Online Instructions or HELP).
3. Both forms of assistance (Online Assistance and HELP).

The results of this adjustment are displayed in Table 10. When the system has explicitly designed online aids, they are indeed used: 34 percent of users in systems with two forms of aid used them, as opposed to 29 percent in systems with no explicit aids. On the other hand, one wonders which "instructions on the terminal screen" were used by the 29 percent of users in the systems with no aids.

TABLE 10   Sources of Help in Systems With and Without Online Assistance

	Systems With No Aids %	Systems With One Aid %	Systems With Two Aids %
I got help in doing this online catalog search from:			
a. Printed material or signs	57	31	38
b. Instructions on the terminal screen	29	29	34
c. Library staff member	26	36	15
d. Person nearby	5	7	5
e. I did not get help	24	27	35
TOTAL*	141	131	128

*Percentage sum to more than 100 due to legitimate multiple responses.

Online Aids Reduce Reliance
on Printed Materials

Online aids reduce reliance on printed materials. In no-aid systems, 57 percent of users used print sources, compared to 31 to 38 percent in systems with aids. This relationship—the more online aid, the less reliance on print—has a relatively strong correlation (the Pearson correlation coefficient, $r = 0.1320$).

Online Aids Can Reduce Reliance
on Staff Assistance

Of some interest here is the pattern of help from library staff. Although there is a mild tendency for reliance on staff to increase as online aid increases, the pattern is not linear. One online aid feature increases reliance on staff, while both features (online instructions *and* HELP) reduce use of staff aid.

Online Aids Increase Users
Self-Reliance

Another interesting offshoot of online assistance is that it appears to increase self-reliance. The greater the number of such aids, the greater the proportion of respondents who say they did not get any help at all ($r = 0.088$). The relationship is not strong, and the finding is open to several interpretations. For example, (a) in systems with online aids, respondents may not *realize* that they have received assistance, or may not have actively sought help, even though they got some (if this is true, the actual incidence of benefit from online aid is greater than Table 10 would suggest), or (b) systems with online aids happen to be easier to use, so that the apparent relationship between online aids and self-reliance is spurious.

Clear Instructions Are Needed

Thus, initially there is a real need for the library to provide clear instructions on how to use the online catalog and how satisfactorily to resolve problems encountered during a search. To minimize dependency on staff, the online catalog should be able to provide online instructions *and* be equipped to respond to user requests for "help" at each possible stage of a search.

Libraries Are Meeting Organizational
Interface Issues Effectively

By and large the libraries included in the study dealt with the organizational interface issues fairly effectively. While there are a few areas that need improvement, the majority of issues, e.g., lighting, glare, terminals, training, signs, etc., have been satisfactorily addressed. Relatively few users, between 11 percent and 15 percent, are dissatisfied with the signs and brochures, staff advice, or the availability of signs.

Online Catalog Terminal Presents
Few Problems

Initially there was some concern that the online catalog terminal, the physical link between the user and the computer system, would play a major role in the success of the online catalog. Yet, based on the survey results as seen in Table 11, the terminal itself presented few problems.

Chief Problem Is Insufficient Writing
Space at the Terminal

The primary problem experienced by users of the online catalog was the lack of sufficient writing space adjacent to the terminal. Slightly more than one-third of the users indicated difficulty in this area. The distribution is consistent across all types of libraries. This indicates the pervasive nature of the problem. Adequate writing space should be provided on *both* sides of the terminal and additional space should be allocated for the temporary storage of personal belongings, e.g., books, tablets, jacket, purse, etc.

Printer Problems

For libraries that provided printers for use in conjunction with the online catalog, users had some difficulty using the printer.[3] To some extent the users may have reported the fact that they did not realize the printer was available rather than printer operational problems per se.

TABLE 11 Organizational Interface Problems

	ARL Libraries %	Other Academic Libraries %	Community College Libraries %	Public Libraries %	State and Federal Libraries %	Aggregate Sample %
Online Catalog Terminal:						
There is not enough writing space	35	30	43	32	45	34
Printer is not easy to use	37	52	31	26	10	29
Nearby noise is distracting	12	15	15	10	9	11
Keyboard is confusing	10	12	10	13	13	11
Letters on screen not easy to read	11	8	5	7	8	10
Table height not right	9	8	11	9	5	8
Lighting is too bright	9	7	8	6	8	8
Too much glare on screen	8	6	4	7	10	8

TABLE 12 Organizational Interface Improvements

	ARL Libraries %	Other Academic Libraries %	Community College Libraries %	Public Libraries %	State and Federal Libraries %	Aggregate Sample %
Online Catalog Service Improvements:*						
More terminals	49	50	56	55	51	51
Terminals outside library	41	40	27	20	31	35
Terminals in other library locations	37	22	26	23	28	31
Command chart posted	28	27	18	33	28	29
Manual at terminal	19	19	10	30	0	20
Training sessions	12	18	12	15	26	14
Audio-visual training session	10	12	12	13	15	11
Manual for purchase	7	8	6	8	18	8
None	15	18	22	17	16	16

*Multiple responses possible; therefore totals may be larger than 100%.

Few Other Terminal-Related Problems

Potential problems with the online catalog terminal exist. They include: nearby noise (from the terminal itself, the printer, and the library setting); the table height supporting the terminal might not be right; the terminal keyboard might be confusing; lighting may be too bright; the size of the characters displayed on the screen may be difficult to read; and there may be glare on the screen from a nearby major light source. Yet these potential problems are, in the aggregate, relatively minor, with only 8 to 11 percent of the users reporting a problem (see Table 11).[4]

Users Would Like More Terminals

In terms of improvements required at the organizational interface, users do have some definite suggestions. First, users would like access to more terminals (51%) both in locations outside the library (35%) and in other library locations (31%) as shown in Table 12 (see Table 12, page 109). Certainly the issue of the number and location of terminals is an important one since it translates into improved service levels for the library patron and into costs for the purchase and maintenance of the terminals for the library.

Estimating the Number of
Online Catalog Terminals

OCLC received a grant from the National Science Foundation to investigate the number of terminals needed for a library's online catalog. A report from this project should be available by summer 1983. Some libraries have gathered and analyzed queuing data in an effort to predict the number of terminals needed.[5] Others have suggested that there may be a correlation between the number of terminals and average daily attendance or average/peak circulation statistics.[6] While it is clear that there is a need for guidelines for estimating the required number of terminals, each library installing an online catalog will no doubt have to experience a certain amount of trial and error before arriving at the "right" number *and* location of online catalog terminals.

Electronically Distribute the Library's Catalog

The fact that the library can electronically distribute the library's catalog (database) to multiple locations is one of the most attractive features of the online catalog. Library users need not come to the library or to the main card catalog area to find needed information. Thus, access to the database is possible wherever a computer terminal is located—the library, faculty offices, homes, dormitories, senior citizen centers, shopping malls, etc. Convenient access to the information stored in the library's catalog, made possible by the combination of computer and telecommunication technology, creates the opportunity to provide library services in new and exciting ways, for example, cable television.

Users Want Commands Charts

Command charts and a manual or brochure assist the inexperienced user in learning how to use the online catalog and aid the infrequent user who needs to "brush up" on online catalog skills. Almost one user out of three (29%) would like a command chart posted at the terminal and one user in five would like a manual or brochure near the terminal (see Table 16, page 120).

Interestingly, 16 percent of the users suggested that *no* organizational improvements are necessary; this is surprising given that online catalogs are really in their infancy. This would suggest that the libraries are aware of and have begun to meet their organizational interface obligations. Or, perhaps, users are simply so delighted with the library services provided via the online catalog and thus have not yet focused on needed improvements.

SUMMARY AND OBSERVATIONS

Overall, libraries with operational online catalogs appear to have done a relatively good job of addressing the organizational interface issues. The majority of users simply observe the terminal in the library and learn to use the online catalog by themselves, using the printed instructions provided by the library via brochures or signs or the instructions displayed on the terminal screen itself. And when users need help, they turn most frequently to printed materials or ask the online catalog for "HELP." Thus, there is a real need for the library to provide clear and concise instructions on how to use the online catalog and how the user can solve problems encountered during a search.

The text layout or format for the presentation of this explanatory information should be suited to, and thus different for, the printed and video media. To be truly effective, the online catalog should provide both brief online instructions on how to use the system *and* online "HELP" assistance to aid the user in solving a problem. In addition to brochures, a summary command chart affixed to the terminal is a feature frequently requested by users.

Libraries must address the issue of support furniture for online catalog terminals. Terminals are typically placed on existing furniture with little thought of the needs of the user, e.g., privacy and comfort, or of the requirements of the terminal itself. The need for adequate writing space on both sides of the terminal is a prime consideration. Other factors for online catalog terminal furniture include temporary storage of personal belongings, provision for and masking of unsightly and potentially dangerous electrical and data cables, glare on the screen, and the need for a terminal "fence" at the rear of the terminal to improve the visual aesthetics and discourage tampering with the switches and cables located at the rear of the terminal.

Providing dial-in ports to the computer to facilitate access to the library's catalog for users with terminals or personal (micro) computers is an encouraging development. However, these dial-in ports require additional CPU communications support equipment and the issues of patron confidentiality and system security must be addressed.

The provision of general dial-up access seems likely to raise some public service issues as well. These issues are of two kinds: 1) extending the "organizational interface" to remote users and 2) developing and providing new forms of technical support.

Dial-in users are far outside the boundaries of what we conventionally think of as the "organizational interface." Using the online catalog from homes, offices, dormitories, and shopping centers, these users are not aided by signs, brochures, and staff assistance available within the walls of the library. Provision to help dial-in users may be made through mailed brochures and announcements of system changes, and by planning for extensive telephone assistance. Probably the best and least expensive form of aid for dial-up users, however, is the provision of online instruction and assistance in the online catalog system itself.

Providing dial-up access may also inundate the library staff with a host of questions about a wide variety of specific terminals and microcomputers and their compatibility with the online catalog, as well as questions about telecommunications equipment, arrangements, and costs. Not only will staff have to cope with these issues when users first arrange for dial-up access, but it seems likely that they will be asked for advice and assistance whenever communication fails. The prospect of preparing the reference staff to provide troubleshooting advice for the entire universe of personal computers, terminals, and modems may appear daunting, but we think libraries would be well advised to plan for dealing with this situation.

NOTES

1. Douglas Ferguson, Neal K. Kaske, Gary S. Lawrence, Joseph R. Matthews and Robert Zich. "The CLR Public Online Catalog Study: An Overview." *Information Technology and Libraries,* 1(2), June 1982, pp. 84–97.
2. Information for this analysis was provided by the participating systems on a standard survey form (*Users Look at Online Catalogs,* Appendix J). System managers were asked to indicate if their systems had "instructions or assistance imbedded in the dialog" or if "separate HELP displays are available on request."
3. It should be noted that, in library systems where no local printers are available, the responses are not included in the tabulations for this response category.
4. For a comprehensive summary of environmental and ergonomic factors associated with CRT terminals, see A. Cakir, D. J. Hart, T. F. M. Stewart. *Visual Display Terminals: A Manual Covering Ergonomics, Workplace Design, Health and Safety, and Task Organization.* New York: John Wiley & Sons, 1980.
5. Christine Borgman and Neal Kaske. "On-Line Catalogs in the Public Library: A Study to Determine the Numbers of Terminals Required for Public Access." *Proceedings of the 43rd ASIS Annual Meeting.* Vol. 17. White Plains, NY: Knowledge Industry Publications, 1980, pp. 273–275; Christine Borgman and Neal Kaske. "Determining the Number of Terminals Required for an On-Line Catalog through Queuing Analysis of Catalog Traffic Data," in J. C. Divilbiss (Ed.) *Public Access to Library Automation* (Clinic on Applications of Data Processing: 1980). Urbana-Champaign, IL: University of Illinois Graduate School of Library and Information Science, 1981, pp. 20–36; A. Whitney Knox and Bruce A. Miller. "Predicting the Number of Public Computer Terminals Needed for an Online Catalog: A Queuing Theory Approach." *Library Research,* 2(1), Spring 1980–81, pp. 95–100; and Charles Sage, Janet Klaas, Helen H. Spalding and Tracey Robinson. "A Queueing Study of Public Catalog Use." *College & Research Libraries,* 33, July 1981, pp. 317–325.
6. Joseph R. Matthews. *Public Access to Online Catalogs: A Planning Guide for Managers.* Weston, CT: Online, Inc., 1982.

CHAPTER FIVE

The Computer System

THE computer system is the sine qua non for the online catalog. The principal components of the computer system are three: *the terminal* used by the user, the *computer* which handles the communications between the terminal and the *database*. In addition to the machine-readable records representing the library's collection of materials, the database also contains indexes to these records designed to facilitate access by the user.

THE TERMINAL

Standard CRT Terminal with Keyboard

Currently there are two types of terminals that a user may encounter when using an online catalog. The first type of terminal is the standard cathode ray tube (CRT) or "TV screen" terminal with a keyboard which resembles that found on a typewriter. The CRT terminal displays both the data input by the user and any messages, prompts, and screens returned to the user by the computer. The keyboard allows the user to enter a search request and send it to the computer. This CRT terminal with keyboard is used by all of the online catalog systems, with the exception of the public access terminal provided by CL Systems, Inc.

Touch-Screen Terminal

The CLSI touch-screen terminal, the second type of terminal, is a CRT terminal that does not have a keyboard. In addition to displaying information, it provides the user with choices or alternatives for further action. Users indicate their choice by pressing their finger on an indicated location directly on the screen of the visual display unit itself; thus, the reference to "touch-screen" terminals. It takes up to seven touches for a user to retrieve and display an individual record.

Labeled Function Keys

Perhaps the two most important aspects of the CRT keyboard terminal are the keyboard used by the patron to input search request and the size of the characters displayed on the CRT screen itself. Keyboards come in a confusing array of configurations. The majority of keyboards resemble a typewriter keyboard, but there the similarities cease. Some keyboards may have a separate numeric keypad to the right of the main group of keys, while other terminals may have a group of special function keys located above the main set of keys. Special function keys enable the user to initiate an entire series of related commands by pressing only one button. The special function keys may be labeled "F1," "F2," etc., as found on some terminals included in this study. It would be perhaps more helpful for an inexperienced user if the special function keys were labeled "Author Search," "Title Search," etc. Note, however, that if the computer system depends on a particular kind of terminal with unique function keys, problems with dial-up support discussed previously may arise. In addition, the RETURN key may be located at different places on the keyboard and may be labeled "SEND" or "NEWLINE" rather than "RETURN."

Terminal Screen Character Size

The character displayed on the screen is created by energizing several dots or spots within a matrix of dots on the face of the CRT screen. A minimum acceptable character size is a 7 x 9 dot matrix.[1] A larger 9 x 11 dot character is preferable since it produces a more natural character—a character more clearly resembling a standard print character. Of the systems studied, only the CLSI touch-screen terminal uses a 9 x 11 character, while all other systems rely on a 7 x 9 dot character size.

Users Have Few Problems with the Terminal Itself

The user questionnaire included two questions dealing specifically with the terminal itself (Question 43A and 43C). As shown in

Table 13, users have few problems with the legibility of letters on a CRT screen (only 10% of all users indicating a problem) or with the keyboard being confusing. Based on this data it would appear that most users have few problems with the terminal itself.

THE COMPUTER

The computer system can be considered to be composed of two components: hardware and software. The hardware—or the computer equipment itself—is important because the size of the computer, i.e., mainframe computer or minicomputer, will influence the number of terminals that may be attached to the computer as well as the number of information retrieval features, e.g., Boolean searching, keyword or term searching, sorting retrieved records, etc. There are two main types of computer software or programs—operating system software and applications software. The operating system software handles the communications between the computer, the disk drives where the bibliographic records and indexes are stored, and the online catalog terminal used by the patron. But while the operating system routinely handles all the necessary computer housekeeping tasks, the applications software is much more important to the ultimate success of the online catalog. The applications software allows records to be added to the database, creates and maintains indexes or access points to the bibliographic records, and provides the necessary and appropriate terminal screen messages, prompts, and information displays. It is this last function, the information displayed to the user and the human-computer communication protocol (or language), which allows the user to send a search request to the computer, that is typically called the "system interface."

Computer System Characteristics
Vary Considerably

The characteristics of both the computer system and the online catalogs that run on each corresponding computer system vary considerably as is seen in Table 2.

Computer System Response Time Is
an Important Factor

Regardless of the size of a computer system and its characteristics, the two most crucial issues relative to the success of an online

TABLE 13 Terminal Problems

	ARL Libraries %	Other Academic Libraries %	Community College Libraries %	Public Libraries %	State and Federal Libraries %	Aggregate Sample %
Terminal keyboard is confusing	10	12	10	13	13	11
Letters on terminal screen are not easy to read	11	8	5	7	8	10

TABLE 14 Computer System Response Time

	ARL Libraries %	Other Academic Libraries %	Community College Libraries %	Public Libraries %	State and Federal Libraries %	Aggregate Sample %
Rate of computer response too slow*	24	25	20	43	40	30

*Percent Agree or Strongly Agree

catalog are system reliability and system response time. System reliability was not addressed by this study but users were asked about response time as a problem. Response time, that interval of time while the user waits for the computer to process the search request, has been shown to affect the user's attitude about a computer.[2] Response time is affected by the number of active terminals connected to the computer, time of day and day of week (busy periods), the type of transaction, and the amount of computer power available to process the user's search request. In particular, as response times increase beyond 10 seconds attitudes become negative. Interestingly, users are really concerned about consistency of response times—even during periods of heavy computer usage. Thus, system designers may wish to measure all transactions and "slow down" some responses during non-peak periods to provide consistent response times.

Almost One-Third of All Users Are
Dissatisfied with Response Time

Almost one-third of all users (30%) indicate a problem with computer system response times (see Table 14, page 117). According to the users, response time seems to be a serious issue at the public and state and federal libraries.

THE DATABASE

A machine-readable database is fundamental to an online catalog. Obviously if the data are not available in machine-readable form then they are not accessible by the patron via the online catalog. As was shown in Table 2, the size of each library's collection and the amount of the collection in machine-readable form vary considerably. The database may contain brief or full MARC records; it may only reflect the monograph holdings of the library, as seen in Table 15, or include journals and other materials. The library may not yet have completed a retrospective conversion project.

Access to the Database

Access to the database is provided through a number of indexes or inverted files which in turn point to or are linked to the appropriate bibliographic records. Again the number of indexes provided to the user varies from a high of 14 to as few as 3 (see Table 2).

TABLE 15   Library Holdings Represented in the Online Catalog

Type of Material/ Library Type	Number of Libraries in Which the Online Catalog Includes:		
	None	*Some*	*All*
Monographs:			
ARL Libraries	0	5	2
Other Academic	0	3	3
Community College	0	2	0
Public	0	0	4
State and Federal	0	1	1
Journals:			
ARL Libraries	1	3	3
Other Academic	2	1	3
Community College	2	0	0
Public	2	1	1
State and Federal	0	1	1
Other Materials (newspaper, films, maps, etc.):			
ARL Libraries	1	4	1
Other Academic	2	1	3
Community College	2	0	0
Public	0	2	2
State and Federal	0	1	1

Users Want Database Coverage Expanded

The user of the online catalog would like the database expanded to include additional kinds of materials. Three out of ten users indicate that they would like access to newspapers and about one-fourth of the users desire access to government publications, more older books, journal titles and dissertations (see Table 16, page 120). Surprisingly, 10 percent of the users felt the database required no additional coverage of materials in the library's collection.

SUMMARY AND OBSERVATIONS

The terminals included in this study contributed few problems for users of the online catalog. A larger character size on the terminal screen will be more pleasing to the user, but users are generally satisfied with the current 7 x 9 dot matrix character size. Yet, substantial improvements can be made in the design of online catalog terminals. Keys with similar functions could be color coordinated and special function keys could be precisely labeled, e.g., Author Search,

TABLE 16 Database Improvements Requested by Users*

	ARL Libraries %	Other Academic Libraries %	Community College Libraries %	Public Libraries %	State and Federal Libraries %	Aggregate Sample %
Newspapers	31	33	30	20	39	30
Government Publications	34	22	19	24	0	28
More Older Books	32	21	17	4	40	26
Journal Titles	17	54	51	34	0	23
Dissertations	23	15	7	10	46	21
Records or Tapes	19	13	22	31	7	20
Maps	13	15	13	21	0	14
Technical Reports	19	15	18	14	21	18
Motion Picture Films	14	23	24	10	17	14
None	10	14	13	15	7	10

*Multiple responses possible so percentages do not total 100%.

Title Search, Subject Search, to facilitate searching by the new and infrequent user of the online catalog. Regardless of the size of the computer system, system reliability and a consistent response time, even during peak periods of use, are two factors pertaining to the computer itself which must be addressed by the system designer.

The issues surrounding the database are complex and involve a number of trade-offs. Should the database contain full MARC records? A full MARC record for all or some of the MARC formats, e.g., monographs, serials, maps? How many indexes should provide access to the database? Should Boolean search capabilities be provided at all, or should they be explicitly or implicitly provided? Should there be term or keyword access to author, title, subject headings, added entries, notes, or series data fields? Should a user be able to limit or restrict search results by date of publication, language, format of material, etc.? All of these issues and more must be faced by librarians and system designers considering an online catalog.

NOTES

1. A. Cakir, D. J. Hart, T. F. M. Stewart. *Visual Display Terminals: A Manual Covering Ergonomics, Workplace Design, Health and Safety, and Task Organization.* New York: John Wiley & Sons, 1980.
2. Robert B. Miller. "Response Time in Man-Computer Conversational Transactions." *Fall Joint Computer Conference Proceedings,* 1968, pp. 267–277.

CHAPTER SIX

Problems With the Online Catalog Interface

THE information displayed to the user, plus the human-computer communication protocol or language—commands, provided to aid the user in sending a search request to the computer—constitute what is typically called the "system interface."

THE USER-SYSTEM INTERFACE

The goal of any human-computer interface, most recently called "user friendly" or "user cordial,"[1] is to make the user most productive while using the computer-based catalog system. The "friendliness" of a particular system or human-computer interface is much like beauty—"it's in the eyes of the beholder." Or, like Justice Potter Stewart's classic pornography definition, "I know it when I see it."

Exactly what constitutes a user-cordial system interface is still difficult to define but some progress has recently been made. Charles Hildreth, in recent work supported by the Council on Library Resources, suggests that a user-oriented system interface is: 1) easy to use; 2) friendly and cordial; 3) protective and forgiving; 4) reliable and responsive; and 5) adaptive and flexible.[2]

Users Have Generally Positive Feelings About Online Catalog Features

The longest portion of the user questionnaire, with 27 Likert-type (agree-disagree) attitude questions, was devoted to issues related to the system interface. This section of the questionnaire asked about general types of searches as well as specific aspects of the search itself. Respondents either "Agreeing" or "Strongly Agreeing" are grouped together to provide an indication of the problems experienced by users with a particular online catalog feature. As shown in Table 17, while a number of users have a significant problem with nine features of the online catalog (more than 25% of the users indicated they experienced a problem with one or more of the nine features), the majority of users have very positive feelings overall about the online catalog (see Table 17, pages 124–25). An additional 16 features were considered problematic by 9 percent to 24.9 percent of the users.

While such a finding is indeed encouraging, especially given the early development state of online catalogs, much work remains to be done to make computer catalogs truly "user friendly." It is surprising that more users did not encounter more problems with a greater number of the available online catalog features. It is anticipated that the continuing feedback of users to librarians and system designers will significantly reduce the number and intensity of problems experienced by future users of online catalogs. However, recall that over one-third of online catalog users have no experience with other computer systems. As general computer literacy increases, library patrons may become more effective online catalog users, and their experience with other computer systems may reduce their tolerance for the shortcomings of existing computer catalogs.

Majority of Problems Are in the Areas of Search Control and Display Control

There are four functional areas which make up the user interface: 1) operation control—for example, stacking or entering multiple commands at one time; 2) search formulation control—for example, limit by date or language; 3) output control—for example, display forward and backward; and 4) support functions—for example, information and instruction.[3] It is interesting to note that the majority of software interface problems are concentrated in the areas of search formulation control and output (display) control.

User Wants to Be in the "Driver's Seat"

Two out of the top five system interface problems pertain to the user's ability to retain control while using the computer catalog.

TABLE 17 System Interface Problems

	ARL Libraries %	Other Academic Libraries %	Community College Libraries %	Public Libraries %	State and Federal Libraries %	Aggregate Sample %
1 Increasing the result (Q 19)*	49	40	28	38	43	46
2 Finding correct subject term (Q 17)	46	38	33	40	34	43
3 Knowing what is in online catalog (Q 33)	37	41	36	33	43	37
4 Computer search by subject (Q 13)	34	19	15	31	26	31
5 Scanning through a long display (Q 18)	29	28	15	25	39	28
6 Entering commands when I want (Q 37)	27	30	16	33	23	28
7 Searching with truncation (Q 25)	28	26	27	31	22	28
8 Reducing the result (Q 20)	28	25	14	24	29	27
9 Interrupting or stopping the display (Q 31)	25	27	29	23	25	25
10 Typing in exact spelling, initials and spaces (Q 32)	21	20	21	29	14	22
11 Using logical terms like AND, OR, NOT (Q 26)	22	22	NA	NA	15	21
12 Remembering commands in the middle of the search (Q 16)	21	20	15	17	30	20

13 Selecting from a list of choices (Q 36)	19	23	12	22	17	20
14 Remembering exact sequence of commands (Q 27)	19	22	13	18	27	19
15 Using codes or abbreviations for searching (Q 22)	14	15	12	27	18	17
16 Understanding abbreviations on the screen (Q 23)	15	18	20	21	22	17
17 Understanding the initial instructions on the screen (Q 28)	11	12	11	19	22	15
18 Computer search by call number (Q 14)	13	23	16	20	15	15
19 Understanding explanations on the screen (Q 21)	13	16	4	17	23	14
20 Locating call number on the screen (Q 24)	14	14	6	15	15	14
21 Computer search by title (Q 11)	13	10	8	15	14	13
22 The order in which items are displayed (Q 34)	13	11	8	13	14	12
23 Combined author/title search (Q 15)	12	12	11	14	13	12
24 Understanding the display of multiple items (Q 30)	11	13	6	14	9	11
25 Displayed messages too long (Q 35)	10	14	5	10	6	10
26 Computer search by author (Q 12)	10	9	8	11	6	10
27 Understanding the display for a single item (Q 29)	9	10	4	11	8	9

NA = Not applicable (system does not offer this feature).
*Q refers to the User Questionnaire number.

These two problems include how to increase the result when too little is retrieved (ranked #1 with 46% of the users indicating this as a problem), and scanning through a long display (ranked #5—28%).

Some Problems Associated with
Subject Searching

As will be shown in Chapter 7, a significant number of online catalog searches being done by users are subject searches. Yet users indicate that they continue to experience problems with subject searching. The second and fourth most frequently cited problems were "finding the correct subject term" (43% of the users indicated a problem) and "computer search by subject" (31%). It should be noted, however, that users experience greater success with subject searching and in finding appropriate subject headings with the online catalog. Users at the card catalog find valid subject headings only about one-half the time.[4]

Improving Controlled Vocabularies
Is Essential

Most of the libraries in this study use *Library of Congress Subject Headings* (LCSH). By virtue of their wide distribution through co-operative cataloging systems and from the Library of Congress card distribution service, LCSH represents the most widely used subject vocabulary for monographs in the U.S. Thus a subject heading search is, almost by definition, a search for an LC subject heading. Much has been written about the limitations of LCSH and will not be repeated nor summarized here.[5] Knowing of the large number of subject searches in online catalogs, knowing that most of the participating online catalogs use LCSH for subject access, knowing of the problems with LCSH, and knowing of users problems with subject searching, there is ample justification to recommend action to improve the utility of LCSH for computer searching.

Online Catalog Can Increase
Number of Access Points

The online catalog has the potential for substantially increasing the number of access points available to the user; computer indexing allows the user to go beyond the first few words of a subject heading to component words or subdivisions through the use of term or keyword searching. Keyword or term searching increases the likelihood of a user's finding one or more subject headings or titles containing the user's "search term." Keyword searching can also retrieve large amounts of irrelevant material, records that happen to use the search term entered by the user. Features to help the user limit overly long search results, e.g., Boolean searching, limiting by date and language, should accompany term searching; "reducing the search result" was the eighth-ranked system problem (see Table 17).

Problems Experienced by Users Are Similar Regardless of Type of Library

When looking at Table 17, the similarities between all types of libraries, including ARL and public libraries, are much greater than the few differences that exist. Users from state and federal libraries do, however, report greater difficulty with scanning through a long display (rank #5), remembering commands in the middle of the search (rank #12), and remembering the exact sequence of commands (rank #14).

Further Analysis of System Features

To obtain reliable information on the problems and benefits of specific system features, it is, in principle, necessary to compare user problems for at least two systems that are alike in every way—features, capabilities, databases, user characteristics—except one: some systems possess the feature of interest, and some do not. The variety of computer catalog systems makes it impossible to meet this "ideal" condition. As Table 18 shows, among the 15 systems included in this study, no two meet the criterion of being alike in all features but one (see Table 18, pages 128–29).

In many cases, it is possible to approach the condition of "holding everything else constant" using various statistical analysis techniques, but the number and variety of system features, database characteristics, and user characteristics to be controlled in this case makes a statistical approach exceptionally complex, and could yield results of limited or questionable validity.

Despite these problems, there are a few measured relationships between system features and user problems, based on an analysis of variance, that are sufficiently strong to merit discussion. It is important to remember, however, that these relationships arise from comparisons between all systems that possess a particular feature

TABLE 18 Functions and Capabilities of 15 Computer Catalogs[6]

						CODE									
Function	A	B	C	D	E	F	G	H	J	K	L	M	N	P	Q
OPERATIONAL CONTROL															
SELFUNC — Selection of function (Search, circulation, etc.)			X	X			X			X				X	X
DISRUPT — Interruption of online output			X	X	X	X				X			X		X
STACKCOM — Command stacking/multiple commands			X									X		X	
BCKSPACE — Correct keying errors before command input (back space)			X	X		X		X		X	X	X	X	X	X
OUTPUT CONTROL															
SELDISP — Can user select preferred display format? (yes or no)			X		X	X	X	X		X	X	X	X		
DISPB/F — Display forward and back			X	X	X		X			X	X	X	X		X
COLPRINT — Hard copy printed results available						X		X	X			X			
SORT — Sort capability									X						
INFORMATION AND INSTRUCTION															
OLINSTR — Instruction or assistance imbedded in dialogue			X	X	X	X	X	X		X	X	X	X	X	X
HELP — Separate HELP displays available on request			X		X	X	X	X		X	X	X	X		X
THESAUR — Related terms, index, or thesaurus available online				X								X	X	X	

SEARCH FORMULATION AND CONTROL

		A	B	C	D	E	F	G	H	J	K	L	M	N	P	Q
DATELIM	Expand or limit results by date	X				X		X					X	X	X	
LANGLIM	Expand or limit results by language				X	X							X		X	
TYPELIM	Expand or limit results by type of material	X							X				X	X	X	
OTHERLIM	Expand or limit results by (please specify)						X						X	X	X	
FREETEXT	Free text term or keyword searching available			X	X				X				X	X		X
BOOLEAN	Use of Boolean operators (and, or, not)			X	X				X				X	X		X
TRUNCATE	Ability to use truncated search terms	X	X	X	X	X	X		X	X	X		X	X	X	X
SAVESET	Ability to create and save sets										X					
SELMODE	Ability to select or change search mode			X	X								X			

TYPE OF COMMAND ENTRY LANGUAGE

		A	B	C	D	E	F	G	H	J	K	L	M	N	P	Q
COMMAND	Formal command language	X	X	X	X	X		X	X	X	X	X				X
MENU	Menu selection	X	X	X	X	X							X	X	X	
OTHERMDE	Other													X		

A = Online Computer Library Center; B = Research Libraries Information Network; C = Northwestern University; D = Dartmouth University; E = Pike's Peak Regional Library System; F = Claremont Colleges; G = CL Systems, Inc; H = DataPhase Systems, Inc.; J = Mankato State University; K = Universal Library Systems; L = Library of Congress; M = University of California; N = Ohio State University; P = Dallas Public Library; Q = Syracuse University.

TABLE 19   Selected Relationships of System Features and Reported Problems

System Feature[1]

System Problem[2]	Command Stacking	User Select Display Mode	Print Results	Related terms, index or thesaurus	Limit by date	Limit by type of material	Limit by other ways	Truncate search terms	Command language	Menu selection	Online inst.	Online HELP
Q 19. Increase Result			+							0		
Q 17. Subject Terms			+		+	0		−	−			
Q 33. Knowing Incl.				−		−	−					
Q 20. Reduce Result	−	+	+	+	+	+	+			−	−	
Q 25. Truncation				+	+	+						
Q 37. Entering Cmds	+	+	0	+	+	0	+		+	0		−
Q 38. Response Rate	0	+	+	+	+	+	+	+	0	0	−	−
Q 18. Long Display			+					−	−			
Q 13. Subject Srchg	−	+	+		+	+	+					
Q 31. Stop Display	−	−			−		−		−			
Q 26. Boolean Opns	0	0			0	0		0		+		
Q 16. Remember Cmds	−			−	0		−		0		+	+

[1] A '+' denotes a statistically significant relationship (.001 level) that improves satisfaction. A 'o' indicates a strong positive relationship (eta > 0.10). A '−' denotes a statistically significant relationship that degrades satisfaction and '0' denotes a strong negative relationship.

[2] Listed in approximate order of importance. Q # refers to the User Questionnaire question number. (See Appendix 1.)

and all systems that do not; within each comparison group are systems with a variety of other features and characteristics. The findings discussed below could easily arise from characteristics other than the ones being directly compared.

The important results of these comparisons are shown in Table 19. From this analysis, we observe that the following "problem variables" appear to be influenced by system features.

a. *Increasing the result when too little is retrieved.* Most system features, as seen in Table 19, seem not to offer much help here. Online printing appears somewhat useful. Menu-driven systems appear to be at a significant disadvantage.

b. *Finding the correct subject term.* Systems with online printing and search-limiting by type of publication seem to be more successful. Truncation appears to present a definite problem. Interestingly, the presence of a searchable term index or thesaurus does not appear to be significantly related to user responses to this question.

c. *Knowing what is included in the catalog.* No system features appear to offer help here. Systems with some forms of search-limiting and with truncation appear to create problems in this area.

d. *Reducing the result when too much is retrieved.* Not surprisingly, limiting features are helpful, though the relationship is not strong. Also, the ability to select among several display formats, searchable indexes and thesauri, and online printing seem helpful.

e. *Searching with the short form of a term (truncation).* The use of truncation appears easier in systems with thesauri and with search-limiting.

f. *Entering commands when I want to.* Menu-driven systems present definite problems here. This kind of user control appears easier in systems with search limiting, command stacking (ability to string commands together), and online printing.

g. *The computer takes too long to respond.* Again, menu-driven systems seem to increase problems. Most other features appear to reduce complaints about perceived response time. An exception is the provision of online instruction or user-controlled online help systems.

h. *Scanning through a long display (forward or back).* Providing truncation and a command mode of interaction appear to increase problems, while online printing reduces them, although none of the relationships are strong. Interestingly, the explicit provision of a forward/backward display control feature (not included in Table 19) is not statistically related to this question.

i. *Searching by subject.* Search limiting and online printing features appear helpful, as does the ability to select display formats.

j. *Interrupting the display.* Several system features have weak negative associations with this question, but the nature of the relationship is not obvious. The presence of a display interruption feature (not included in Table 19) is not statistically related to this question.

k. *Using logical terms (and, or, not).* There are several strong positive relationships—selection of display formats, searchable thesauri, and limiting by date or by another element. Menu-driven systems appear to have a mild advantage here (perhaps because they do not require users to construct explicit Boolean arguments), and the command stacking feature appears to represent a definite disadvantage in this regard.

l. *Remembering commands in the middle of a search.* Most of the features included in Table 19 present problems in this respect. Two of them (limiting by date and by another element) are relatively important problems. The exceptions are the provision of online instruction and user-directed help screens, which are positively (although not strongly) related to the ability to remember commands.

Another way to look at the data is to note those system features that reduce or increase reported problems:

a. *Online printing* is almost universally helpful, aiding users in increasing and reducing retrieval results, finding the right subject term, and so on. The one negative correlation, with "interrupting the display," may suggest problems in user control of the printing process.

b. *Search limiting features,* including limiting by date, type of material, and other elements, are generally helpful, but apparently make the online catalog appear more difficult to master. This is indicated by strong negative relationships with the ability to remember commands in the middle of a search. Limiting by language was not a statistically important variable in this analysis.

c. *Searchable indexes and thesauri* also appear to be generally helpful in searching, but add to confusion in using the interface.

d. *User-selected display formats* are also helpful on the whole, but seem to be confusing to some users.

e. *Command stacking,* for systems with this feature, seems to make it easier to enter commands, and contributes to a faster perceived response rate, but contributes to problems in other areas.

f. *Truncation* is very nearly a universal problem for users; the only exception is an apparent positive contribution to perceived response rate.

g. *Command language and menus,* the two principal methods of search control, get somewhat mixed reviews. Command language systems receive some positive votes, including a strong relationship to perceived system response, but appear to have some mild drawbacks as well. Menu-driven systems, on the other hand, rack up some important disadvantages, most notable in perceived response time and in ability to control the search session. There are apparently some offsetting advantages as well. For instance, menu systems appear to engender fewer problems in using Boolean operators.

h. *Online help and instruction features* either do not provide help where it's needed (e.g., in reducing search results) or add problems of their own (e.g., response time), but provide significant aid to users who are not sure what to do next, or how to do what they want.

The point of the foregoing sections is not to identify those features that are specifically desirable or undesirable in online catalogs. As previously indicated, the evidence is not strong enough to demonstrate the clear superiority of any particular feature.

Online Catalog Design Trade-offs

It is, however, our intention to introduce the notion of design trade-offs into the discussion of online catalog development. To support the idea that a particular feature or design choice, implemented to improve one aspect of the catalog, may have undesirable consequences in another aspect, consider the following observations that might be drawn from the previous discussion.

1. When features are added to address specific searching problems (e.g., limiting features), they often work in that context, but add to the complexity of the catalog and make it difficult for users to remember what command among many to use, and when and how to use it.
2. With online instruction or user-addressable help functions, people can find and use the right command in a complex catalog, but these aids are often perceived as slowing down the catalog's response time.
3. When a menu-driven system is instituted to avoid the problems of complexity and syntax in command-driven systems, some operations become easier; however, users perceive that flexibility is lost and that the catalog becomes slower.

It is also not our intent to suggest solutions to these design dilemmas. For the present, we can only highlight the fact that there is no uniquely right answer to the question of how to design an online catalog, and encourage efforts to investigate and define the dimensions of these trade-offs.

Improvements Sought for Subject or Term Searching

While more will be said about the improvements sought by the users of online catalogs later in this chapter, it is important to note here that the first, second, fifth, and eighth ranked improvements relate directly to subject or term searching (see Table 20, page 134). Almost one-half of the users would like to be able to "view a list of related words" (45%). In addition, users indicate a desire to be able to "search the table of contents/index" (42%), "search by subject word" (24%), and "search by title word" (18%). There is considerable broad-based support for these improvements and the ability to browse the authority control file and the ability to use term or keyword searching are almost mandatory requirements for any online catalog—whether located in an academic or public library. While it is true that keyword searching may add as much as 50 percent to the cost of disk data storage requirements, these costs are continuing to decline. The issue of cost is an important consideration,[7] but should only be one of several factors in deciding upon the capabilities of an online catalog.

Importance of Authority Control Records Yet to Be Realized

The issues raised by the first ranked improvement—ability to view related words—are serious and have yet to be fully recognized either by system providers or by librarians. Two of the most important

TABLE 20 Additional System Features Desired by Users*

	ARL Libraries %	Other Academic Libraries %	Community College Libraries %	Public Libraries %	State and Federal Libraries %	Aggregate Sample %
View related words	48	41	47	39	42	45
Search table of contents/index	44	44	39	35	47	42
Determine if book checked out	25	47	18	19	44	26
Print search results	27	26	28	29	0	25
Search by subject word	23	28	28	31	0	24
Step by step instructions	18	29	14	34	30	24
Search by journal title abbreviation	25	20	12	10	15	20
Search by title word	16	22	19	25	0	18
Search by illustrations & bibliography	19	16	18	15	18	17
Limit search by language	14	5	2	4	0	13
Change display order	11	11	10	13	12	12
Limit search by date of publication	13	12	9	10	0	11
Location of book in library	13	24	12	14	30	10

*Multiple responses allowed so total may exceed 100%.

of these issues are: 1) what should be the source of the list of related words—read, "authority control file with SEE and SEE ALSO cross references," and 2) at what level—the local library, a regional consortium, a state or multi-state network, or a national bibliographic utility—should these authority control records be maintained? The answers to these questions are likely to vary for each individual library.

Augmenting the MARC Record

The second most sought improvement is the ability to search a book's table of contents and/or index. Such an ability implies that the online catalog should provide term or keyword searching and that the bibliographic record should be augmented or enhanced to provide the additional information. Pauline Atherton (Cochrane), in her study of similarly augmented records, *Books Are for Use,*[8] found that users were able to search faster, cheaper, and with a "greater degree of recall using the augmented record in comparison to a full MARC record." Clearly such an augmented record will require additional disk storage capacity but such storage costs continue to decline dramatically and so may not always be such a serious concern. However, the intellectual time necessary to select and input the additional terms from the index and/or table of contents will be quite expensive. In the not too distant future, automated data input machines may be able to read the table of contents and/or index of a work, selecting which phrases and terms should be indexed and automatically added to the MARC record to create an "Augmented MARC" (AUGMARC) record. It is possible that at some point the Library of Congress Cataloging in Publication Office may be able to solicit accurate, succinct descriptions of new books from publishers and to make these descriptions part of the bibliographic record. The library community itself may undertake a cooperative project to manually input such additional data for "important" titles. The improved searching capabilities resulting from such an augmented record may well be worth the costs involved. Use of an AUGMARC record is clearly an issue that deserves additional study and experimentation.

COMPUTER SYSTEM INTERFACE ISSUES

Much as the list of features shown in Table 18 will be helpful for system designers and librarians in making necessary improvements to the online catalog, a grouping of these features would likely provide even more guidance.

Further Analysis of System Features

Using a statistical technique called factor analysis, which groups questions which are response-related (i.e., when this feature is reported as a problem, the other features in this group tend to be reported as a "problem" also), an interesting clustering of features emerges. Seven factors were extracted[9] from the 28 variables in the factor analysis and each seems to have a plausible explanation and a sensible relationship to the use of the online catalog. It is not uncommon for factor analysts to engage in a pastime called "naming the factors." The desire to interpret the factor analysis substantively and to give the results labels more meaningful than "Factor 1" and "Factor 2" is understandable, but it should be recognized that factor weights are statistical artifacts, rather than direct measures of the named phenomenon, and that the "names" of factors come solely from the interpreters of the data in most cases. The factor-weighting results from this analysis are remarkably consistent and unambiguous, with few "stray" variables; the "names" to be discussed below derive considerable support from the data themselves. Because each factor is composed of both positively and negatively phrased Likert questions, the signs of the factor weights are important in understanding the "sign" or direction of the factor itself, a point that will become clear when we discuss each factor below. Our "factor names" are therefore useful to indicate the "sign" of each factor as well as its general subject.

Use of Codes or Abbreviations

As shown in Table 21, the first group of features pertains to the use of codes or abbreviations. This area pertains both to the user's ability to understand abbreviations on the terminal screen and to use codes or abbreviations to conduct a search. Research into human-computer interaction shows that it is helpful for the user if search command abbreviations or codes are mnemonic, and are rule-derived, i.e., uniform and of fixed length.

Display of Information on the Terminal Screen

The second area concerns the display of information on the terminal screen. This factor groups together problems in coping with and

TABLE 21   System Interface Issues

Factor	Factor Name	Factor Weight*
1	Codes and Abbreviations Are Easy to Understand and Use	
	Abbreviations are easy to understand (Q 23)	.719
	Using codes or abbreviations is easy (Q 22)	.584
	Understanding explanations on the screen is difficult (Q21)	−.358
2	Displays Are Hard to Understand	
	Understanding the initial instructions on screen is difficult (Q 28)	.512
	Understanding a multiple record display is difficult (Q 30)	.496
	Understanding explanations on screen is difficult (Q 21)	.488
	Locating call numbers is difficult (Q 24)	.369
	Understanding the display of a single record is easy (Q 29)	−.332
	Remembering sequence of commands is easy (Q 27)	−.305
3	Command and Control Is Easy	
	Remembering the exact sequence of commands is easy (Q 27)	.522
	Remembering commands in middle of search is easy (Q 16)	.486
	Scanning through long display is easy (Q 18)	.419
	Knowing what is in the computer catalog is easy (Q 33)	.410
	Reducing the result when too much is retrieved is easy (Q 20)	.358
	Interrupting or stopping the display is easy (Q 31)	.337
	The order (of bibliographic display) is easy to understand (Q 34)	.329
4	Subject Searching Is Difficult	
	Finding the correct subject term is difficult (Q 17)	.659
	A subject search is difficult (Q 13)	.599
	Increase the result when too little is retrieved is difficult (Q 19)	.401
	Searching with truncation is easy (Q 25)	−.311
5	Known-Item Searching Is Difficult	
	A search by title is difficult (Q 11)	.506
	A search by author/title is difficult (Q 15)	.486
	A search by author is easy (Q 12)	−.479
	A search by call number is easy (Q 14)	−.455
6	The Computer Tries My Patience	
	Selecting from a list of choices takes too much time (Q 36)	.497
	Displayed messages are too long (Q 35)	.482
	The response rate is too slow (Q 38)	.408
	It is hard to find a free terminal (Q 42)	.312
7	Library Services Are Not Helpful	
	Signs and brochures are not very useful (Q 40)	.579
	Availability of signs and brochures is adequate (Q 39)	−.389
	The staff advice is often not helpful (Q 41)	.343

*Positive numbers indicate agreement; negative numbers are questions to which the user disagreed.

understanding the initial instructions displayed on the screen, single record and multiple record displays, understanding explanations on the screen, and finding a specific data element on the screen, e.g., the call number. Problems with information displays are apparently not very serious; the most important "problem variable" in this group is "remembering the exact sequence of commands" (a somewhat curious variable to be found in the company of display problems), which was the 14th-ranked problem in Table 17. The most serious problem directly related to screen displays was "understanding abbreviations," ranked 16th of 27 in Table 17.

This result notwithstanding, much remains to be learned about the display of bibliographic information on the screens of CRT terminals. The terminal itself offers some new ways in which information can be displayed and highlighted. For example, characters can be underlined, enlarged, blinked, made bold, and displayed on a reverse video background. Thus the terminal technology offers a considerable amount of flexibility not possible with 3 x 5 cards. In addition, the increased amount of space—typically 80 characters in width and a minimum of 24 lines—offers the prospect for utilizing "white" or blank space. Data elements can be identified with words and not abbreviations. The layout or typography of the screens can be based on the frequency of use of data elements by patrons rather than the tradition of an older form of the (card) catalog.

Command and Control of Search by the User

The third area identifies the fact that the user is (or should be) in command and control of the search process. The majority of users report little difficulty in remembering commands and when to use them, scanning a long display and understanding the display order, reducing the initial search result, or interrupting or stopping the display. Nonetheless, four of the seven questions that define this factor are among the "top ten" system problems as shown in Table 17, suggesting that problems with command and control are definitely important to users.

Difficulty with a Subject Search

The fourth major factor involves subject-searching problems. As Table 17 shows, all four variables in this group are among the "top ten" problems, and three are in the "top five," suggesting that subject searching should be a high priority for improvement.

Known-Item Searching

The fifth area of interest is known-item searching. Problems are apparently much less prevalent here: the most serious problem in this group, "searching by call number," ranks 18th of the 27 problems in Table 17.

Delays Lead to User Frustration

The delays users experience in using or attempting to use the online catalog are a source of frustration. Extensive use of menus, long messages displayed on terminal screens, and poor system response time all contribute to this problem.

Helpfulness of Library Services

The helpfulness of library services is related to the quality of the interaction with library staff and to the quality and quantity of printed materials provided by the library. The findings merely emphasize this commonsense approach.

SUMMARY AND OBSERVATIONS

Although users appear to have little difficulty understanding the information displays used by this group of online catalogs, standardization and consistency in the area of the display of information and use of codes or abbreviations on terminal screens may be beneficial. For example, should bibliographic data elements be labeled? Where should the call number be located? Should the call number be a multi-line display similar to what is found on the spine of the item? Should system messages and options be presented at the bottom of the CRT screen? Should the previous command, used to generate the current display, be included on the current display? Those involved with online catalogs must remember that much of what worked with the 3 x 5 card technology will not work with CRT technology. As the number of online catalogs proliferate and the number of separate online catalogs multiply, this area may become increasingly important. Notably the work underway by an ANSI Z39 committee (American National Standards Institute) chaired by Pauline Cochrane is beginning to address this area.

The chief reason for considering standards in this area at present is to spare the user the learning time and frustration associated with learning to use and interpret the information displays as they use different online catalogs. Certainly there would be a cost associated with the adoption of these standards[10] for those few libraries with operational online catalogs, but it may be preferable to minimize these costs by acting before the number of functioning catalogs becomes too great.

The display of bibliographic information on a CRT terminal screen is rarely evaluated from the perspective of the online catalog user. What data elements are needed for different types of displays? With what frequency do most patrons examine bibliographic data elements? What do a majority of patrons call each specific data element? The variations for displaying data on a CRT terminal screen are vast indeed. CRT terminals can display data in a number of ways: reverse video, brightness, blinking, size, and underlining. However, it is important to prevent the tyranny of the constraints imposed by the 3 x 5 card from spilling over and forcing their way, either intentionally or accidentally, onto an 80 character by 24 line CRT terminal screen (which also imposes some limitations).

Users of online catalogs need improved user-cordial ways of retaining control and managing the information that they retrieve. Improvements are needed with the interface itself and consistent and meaningful command languages are of paramount importance.

Given the amount of subject searching that is occurring with online catalogs and the problems experienced by users with subject searching, this area commands serious attention. What solutions might be implemented by designers of online catalogs or by the library community to improve subject searching? Systems might systematically "capture" terms entered by users to build a list of "aliases" (SEE References) to aid the user in moving from words entered by the user to LCSH terms. The subject authority files, with extensive scope notes that can be searched and displayed, could be placed online. The Dewey and LC Classification Tables, including the defining words and phrases tied to the class numbers, might be placed online and made available for searching and browsing.[11] In addition, the Library of Congress might begin to assign more subject headings to each MARC record to improve the likelihood of a user finding valid subject headings.

The ability to view and browse an authority control file or an authority-based index is perhaps crucial to the success of the online catalog. The authority control file, given sufficient SEE and SEE ALSO cross references, can link the users' vocabulary to the pre-coordinate subject headings usually employed by libraries.

Keyword access for words contained in the corporate author, conference name, title, subject headings, notes, and added entries *combined* with controlled vocabulary searching will prove a powerful tool. For example, a significant topic word may retrieve a number of useful works from the title or subject heading fields; a look at the subject headings and call numbers assigned to the retrieved records can lead to subject searches that bring together additional related works not having the initial keyword in their titles or subject headings.

Perhaps the only realistic solution to the shortcomings of the *Library of Congress Subject Headings* is to provide users of the online catalog with term or keyword searching. Such a technique substantially increases the number of access points and thus the number of records retrieved by a system. The use of keyword searching need not be restricted to subject headings but can also be used for author, title, notes, series, etc. searches. Additional techniques, such as the "keyword approximation search" used at the Washington University School of Medicine in St. Louis, Missouri, can be used to improve the likelihood of a user's being successful at the online catalog. A keyword approximation search index is created for each term following specific rules, e.g., delete all vowels and selected consonants. Should a search be unsuccessful using the regular indexes, the computer modifies the users' search request, following the same rules used to create a keyword approximation search index, as an aid in overcoming spelling errors input by the user.

Another promising approach is the use of "soundex algorithms" (rules that direct the computer to search for words whose spelling would cause them to "sound like" the terms entered by the user) to compensate for typing errors and broaden search results.

Owing to the improved searches likely to result from an augmented MARC record, i.e., MARC plus the addition of the table of contents and/or index terms, serious attention should be paid to the creation, distribution and use of augmented records for use in online catalogs.

Signs and brochures need to contain clear and nontechnical language. The terminology must be consistent with the online explanations provided by the online catalog. Explanations provided by staff should also be consistent with the signs, brochures, and the online instructions or help screens.

NOTES

1. Charles M. Goldstein and William H. Ford. "The User-cordial Interface." *Online Review,* 2(3), 1978, pp. 269–276.

2. Charles Hildreth. *Online Public Access Catalogs: The User Interface.* Dublin, OH: Online Computer Library Center, 1982.
3. Hildreth, *op. cit.*
4. American Library Association. *Catalog Use Study.* V. Mostecky (Ed.) Chicago: American Library Association, 1958 and University of Chicago. *Requirements Study for Future Catalogs.* Chicago: University of Chicago, Graduate Library School, 1968.
5. Carol A. Mandel with the assistance of Judith Herschman. *Subject Access in the Online Catalog.* Washington, DC: The Council on Library Resources, August 1981 and Pauline A. Cochrane and Monika Kirtland. "I. Critical Views of LCSH—The Library of Congress Subject Headings; A Bibliographic and Bibliometric Essay." "II. An Analysis of Vocabulary Control in the Library of Congress List of Subject Headings (LCSH)." Syracuse, NY: ERIC/Information Resources Clearinghouse, 1981 ERIC ED 208 900.
6. Several of the functions included here are described in greater detail in later chapters. A more complete description of all functions will be found in *Users Look at Online Catalogs,* (University of California, 1982). Data for Table 18 were obtained from the Computer System Profile Questionnaire discussed in Appendix J of *Users Look at Online Catalogs.* An extended analysis of the functions and features of computer catalogs is contained in Charles Hildreth's *Online Public Access Catalogs, op. cit.*
7. Margaret M. Beckman. "Online Catalogs and Library Users." *Library Journal,* 107 (19), November 1, 1982, pp. 2043–2047.
8. Barbara Settel and Pauline Cochrane. "Augmenting Subject Descriptions for Books and Online Catalogs." *Database,* 5(4), December 1982, pp. 29–37 and Pauline Atherton. *Books Are For Use.* Final Report of the Subject Access Project to the Council on Library Resources. Syracuse, NY: Syracuse University, School of Information Studies, February 1978. (Available from ERIC, ED 156 131).
9. Using the principal factoring method with iterations, and equimax orthogonal rotation. See Harry H. Harman, *Modern Factor Analysis* (Chicago: University of Chicago Press, 1967) for a general introduction to factor analysis techniques, and Chapter 24 of Norman H. Nie et al, *SPSS: Statistical Package for the Social Sciences,* Second Edition (New York: McGraw-Hill, 1975), for a detailed description of the techniques used for this analysis.

   Each of the 28 variables has a "factor weight" for each of the seven factors. The "factor weight," which ranges in value from +1 to −1, can be thought of as a correlation coefficient indicating the strength of the relationship between each variable and the factor as a whole. A large factor weight (either positive or negative) suggests that the variable makes a large contribution to the factor. Conventionally, factor weights greater than 0.30 (positive or negative) are considered to be "important" variables, and only variables with factor weights greater than this value are shown.

10. Beckman, *op. cit.*
11. Pauline A. Cochrane, "Classification As a User's Tool in Online Public Access Catalogs." *Universal Classification. Proceedings of the 4th International Study Conference on Classification Research, June 28–July 2, 1982.* Augsburg, Frankfurt: Indeks Verlag, 1982, pp. 260–267 and Karen Markey. *The Process of Subject Searching in the Library Catalog: Final Report of the Subject Access Research Project.* OCLC/OPR/RR-83/1. Dublin, OH: OCLC Online Computer Library Center, February 4, 1983.

CHAPTER SEVEN

Online Catalog Use and Satisfaction

T HIS section will examine the use patrons make of the online catalog, the success they experience in using it, and their expressed levels of satisfaction with the online catalog.

USE

Most Users Search by Subject or Topic

Most users, as indicated in Table 22, use subject headings or topic words in their search: 43 percent "searched by subject headings" and 30 percent "searched by topic word or words." The amount of subject searching is considerably higher in the community college libraries. It is important to remember that a subject heading search is the only kind of subject searching allowed by ten of the fifteen online catalogs. When data for the systems that do not provide subject access are removed and the searches are further classified as known-item and subject searches, about 59 percent of all searches are for subject information (see Table 23, page 146).

Slightly less than one-third of all users (30%) reported that they used a topic word or words for their search. In fact, the user may have used a topic word or words and entered this phrase as a partial subject-heading search and achieved satisfactory results.

Keyword or Term Searching Preferred by Users

It is interesting to examine closely the data from the Mankato State System which allows users to conduct *either* a keyword or term

TABLE 22 Type of Search Reported by Users*

	ARL Libraries %	Other Academic Libraries %	Community College Libraries %	Public Libraries %	State and Federal Libraries %	Aggregate Sample %
A subject heading or headings	40	37	67	47	56	43
A complete author's name	39	36	27	37	36	38
A complete title	36	40	31	36	26	36
Topic word or words (keyword or term searching)	28	37	24	29	45	30
Part of an author's name	18	15	10	10	13	15
Part of a title	16	16	13	12	11	14
Part for a complete call number	7	0	3	4	4	5

*User was reporting on his or her last search, not all searches performed in the session. Multiple responses may be chosen so total may exceed 100%.

TABLE 23   "Known Item" and Subject Searches in Catalogs with
Subject Search Capacity

Type of Search	Frequency
Author	14%
Title	12%
Author-Title	15%
Subtotal, Known Items	41%
Subject	36%
Author-Subject	7%
Title-Subject	6%
Author-Title-Subject	10%
Subtotal, Subject Information	59%

search or a subject heading search. Almost two-thirds of the Mankato users (64%) indicate they use the term searching capability of the online catalog and slightly less than one-half of the users (48%) use a subject-heading search (see Table 25, page 148). Given a choice, users report they will more often utilize the information retrieval capabilities of a computer system through the use of keyword and term searching than choose a controlled vocabulary (subject heading) search.

Term Searching Can Complement
LC Subject Headings

The extensive use of term searching by the users at Mankato State should not be too surprising. Term searching more closely approaches the "real or natural" language people actually use in daily conversation. It is the same natural language that users bring with them as they approach and use the online catalog terminal rather than the pre-coordinated phrases used in the Library of Congress Subject Headings. However, the combination of term searching and subject-heading searching provides a powerful tool for library patrons since term searching can aid the user in identifying one or more highly useful or relevant records. The subject headings assigned to these "relevant records" can in turn lead to records which may have been overlooked by the user because appropriate or alternative subject headings were not known or remembered by the online catalog user. Within the DIALOG system, such a capability can be employed by the searcher through the use of an "EXPAND" command. A similar command would be extremely useful to online catalog users.

Multiple Access Points are Used

Since the questionnaire respondent was allowed to indicate multiple responses, the totals for the question on types of searching are larger than 100% (see Table 22), it is clear that users are employing multiple types of searches to obtain their desired information from the online catalog. In fact, slightly more than one-third of online catalog searches result in the use of more than one index in the database (see Table 24).[1]

When information brought to the search (Question 1) is compared with information used in the search (Question 3), we find that about 41 percent of users come with only known-item information, but almost 44 percent use only known-item access points in the search. When the responses for systems that do not provide subject searching are removed, the patterns of information brought and used match more closely (Table 24). This offers some confirmation for the belief that in systems without subject access or with limited subject access (including card catalogs), some author and title searches may in fact be "disguised" subject searches.

Relationship Between Bibliographic
Information and Search Method

In Table 24, we see that although 56 percent of users bring information for only single access points, 60 percent search only a

TABLE 24   Information Brought to and Used in the Search

Category[1]	Information Brought	Information Used
Author	11%	14%
Title	9%	12%
Subject	36%	34%
Subtotal, Single Element	56%	60%
Author-Title	22%	17%
Author-Subject	6%	7%
Title-Subject	5%	6%
Author-Title-Subject	12%	10%
Subtotal, Multiple Elements	45%	40%
Totals[2]	101%	100%

[1]Derived from User Questions 1 and 3. Users who came with or searched by call number information only are excluded.
[2]Totals may deviate from 100 percent due to rounding.

TABLE 25 Types of Searches Performed On Online Catalogs*

Search	Northwestern University[1] # %	University of Calif. (Command Mode)[2] # %	University of Calif. (Lookup Mode)[2] # %	Claremont Colleges[3] # %	Mankato State[4] # %	Mission/[1] West Valley # %	Pikes Peak[5] # %
Term	SNA	SNA	SNA	SNA	40,206 (36.8)	SNA	SNA
Subject Heading	60,898 (31.1)	SNA	SNA	1,957 (41.7)	20,421 (18.7)	17,589 (62.4)	26,424 (37.6)
Subject Term	SNA	58,266 (46.2)	111,308 (29.6)	SNA	5,423 (5.0)	SNA	SNA
Title	74,437 (38.1)	SNA	SNA	862 (18.4)	16,936 (15.5)	5,263 (18.7)	28,371 (40.4)
Title Term	SNA	30,309 (24.1)	152,017 (40.5)	SNA	2,849 (2.6)	SNA	SNA
Author	60,294 (30.8)	SNA	SNA	1,661 (35.4)	12,732 (11.6)	4,397 (15.6)	9,287 (13.2)
Author Term	SNA	35,328 (28.0)	112,475 (29.9)	SNA	373 (.3)	SNA	SNA
Author/Title	—	—	—	SNA	7,211 (6.6)	32 (.1)	SNA
Call Number	—	SNA	SNA	107 (2.3)	SNA	459 (1.6)	SNA
Course, Instructor	SNA	SNA	SNA	SNA	SNA	440 (1.6)	SNA
Other	—	2,099 (1.7)	0 (0.0)	101 (2.2)	3,235 (3.0)	—	3,954 (5.6)
Totals	195,629 (100)	126,002 (100)	375,800 (100)	4,688 (100)	109,386 (100)	28,180 (100)	70,282 (100)

SNA = Search Not Available
— = Data Not Available
[1] = Data for months of April and May, 1982.
[2] = Data from February 28–April 25, 1982.
[3] = Data for month of April, 1982 for branch Science libraries; Sept. 15–Oct. 15, 1982 for Sprague Library.
[4] = Data for month of April, 1982.
[5] = Data for month of April, 1982.

single access point. Although the difference is not large, the gap is over twice as great as that between known item and subject information brought and used. The implication is that *users do not use as much information as they bring to the search*. This apparent phenomenon may be explained either of two ways:

• Users are able to complete their online catalog searches successfully with only part of the information they bring to the search; or
• Present online catalog systems make it difficult for users to apply all the information they bring to the search, either by failing to provide the necessary access points and features, or by failing to communicate to users how to use those features.

Users Employ Subject Searching Extensively

Available data from the online catalogs themselves (see Table 25) confirm the large amount of subject searching being done by users. The amount of subject heading searching ranges from 37.6 percent at Pikes Peak to a high of 62.4 percent at Mission/West Valley Colleges. Title searches range from a high of 40.4 percent at Pikes Peak to 15.5 percent at Mankato State. Author searches account for no more than 15 percent in all systems.

Actual search statistics indicate that title and author searches are used considerably less than the typical user employs these search approaches when at the card catalog.

Keyword Searching Is Heavily Used When Available

The users at Mankato State have the ability to search with keywords and terms. As shown in Table 25, the users frequently use term searching, with about 45 percent of all searches being keyword or term searches. A term search is employed more than twice as frequently as a subject heading search.

Data collected and analyzed at Mankato State indicate that about 60 percent of the title terms entered by users are found in the subtitle portion of the title field. Therefore, keyword/term access is important in fields other than subject headings.

SUCCESS

The online catalog has the potential of "failing" the user for one of three reasons: 1) the user cannot find an item that is in fact in the catalog, 2) the sought item is not in the collection—a collection failure (some think that the collection failure should not be considered a catalog failure since the catalog correctly indicated that the sought item was not in the collection), or 3) the item is in the collection but not yet in the online catalog, e.g., nonprint media, older materials, etc.

While the study was not able to collect objective data about the success rates enjoyed by users of the online catalog, two questions did focus on the user's perception of the utility of the retrieved information.

Eighty-five Percent of Users Find Some
Relevant Material in Their Search

Seventeen percent of all users found more than what they were looking for; slightly less than one-half of all users (40%) found some of what they were looking for and an additional one-quarter of all users (28%) found all or most of what they were looking for (see Table 26). Thus, it is possible to say that eight out of ten users were "successful" in their search. The remaining 16 percent of users found nothing. This distribution was consistent across all types of libraries. Given that the majority of libraries in this study have yet to complete retrospective conversion of their bibliographic records into machine-readable form, the fact that about 15 percent of the users found nothing is not too discouraging. But total "recon" must be completed, it is assumed, to reduce the number of users finding nothing.

Half of All Users Discover Interesting
Material They Were Not Seeking

In addition, the online catalog seems to be playing a serendipitous role in that one-half of all users are finding things of interest other than what they had anticipated (see Table 26). As online catalogs continue to mature and evolve, providing features such as the ability to browse indexes and authority files and to automatically link and display all records associated with a particular index term (as with the "Expand" command on DIALOG), serendipity will no doubt increase. Yet, the number of pleasant "surprises" now found by users of the online catalog is indeed encouraging. And, the more frequently the online catalog is used, the more likely the user will find other things of interest.

TABLE 26 User Success with the Online Catalog

	ARL Libraries %	Other Academic Libraries %	Community College Libraries %	Public Libraries %	State and Federal Libraries %	Aggregate Sample %
In this computer search I found:						
Some of what I was looking for	40	41	41	34	54	40
All or most of what I was looking for	26	30	28	32	19	28
Nothing I was looking for	19	12	11	15	9	16
More than I was looking for	15	18	20	20	18	17
I came across things of interest other than what I was looking for*	46	52	51	54	64	50

*Percent responding Yes.

SATISFACTION

Eighty Percent of Users Are Satisfied with Results of the Search

An online catalog could facilitate searching and the library could provide all the necessary training aids and physical facilities, yet the user still might not be satisfied. The operative word is "might." How satisfied are users with the computer catalog? To say that users have very positive attitudes towards the online catalog is perhaps the understatement of the year. As shown in Table 27, 80 percent of all users found their most recent search either very satisfactory or somewhat satisfactory. This high level of satisfaction is consistent across all types of libraries.

Over Ninety Percent of Users Like the Online Catalog

There is even more positive overall support for the online catalog itself. More than 90 percent of all users indicated that their general attitude toward the online catalog was very favorable or somewhat favorable. Again, the high level of support is consistent across all types of libraries.

Three-Quarters of Users Prefer the Online Catalog to the Card Catalog

Not surprisingly, three-fourths of all users (75%) rated the online catalog better than the card, book, or microform catalog in the host library (see Table 27). Less than ten percent (9%) favored the non-online form of the catalog.

Preference for the Online Catalog Is Related to Search Satisfaction and Retrieval Results

As with overall attitudes toward the online catalog, users' preferences for the online or the card catalog are rather strongly related to search satisfaction and retrieval results, but even those who had unsuccessful or unsatisfactory searches seem to prefer the online catalog.

- There is a relatively strong correlation between the amount retrieved and catalog preference ($r = 0.230$), with those who retrieved the most being

TABLE 27 User Attitudes Towards the Online Catalog

	ARL Libraries %	Other Academic Libraries %	Community College Libraries %	Public Libraries %	State and Federal Libraries %	Aggregate Sample %
This computer search was:						
Very satisfactory	44	53	50	50	50	46
Somewhat satisfactory	34	32	39	32	38	34
Somewhat unsatisfactory	11	9	8	10	8	10
Very unsatisfactory	12	6	3	8	4	10
Overall or general attitude toward the online catalog is:						
Very favorable	68	73	78	60	78	67
Somewhat favorable	26	22	19	28	18	25
Somewhat unfavorable	5	4	3	8	4	5
Very unfavorable	1	0	0	1	0	2
Compared to the card, book, or microfiche catalog in this library, the online catalog is:						
Better	74	82	91	70	84	75
Equal	17	15	8	17	12	16
Worse	9	3	1	13	4	9

most likely to prefer the online catalog. Nevertheless, 55 percent of those who found nothing in their search think the online catalog is better than the card catalog.

- There is even a stronger correlation between search satisfaction and catalog preference (r = 0.383). Naturally, those most satisfied with the results of their search are more likely to prefer the online catalog. However, of those who were unsatisfied or very unsatisfied with their last search, 47 percent prefer the online catalog, and 29 percent prefer the card catalog.
- There is a mild relationship between instances of serendipity and catalog preference (r = 0.172). Of those who found something unexpected in the course of the search, 81 percent prefer the online catalog, and 5 percent prefer the card catalog; of those who did not, 68 percent prefer the online catalog and 13 percent prefer the card catalog.
- Users with a favorable attitude toward the online catalog are more likely to prefer it to the card catalog. The strength of this relationship (r = 0.602) is among the strongest bivariate correlations found in the data analysis. This is not surprising. What is of interest is that the relationship is not even stronger. About 9 percent of those with a very unfavorable attitude toward the online catalog *nevertheless prefer the online catalog* to the card catalog.

Further Analysis of Satisfaction

The factor analysis described in the preceding chapter succeeds in reducing 28 questions about system problems to seven interpretable factors. It is possible to compute a "factor score" for each respondent for each of the seven factors. The "factor score" is computed by multiplying the user's response to each component question by the factor weight for each question, and summing the results. Using the seven factor-score variables in place of the 28 Likert variables, it is possible to consider methods of relating system problems to search satisfaction. The statistical technique of multiple linear regression was chosen, in part because the data themselves are in a form to permit use of this powerful statistical method, and in part because of the technique's ability to control for other characteristics of the user and the system.

A stepwise multiple linear regression analysis was performed using the seven factor scores, seven demographic variables, three database variables, and a number of system features as independent variables, and the five satisfaction measures as dependent variables, as shown in Table 28 (see Table 28, pages 156–57). In the sections that follow, regression results are displayed and discussed for each of the five measures of satisfaction. Results are displayed in the order that variables entered into the stepwise regression procedure, which is generally ordered from the greatest to the least important. Only statistically reliable variables (significant at the 0.05 level or better) are shown. Variables that are not included in an equation have no statistically reliable relationship to the measure of interest. Thus, what is not included in the regression analysis is in many ways as important as what does appear in each equation.

Each of the following tables also presents an R^2 statistic for the regression equation. R^2 is a measure of multiple correlation, generally interpreted as "the percentage of variance in the dependent variable accounted for (or 'explained') by the independent variables." When, for example, we see that the 16-variable regression on Question 5, "In this computer search I found. . . ." has an R^2 of 0.0961, we can interpret the result as showing that these 16 variables, taken together, account for about 9.6 percent of the variance in responses regarding retrieval results. The remaining 90.4 percent is not accounted for in the analysis. Adding additional variables would not add appreciably to R^2; they would not be "statistically significant." The "unexplained" variance is exactly that: unexplained. Thus we may say that the 16 variables in that equation have a proven statistical relationship to retrieval results, but that most of the variance in users' retrieval success is caused by factors that are not included in this analysis.

The Easier It Is to Do Subject Searching,
the Greater the Quantity of Relevant
Material Is Retrieved

Table 29 shows the result of regressing the group of independent variables on Question 5, "In this computer search I found:." (See Table 29, page 158). As noted in the previous examples, the 16 variables included here, taken together, explain only about 10 percent of the variance in retrieval success (R^2 = 0.0916). Clearly, an attempt to describe the determinants of retrieval success in detail must include more information about the system, the user, and the search than was obtained in the present study.

The variables shown by regression analysis to be important to the amount of material retrieved are discussed below, in their order of importance.

1. *Factor 4, "Subject Searching Is Difficult."* Factor 4's positive coefficient indicates that the greater the difficulty with subject searching, the less was retrieved. The converse, of course, is also true: the less difficulty with subject searching, the more is retrieved.

TABLE 28 Variables Used in the Regression Analysis

Dependent Variables

	System Variables (from Table 18)	*Seven Factors* (from Table 21)
	OPERATIONAL CONTROL	Factor 1. Codes and Abbreviations are Easy
SELFUNC	Selection of function (Search, circulation, etc.)	Factor 2. Displays Are Hard to Understand
DISRUPT	Interruption of online output	Factor 3. Command and Control Is Easy
STACKCOM	Command stacking/multiple commands	Factor 4. Subject Searching Is Difficult
BCKSPACE	Correct keying errors before command input (back space)	Factor 5. Known-Item Searching Is Difficult
		Factor 6. The Computer Tries My Patience
	OUTPUT CONTROL	Factor 7. Library Services Are Not Helpful
SELDISP	Can user select preferred display format (yes or no)	
DISPB/F	Display forward and back	*Demographic Variables*
OLPRINT	Hard copy printed results available	Q 48. Frequency of Library Use
SORT	Sort capability	Q 49. Frequency of Online Catalog Use
		Q 50. Frequency of Other Catalog Use
	INFORMATION AND INSTRUCTION	Q 51. Frequency of Computer Use
OLINSTR	Instruction or assistance imbedded in dialogue	Q 54. Age
HELP	Separate HELP displays available on request	Q 55. Sex
THESAUR	Related terms, index, or thesaurus available online	

SEARCH FORMULATION AND CONTROL

DATELIM — Expand or limit results by date
LANGLIM — Expand or limit results by language
TYPELIM — Expand or limit results by type of material
OTHERLIM — Expand or limit results by (please specify)
FREETEXT — Free text term or keyword searching available
BOOLEAN — Use of Boolean operators (and, or, not)
TRUNCATE — Ability to use truncated search terms
SAVESET — Ability to create and save sets
SELMODE — Ability to select or change search mode

TYPE OF COMMAND ENTRY LANGUAGE

COMMAND — Formal command language
MENU — Menu selection
OTHERMDE — Other

Database Variables (from Table 15)
1. Monographs (None, Some, All)
2. Journals (None, Some, All)
3. Other Materials (None, Some, All)

Independent Variables

1. Q 5. In this computer search I found:
2. Q 6. In relation to what I was looking for this search was:
3. Q 7. I came across things of interest other than what I was looking for:
4. Q 9. My overall or general attitude toward the online catalog:
5. Q 10. Compared to the card, book or microfiche catalog in this library, the computer catalog is:

TABLE 29   Determinants of Amount Retrieved

DEPENDENT VARIABLE:

In this computer search I found:

1. More than I was looking for
2. All that I was looking for
3. Some of what I was looking for
4. Nothing I was looking for

Step	Variable	Coefficient	Significance of t	Cumulative R^2
1	FACTOR04	0.20179	0.0000	0.0309
2	SELMODE	0.24564	0.0000	0.0504
3	FACTOR03	−0.10336	0.0000	0.0603
4	DISPB/F	0.11636	0.0242	0.0670
5	FACTOR07	0.09579	0.0000	0.0743
6	Q49	0.05536	0.0000	0.0799
7	FACTOR06	0.08719	0.0000	0.0833
8	FACTOR05	0.07698	0.0000	0.0860
9	Q48	0.04683	0.0000	0.0884
10	SUBJECT	0.28033	0.0000	0.0898
11	DISRUPT	0.09927	0.0013	0.0911
12	FACTOR01	−0.05353	0.0009	0.0925
13	Q51	0.01676	0.0078	0.0935
14	Q50	−0.02868	0.0068	0.0944
15	OTHERMDE	−0.15384	0.0106	0.0953
16	FACTOR02	−0.04389	0.0191	0.0961
	(CONSTANT)	1.88306	0.0000	

*The significance of the T statistic is a measure of the statistical reliability of the coefficient. Coefficients that are not significant at the 0.05 level or better are generally not reported in these tables.

2. *SELMODE, the ability to select search modes.* Because the coefficient of SELMODE is positive, the presence of this feature would appear to lead to a reduction in retrieval results. Only five systems in the group possess this capability, and 65 percent of the questionnaires representing these systems come from the University of California. It may be that the database limitations of the UC prototype system constrain retrieval results, and that the UC data thereby indirectly affect the relation of SELMODE to retrieval results.

3. *Factor 3, "Command and Control Is Easy."* The negative coefficient indicates that the more difficulty users experience with command and control, the less relevant material they retrieve.

4. *DISPF/B, the capability to move forward and backward in a long display.* The sign of the coefficient indicates that systems having this feature offer less adequate retrieval results.

5. *Factor 7, "Library Services Are Not Helpful."* The less adequate the library support services, in the judgment of the user, the less relevant material is retrieved.

6. *Question 49, frequency of computer catalog use.* As the use of the online catalog is less frequent, the less is found. The greater the user's experience with the online catalog, the greater the likelihood of finding relevant material.

7. *Factor 6, "The Computer Tries My Patience."* The result shows that, the fewer problems users have with gaining access to a terminal or waiting for the computer to respond, the greater their retrieval results.

8. *Factor 5, "Known-Item Searching Is Difficult."* The sign of the coefficient shows that the more difficulty users have with known-item searching, the less is retrieved.

9. *Question 48, frequency of library use.* Frequent library users are more likely to find relevant material than infrequent users.

10. *SUBJECT, the system capability to search by subject.* The finding indicates, somewhat paradoxically, that users find less in systems that have subject searching capability than in systems that do not. It should be noted, however, that the only participating system for which subject searching capability is not present is OCLC. It may be that the effect of the large OCLC database on retrieval success, rather than the effect of subject search capability, is what is measured here.

11. *DISRUPT, the ability to interrupt the online display.* The ability to interrupt output has an adverse effect on retrieval results. It should be noted that about 83 percent of the observations for systems having this capability are from two places, the University of California and Syracuse University, both of which have incomplete databases. The inclusion of this variable, like that of SUBJECT, may simply be an artifact of database size.

12. *Factor 1, "Codes and Abbreviations Are Easy to Understand and Use."* The easier it is to use codes and abbreviations, the more relevant material is retrieved.

13. *Question 51, computer experience.* Users who have more experience with computers other than the online catalog tend to retrieve more of what they are looking for.

14. *Question 50, frequency of use of the card catalog.* Frequent users of the card catalog are less likely to find what they want in the online catalog than are infrequent card catalog users.

15. *OTHERMDE, the system capability to search other than by command or menu modes.* The provision of search modes other than command or menu aids retrieval. Only one participating system, Dallas Public Library, indicated to us that they provided an "other" search mode, so this result may be an artifact of other characteristics of the Dallas Public system that provide larger retrieval results for its users.

16. *Factor 2, "Displays Are Hard to Understand."* Where displays are difficult to understand, more relevant information is retrieved by users. We have no interpretation for this curious finding.

TABLE 30   Determinants of Satisfaction with the Search

DEPENDENT VARIABLE:
In relation to what I was looking for, this computer search was:

1. Very satisfactory
2. Somewhat satisfactory
3. Somewhat unsatisfactory
4. Very unsatisfactory

Step	Variable	Coefficient	Significance of t	Cumulative R^2
1	FACTOR04	0.22600	0.0000	0.0439
2	FACTOR07	0.14322	0.0000	0.0619
3	FACTOR03	−0.12250	0.0000	0.0789
4	FACTOR05	0.14995	0.0000	0.0923
5	SELMODE	0.36817	0.0000	0.1041
6	FACTOR06	0.12492	0.0000	0.1112
7	STACKCOM	0.24629	0.0000	0.1178
8	Q49	0.06999	0.0000	0.1233
9	Q50	−0.05231	0.0000	0.1277
10	FACTOR01	−0.08209	0.0000	0.1312
11	SORT	−0.24755	0.0001	0.1339
12	OLINSTR	0.13841	0.0002	0.1352
13	ACCESS#	0.07149	0.0311	0.1359
	(CONSTANT)	1.49389	0.0000	

Easy Subject Searching Improves Search Satisfaction

Table 30 displays the regression results with Question 6, "In relation to what I was looking for, this search was," as the dependent variable. The fourteen variables included in the regression explain about 14 percent of the variance in satisfaction with the search (R^2 = 0.1359). This is not, of course, a large amount of explained variance, but R^2 is greater for this regression model than for the previous model related to retrieval results.

The variables that are related to satisfaction with the search just completed, in their order of importance, are:

1. *Factor 4, "Subject Searching Is Difficult."* The fewer problems users experience with subject searching, the more favorable is their evaluation of the most recent search.
2. *Factor 7, "Library Services Are Not Helpful."* The less satisfying users found library support services, the less satisfactory is their evaluation of the search.
3. *Factor 3, "Command and Control Is Easy."* The fewer problems users had with command and control, the more likely they are to rate their search as satisfactory.

4. *Factor 5, "Known-Item Searching Is Difficult."* The fewer problems users had with known-item searching, the better they rated the most recent search.
5. *SELMODE, the ability to select search modes.* The presence of this capability tends to lead to unsatisfactory evaluations. As noted in the previous discussion of this variable, its effect may be attributable to the database limitations of the University of California system.
6. *Factor 6, "The Computer Tries My Patience."* Users who had problems with computer response time or terminal accessibility tend to rate their last search as unsatisfactory.
7. *STACKCOM, the catalog feature that allows the user to "stack" a series of commands for sequential execution.* The command-stacking feature has a negative effect on user evaluations. It may be that applying this feature confuses online catalog users, but it should be noted that only three systems, Ohio State, Stanford (RLIN II), and Syracuse, have this capability. It may be that the negative effect measured here is caused indirectly by other aspects of those three systems that lower user ratings.
8. *Question 49, frequency of online catalog use.* Frequent online catalog experience leads to higher evaluations of the most recent search.
9. *Question 50, frequency of use of the card catalog.* People who use the card catalog frequently appear to have a less satisfactory experience with the online catalog.
10. *Factor 1, "Codes and Abbreviations Are Easy to Understand and Use."* The less difficulty people experience with codes and abbreviations, the more satisfactory their search.
11. *SORT, the ability to resort and redisplay retrieval results.* The sorting capability appears to be associated with search satisfaction. It should be noted, though, that only one system, Mankato State, has this feature, so its appearance here might be caused indirectly by significantly high overall satisfaction with that one system, rather than by the feature itself.
12. *OLINSTR, the provision of interactive instruction in online catalog use as part of the catalog.* Online instruction seems to reduce user satisfaction. The results lead to several possible interpretations, among them (1) that online instruction is time-consuming, and tries the patience of users, especially those who do not need instruction, or (2) that the manner in which instructions are presented, rather than the mere provision of the feature, causes more harm than good. We note, however, that this variable does not indicate whether online instruction was used, only that the feature is present. Explication of this finding will require more detailed analysis of the data.
13. *ACCESS#, the capability to search by local accession number.* The provision of this capability has a negative effect on user evaluations. Six systems offer this capability, suggesting that the finding is not merely an artifact of otherwise unmeasured system differences. This result may suggest that providing explicit access to technically-defined fields in a public access system creates confusion for catalog users, but only further analysis could illuminate this possibility.

TABLE 31   Determinants of Unexpected Discovery of Relevant
Material

DEPENDENT VARIABLE:
I came across things of interest other than what I was looking for:

1. Yes
2. No

Step	Variable	Coefficient	Significance of t	Cumulative R^2
1	FACTOR04	0.07078	0.0000	0.0163
2	AU/TI	−0.15221	0.0000	0.0230
3	DISRUPT	0.02960	0.0714	0.0300
4	FACTOR03	−0.04121	0.0000	0.0338
5	Q49	0.02618	0.0000	0.0365
6	STACKCOM	0.04716	0.0052	0.0397
7	TERMTOT	−0.00006	0.0001	0.0412
8	Q55	−0.03376	0.0102	0.0424
9	DISPB/F	0.05691	0.0030	0.0435
10	FACTOR06	0.02705	0.0047	0.0447
11	Q51	0.00827	0.0169	0.0456
12	Q54	0.01309	0.0197	0.0464
13	FACTOR02	−0.02501	0.0133	0.0473
14	FACTOR07	0.02445	0.0176	0.0482
	(CONSTANT)	1.48040	0.0000	

When Subject Searching Is Easy, Users Are More Likely to Come Across Other Things of Interest

Table 31 shows the regression results with Question 7, "I came across things of interest other than what I was looking for," as the dependent variable. This is the least successful of the group of regressions in explaining the phenomenon of interest; the 14 variables in the regression together explain only about five percent of the variance in "serendipity" (R^2 = 0.0482). Clearly, factors other than system problems, system capabilities,and demographic characteristics play the predominant role in determining whether users find relevant but unexpected material.

The variables explaining "serendipity," in order of entry into the stepwise equation, are:

1. *Factor 4, "Subject Searching Is Difficult."* The more difficult the subject-searching experience, the less likely that users will find unexpected things of interest.
2. *AU/TI, the capability to conduct combined author/title searches.* The

presence of a combined author-title search capability appears to enhance the chances of a serendipitous experience. Given that an author/title search is by definition more precise than either of its components, the fact that this feature promotes accidental discovery is surprising.

3. *DISRUPT, the ability to interrupt the online display.* As with the amount of material retrieved (Table 28), the presence of the capability to interrupt output appears to have a negative effect. About 83 percent of the observations for systems having this capability are from two places, the University of California and Syracuse University, both of which have incomplete databases. The inclusion of this variable may simply be an artifact of database size.

4. *Factor 3, "Command and Control Is Easy."* The fewer problems users have with command and control, the more likely they are to find unexpected things of interest.

5. *Question 49, frequency of online catalog use.* People who use the online catalog frequently are more likely to discover relevant material by serendipity.

6. *STACKCOM, the catalog feature that allows the user to "stack" a series of commands for sequential execution.* The presence of the command stacking feature appears to have a negative effect on serendipity, just as it did with evaluation of the most recent search (Table 29). As noted previously, the presence of this variable may be related to other characteristics of the three systems supporting this feature, rather than to the feature itself.

7. *TERMTOT, the total number of public-access terminals available.* The more terminals, the more serendipity. The reasons are unclear, but it is possible that more terminals mean less queuing, and users who are not pressured to leave the terminal to the next user in line may take more time for their session and be more likely to discover unexpected items.

8. *Question 55, the sex of the user.* Men are more likely than women to discover unexpected things of interest.

9. *DISPF/B, the capability to move forward and backward in a long display.* The ability to control long displays has a negative effect on serendipity. Systems having this feature offer less adequate retrieval results.

10. *Factor 6, "The Computer Tries My Patience."* Users who are impatient with the online catalog or unable to find a free terminal are less likely to find unexpected things of interest.

11. *Question 51, computer experience.* Experience with computer systems other than the online catalog promotes serendipity.

12. *Question 54, the age of the respondent.* Older respondents are less likely to find unexpected things of interest, perhaps due to their familiarity with the literature.

13. *Factor 2, "Displays Are Hard to Understand."* The more problems users have understanding the display, the more likely they are to find unexpected items. Perhaps, perversely, the time and effort required to decipher confusing displays promotes serendipity; when displays are clear

and simple, the needed item may be found easily and other, potentially relevant, items overlooked.

14. *Factor 7, "Library Services Are Not Helpful."* The more frequently that library users perceive library support services as helpful, the more likely they are to find unexpected things of interest.

Subject Searching Problems Have an Important Effect on Overall Attitude Toward the Online Catalog

The results of a regression analysis with Question 9, "My overall or general attitude toward the online catalog," as the dependent variable are shown in Table 32. The 18 variables included in the regression account for over 20 percent of the variance in expressed attitudes toward the online catalog ($R^2 = 0.2044$). The first five variables in the equation are all system factors; together they ac-

TABLE 32   Determinants of Overall Satisfaction with the Online Catalog

DEPENDENT VARIABLE:
My overall or general attitude toward the online catalog is:

1. Very favorable
2. Somewhat favorable
3. Somewhat unfavorable
4. Very unfavorable

Step	Variable	Coefficient	Significance of t	Cumulative R^2
1	FACTOR04	0.17399	0.0000	0.0542
2	FACTOR05	0.16354	0.0000	0.0923
3	FACTOR07	0.14155	0.0000	0.1225
4	FACTOR01	−0.09348	0.0000	0.1447
5	FACTOR06	0.09625	0.0000	0.1547
6	Q50	−0.06531	0.0000	0.1632
7	Q49	0.05597	0.0000	0.1714
8	ACCESS#	0.06252	0.0422	0.1814
9	FACTOR03	−0.06343	0.0000	0.1887
10	Q54	0.02865	0.0000	0.1935
11	FACTOR02	0.05096	0.0000	0.1957
12	THESAUR	−0.07770	0.0007	0.1976
13	Q55	−0.05218	0.0007	0.1995
14	SUBJECT	0.11420	0.0845	0.2011
15	OTHERAC	−0.11751	0.0000	0.2026
16	BCKSPACE	−0.10767	0.0001	0.2031
17	OLINSTR	−0.07828	0.0250	0.2038
18	CALL#	0.06725	0.0274	0.2044
	(CONSTANT)	1.45633	0.0000	

count for three-fourths of the explained variance in the 18-variable regression (cumulative R^2 for variables 1-5 is 0.1547). Obviously, the perceived quality of the system and the user interface is an important factor in users' judgment of the catalog.

The variables in the regression equation related to overall satisfaction, in order of importance, are:

1. *Factor 4, "Subject Searching Is Difficult."* When subject searching is perceived as easy, evaluations of the online catalog tend to be more positive.
2. *Factor 5, "Known-Item Searching Is Difficult."* When known-item searching is easy, evaluations are more favorable.
3. *Factor 7, "Library Services Are Not Helpful."* When library support is judged adequate, evaluations improve.
4. *Factor 1, "Codes and Abbreviations Are Easy to Understand and Use."* The less difficulty users have with the catalog's abbreviations and codes, the more positive is their overall attitude toward the catalog.
5. *Factor 6, "The Computer Tries My Patience."* Users' patience with the time-consuming interactions of some online catalogs is an important factor in overall satisfaction. The more impatient users become, the lower their overall evaluation.
6. *Question 50, frequency of use of the card catalog.* Frequent experience with the card catalog has a negative effect; heavy card catalog users tend to make more negative evaluations of the online catalog.
7. *Question 49, frequency of online catalog use.* As in previous cases, the more frequently the online catalog is used, the more favorable is the user's evaluation of it.
8. *ACCESS#, the capability to search by local accession number.* The presence of this capability has a negative effect on the overall evaluation of the catalog.
9. *Factor 3, "Command and Control Is Easy."* The ability to control the computer session easily leads to a more positive evaluation of the online catalog.
10. *Question 54, the age of the respondent.* Older users are less likely to evaluate the online catalog positively.
11. *Factor 2, "Displays Are Hard to Understand."* Good displays have good results in terms of overall evaluation. When users have trouble understanding displays and messages, evaluations drop.
12. *THESAURUS, the provision of thesauri or indexes that can be searched and displayed.* The thesaurus feature appears for the first time in this regression, and it appears in an affirmative way. Systems that provide this feature tend to get higher overall evaluations than systems that do not.
13. *Question 55, the sex of the user.* Male respondents are significantly more likely to give the online catalog a favorable rating than female respondents.

14. *SUBJECT, the system capability to search by subject.* Systems offering subject search capabilities get lower evaluations than systems without this feature. A potential bias exists with regard to this feature (only one system—OCLC—lacks this capability) and it may be that the effect of the large OCLC database on retrieval success, rather than the effect of subject search capability, is what is measured here. Note also, that the significance of the T statistic for this variable is relatively low (t = 0.0845), and by most standards this variable would be rejected as a statistically insignificant regressor.
15. *OTHERAC, the provision of access points other than those named in the system profile questionnaire.* The seven systems that offer access points in addition to author, title, subject, call number, accession number, ISSN and ISBN, LC card number, series, or added entries generally receive higher evaluations.
16. *BCKSPACE, the provision of a means to edit or correct keying errors.* The five systems that make no provision to correct typing errors (typically by spacing back and typing over) are generally evaluated less favorably.
17. *OLINSTR, the provision of interactive instruction in the online catalog use as part of the catalog.* With respect to overall evaluation of the online catalog systems with online instruction are generally more favorably received than those without this feature.
18. *CALL#, the capability to search by call number.* Systems that provide call-number searching are generally rated less highly than those without this feature.

Catalog Preference Is Chiefly Determined by Frequency of Use of the Card Catalog

As Table 33 shows, the most important determinant of preference for the card catalog as opposed to the online catalog is frequency of card catalog use (Question 10). Frequent users of the card catalog prefer it to the online catalog. This is the only regression equation in which Factor 4, subject searching, is not the most important single variable, but in this case Factor 4 does come in a close second. The 16 variables in this regression account for about 16 percent of the variance in card/online catalog preference ($R^2 = 0.1580$).

The sixteen variables explaining preference for the online catalog are:

1. *Question 50, frequency of use of the card catalog.* Frequent users of the card catalog are less likely to prefer the online catalogs.
2. *Factor 4, "Subject Searching Is Difficult."* Where subject searching is perceived as a problem, users tend to prefer the card catalog.
3. *Factor 7, "Library Services Are Not Helpful."* When library support

TABLE 33   Determinants of Preference for Online and Card Catalogs

DEPENDENT VARIABLE:
Compared to the card, book, or microfiche catalog in this library, the computer catalog is:

1. Better
2. About the same
3. Worse

Step	Variable	Coefficient	Significance of t	Cumulative R^2
1	Q50	−0.10240	0.0000	0.0469
2	FACTOR04	0.12999	0.0000	0.0794
3	FACTOR07	0.10772	0.0000	0.1013
4	FACTOR05	0.09570	0.0000	0.1139
5	Q49	0.04987	0.0000	0.1223
6	FACTOR06	0.08569	0.0000	0.1310
7	FACTOR01	−0.06384	0.0000	0.1377
8	SAVESETS	−0.60438	0.0000	0.1418
9	Q54	0.03400	0.0000	0.1455
10	SUBJECT	0.33968	0.0000	0.1479
11	LCCARD	0.10971	0.0000	0.1494
12	SORT	−0.47652	0.0000	0.1520
13	OTHER	0.09061	0.0000	0.1543
14	FACTOR03	−0.03197	0.0029	0.1558
15	LANGLIM	0.31051	0.0032	0.1568
16	SERIES	0.05071	0.0032	0.1580
	(CONSTANT)	0.84943	0.0000	

services for online catalogs are deemed inadequate, the card catalog gets a higher rating.

4. *Factor 5, "Known-Item Searching Is Difficult."* Where searching for known items is judged difficult, the card catalog is preferred.

5. *Question 49, frequency of online catalog use.* People who use the online catalog frequently are more likely to prefer it to the card catalog.

6. *Factor 6, "The Computer Tries My Patience."* Users who have difficulty finding a free terminal or who feel that the computer takes too long to respond tend to prefer the card catalog.

7. *Factor 1, "Codes and Abbreviations Are Easy to Understand and Use."* Users who do not have problems understanding and using codes and abbreviations tend to prefer the online catalog.

8. *SAVESETS, the capability to save and recombine intermediate search results.* This capability appears to result in a greater preference for the online catalog. Only the Library of Congress system has this feature, so there may be other conditions at LC that affect this preference for the MUMS/SCORPIO system, rather than the virtues of the SAVESETS feature itself.

9. *Question 54, the age of the respondent.* Older respondents are more likely to prefer the card catalog.

10. *SUBJECT, the system capability to search by subject.* The presence of the subject-searching feature appears to result in a greater preference for the card catalog. As noted earlier, this may be an artifact associated with the one system (OCLC) that does not offer subject searching.

11. *LCCARD, the capability to search by Library of Congress card number.* In systems that offer the capability to search by LCCN, users tend to prefer the card catalog. About half the systems in the study offer this feature, so it is apparently not an artifact. It may be that, as with accession-number searching, the provision of access to this rather esoteric entry point in a public system lends some complexity and confusion from the user's point of view.

12. *SORT, the ability to resort and redisplay retrieval results.* In systems having this feature, the online catalog tends to be preferred over the card catalog, as was the case with search satisfaction (Table 29). As noted there, only one system has this feature, so the positive relationship may be a system-specific artifact.

13. *OTHER, the amount of material in formats other than books and serials included in the online catalog.* This is the only instance when a measure of completeness of the database enters directly into a regression model, and its effect, surprisingly, is negative. It should be noted that only seven libraries, representing four participating catalog systems, claim to have all their "other" material in their database, so the effect measured here may be an artifact. It may also be the case that, while including multiple formats in the catalog is good, the provisions of specific systems to aid users in locating materials in multiple formats are not adequate, leading to some frustration when they actually try to search for holdings of, say, sound recordings or musical scores.

14. *Factor 3, "Command and Control Is Easy."* When users find it easy to control their catalog session, they tend to prefer the online catalog.

15. *LANGLIM, the capability to limit search results by language of publication.* Systems with language-limiting capabilities apparently are not as preferred by users as systems without this feature. The three systems with this capability (Mankato, Dartmouth, and Library of Congress) are principally academic and research libraries, however, so the measured effect may be an artifact of a more general preference of academic users for the card catalog.

16. *SERIES, the capability to search by series name.* The presence of this feature depresses user preference for the online catalog. About half the participating systems offer this capability, so it is unlikely to be an artifact. As with some other system features appearing in the regression analyses, it may be that providing this search point serves to confuse, rather than aid, the general public.

SUMMARY OF THE FACTOR/REGRESSION ANALYSIS

In the five regression analyses reported here, the seven factor variables measuring problems with online catalog systems and with library support for the online catalog have played a major role. All or most of the factors appear in every regression equation, and in most cases the results show that where interface and support problems are perceived as serious, the user's evaluation of the online catalog suffers.

The analysis shows that, when other factors are controlled, demographic characteristics of users (age and sex) have a small but significant predisposing influence on user evaluations. Specifically, older adult users and women are less likely to evaluate the online catalog highly or prefer it to the card catalog.

Other demographic characteristics (education level, academic status and affiliation in academic libraries) were not included in this analysis because the scaling of these data was not suitable for direct inclusion in a regression analysis, but the predisposing influence of sex and age suggests that additional analytical work with these demographic variables would be worthwhile.

All four characteristics of library and computer use (frequency of library use, online catalog use, card catalog use, and use of non-library computers) appear in the analysis at one place or another. Of these four, the most important appears to be frequency of use of the online catalog—in which more frequent users tend to favor the online catalog, and frequency of use of the card catalog—in which more frequent users of the card catalog tend to prefer the card catalog. There are obvious elements of self-selection here, and perhaps the best we can say is that users tend to prefer the catalog they know best. It is, however, important to note that the demographic factors have an influence on satisfaction and preference that is independent of the effect of system quality, suggesting that, while system improvements will certainly improve user satisfaction, there is an element of "bibliographic predisposition" that perhaps cannot be directly reached by improved systems or support services.

In most cases where the availability of specific system features enters into the regression equations, the interpretation of the effects has been unclear, and the measured relationship often appears to be confounded by other characteristics of the systems that support those specific features. It may be that a "post-controlled" approach like that necessarily used here, in which systems with and without particular features are compared in the aggregate, cannot address the issue, and it will be necessary to conduct detailed "micro-studies" of the actual use of these features, case by case, to illuminate their advantages and disadvantages.

The five regression analyses provide interesting but somewhat piecemeal evidence about problems of user satisfaction. To draw together the salient results from all five measures of satisfaction, the "top five" variables appearing in each of the five regression analyses are examined.

Difficulty in Subject Searching Is the Most
Important Single Factor in User Satisfaction

We found that:

1. *"Subject Searching Is Difficult,"* Factor 4, appeared in the top five in all five regressions, and was the most important single explanatory variable in four of the five equations. In all cases, improved subject searching (in the eyes of the users) leads to improved satisfaction.
2. *"Library Services Are Not Helpful,"* Factor 7, appeared in the top five four times. Improvements in the quality of staff assistance, and particularly in the availability and quality of printed aids (given our earlier findings about the sources of assistance that users prefer) can be expected to improve user satisfaction with the catalog.
3. *"Command and Control Is Easy,"* Factor 3, appears in the top five three times. Improvements in command language and in capabilities for controlling the session and the displays would tend to increase satisfaction with the online catalog.
4. *"Known-Item Searching Is Difficult,"* Factor 5, also appears in the top five three times. Enhancing capabilities to conduct known-item searches will enhance the success and satisfaction of the catalog's users.
5. *Frequency of online catalog use,* Question 49, appears in the top five twice. As noted previously, frequent online catalog users are more satisfied users.
6. *The ability to select search modes,* SELMODE, also appears twice in the top five. The previous discussion of this finding emphasized that its significance is unclear, but its importance to user satisfaction would appear to warrant further investigation.
7. The following variables appeared in the "top five" once:
    a. *"Codes and Abbreviations Are Easy to Understand and Use,"* Factor 1: Improvements in this problem area improve user satisfaction.
    b. *"The Computer Tries My Patience,"* Factor 6: Improvements in terminal availability and response time, and revision of verbose menus, instructions and messages will improve user satisfaction.
    c. *Frequency of use of the card catalog,* Question 50: Frequent users of the card catalog are less satisfied with the online catalog.
    d. *The system capability to conduct combined author/title searches,* AU/TI: This capability appears to enhance user satisfaction.
    e. *The ability to interrupt the online display,* DISRUPT: Systems that have this capability appear less satisfactory to users. As discussed previously, this result may be an artifact, resulting indirectly from other, apparently unmeasured, system characteristics.
    f. *The capability to move forward and backward in a long display,* DISPF/B: The presence of this feature also appears to degrade satisfaction. This result may also be an artifact.

Many Problem Areas and System Features
Have No Significant Effect on User Satisfaction

Of equal interest is consideration of the variables that do not appear in the top five, or at any point in the regression analysis. Among these are:

- *"Displays Are Hard to Understand,"* Factor 2. This variable enters the regressions three times, although never in the top five. In two of the three cases, hard-to-understand displays paradoxically lead to better results. In any case, the quality of display formats, while a significant variable, apparently is not of paramount importance to users.
- Age and sex have been noted as important predisposing variables, but they are not of dominant value in user acceptance of the online catalog.
- Numerous system features do not appear in the regressions at all, notably features like keyword searching, Boolean searching, and truncation. This may be due to the confounding effects discussed above, and the problems in analyzing system features. It may also be the case that system features work "indirectly" to influence the problems measured by the seven factor analysis variables. If so, the difficulties regarding the relationship between system features and system problems continue to obtain, and different forms of analysis and different kinds of research designs will be required to address these issues.
- While frequency of catalog use is important, neither frequency of library use nor familiarity with computers in general seems to have a dominant influence on evaluation of the online catalog.

INCREASED USE OF THE CATALOG
AND COLLECTION

While not a part of this study, there is some evidence to suggest that use of the catalog and use of the collection (both in-library use and annual circulation figures) increase after the online catalog is installed. Circulation increases have been noted at Mission/West Valley Colleges, Mankato State, Pikes Peak Library and the Evanston Public Library. Similar experiences in other libraries have been reported.[2]

NOTES

1. This assumes that an author/title search is a "single index" search, which is true, at least from the user's viewpoint, in many of the participating

systems. Some systems require author/title searches to be constructed with Boolean arguments. If author/title searches are counted as using more than one index, then "multiple index" searches constitute 40 percent of search activity.

2. Carol Weiss Moore. "Reactions to Online Catalogs." *College and Research Libraries,* July 1981, pp. 295–302; Connie Tiffany. "An Electronic Public Library for Iowa City." *Library Journal,* 107(17), October 1, 1982, pp. 1816–1820; and Margaret M. Beckman. "Online Catalogs and Library Users." *Library Journal,* 107 (19), November 1, 1982, pp. 2043–2047.

CHAPTER EIGHT

Implications of the Survey Findings

In this chapter some of the salient findings are pulled together and an assessment of their implications is made. The observations discussed below are all drawn from the data and analyses reported in previous chapters; the discussion that follows, however, is based on our interpretation of those findings.

The discussion is divided into four parts:

- Implications that are within the action scope of library managers (directors, department heads, etc.).
- Implications for library reference staffs.
- Implications that are within the scope of system designers.
- Implications that must be acted upon by the library profession.

IMPLICATIONS FOR LIBRARY MANAGERS

While financial and other considerations may prevent a library from installing an online catalog, there are no public service barriers: patron acceptance of the online catalog can be counted upon. The evidence shows that those who have used the online catalog love it, and that those who have not used the online catalog like it almost as well. It is certainly true that some online catalogs will provide more satisfaction than others, but users (and non-users for the most part) prefer the online catalog to the catalog forms it replaces, regardless of the level of sophistication or quality of the online catalog.

Assume that online catalog adoption rates will vary among different patron groups. Within academic libraries the different rates of use by undergraduates and graduates may reflect different rates of library use or perhaps greater familiarity with the online catalog. Faculty and staff may represent a group of users among whom there is greater user resistance to the online catalog. For public libraries, the age of the patron will likely influence use of the online catalog.

Don't be shy. Put the computer catalog terminals where users can't miss them. The evidence shows that this is the best form of publicity for the online catalog and (as we will discuss below), the catalog tends to "sell itself": those who see it use it, and those who use it continue using it.

Over half of our respondents want more terminals: terminals throughout the library, and terminals in places other than the library. This tends to be true of both "opening day" online catalogs and "mature" catalogs that have been available for years and already support hundreds of public-access terminals. It would appear that the driving force here is not the inconvenience of waiting for an available terminal (about 28 percent of respondents said this was a problem—a large number, but smaller than the number who want more), but the convenience of having access to the catalog where the users are, rather than where the catalog card cabinet has always been. This suggests that although it is necessary to supply enough terminals initially to keep queuing to acceptable levels, in the long run the demand for terminals may be nearly infinite. Because users find terminal access important, significant expenditures are necessary to provide optimal terminal access. It would be sensible to prepare well in advance to deal with this demand.

Over one-third of users complained about the lack of adequate writing space at the terminal. Providing space to take notes and stash belongings seems like an obvious design factor, but it is often overlooked.

Taking notes from computer catalog searches is always a problem, even with enough writing space. About 30 percent of users want a printing capability in systems that do not now have it, and analysis shows this feature can help ameliorate a number of searching problems. As a corollary, make sure the printer is easy to use—this was a significant source of complaint among respondents who used printers.

User preferences for adding to the database vary widely, but most respondents want the database expanded in some way; only 11 percent could think of no additional material they wanted included. Expansion includes both retrospective conversion of card catalog records and the addition of a variety of formats, e.g., microforms, films, not now in the online catalog. Users' inability to remember what was included in the scope of the online catalog was among the top three searching problems. Given the well-documented intolerance of library users to search multiple files, the only solution may be to include everything.

Before proceeding to our observations on how libraries can assist online catalog users and attract non-users, we would like to briefly review the principal findings in this area:

1. The chief reason for non-use of online catalogs appears to be that respondents are not frequent users of either the library or the library catalog (in any form).
2. The majority of users (70 percent) learn to use the online catalog without staff help.
3. First-time users are generally enthusiastic about the online catalog; satisfaction drops with increased use, then rises again as frequency of use increases.
4. Non-users think the online catalog is great: 90 percent have a favorable attitude toward the online catalog, and (of those who could decide), 63 percent think the online catalog is better than the catalog it replaces.

If, as the evidence shows, most users discover the online catalog by seeing it in the library, most learn to use it with the help of printed and online aids, and most non-users of the online catalog are less frequent users of libraries and library catalogs, it would appear that the best expenditure of staff effort to increase online catalog use is to make frequent library users of infrequent ones. For fairly frequent library users, the online catalog sells itself, and groups who do not now use it would not, for the most part, take advantage of training or promotional programs targeted at the catalog itself.

Most users learn to use the catalog from print sources, and most turn to printed guides and brochures when they need help. This is not to say that public service staff are unneeded or should themselves be untrained (recall that the quality of library support services was, overall, the second most important determinant of satisfaction in the factor/regression analysis), but it does imply that effective printed materials should be a priority.

One factor that ameliorates reliance on both printed aids and staff assistance is online help, but it is evident that halfway measures will not do: a few instructions or help screens, especially if they are "mandatory," may try users' patience, and the evidence suggests that a little online help may add to the load on public service staff, while a lot of online help substantially reduces it.

First-time users of the online catalog generally walk away happy, with or without prior training. Levels of satisfaction drop with further experience, as though initial expectations had been let down. We also know that "success breeds success"—users who find what they are looking for are not only happier with the search, but with the online catalog in general. It looks as if the best way to improve user satisfaction is not to train users in ways to deal with problems or get around them, but to remedy the system's inadequacies.

Finally, add records, terminals, and printers; give printed and online assistance. Press system designers to improve and simplify the interface, and to add useful features. Since the public service staff sees the users and helps them with their problems it is essential to involve staff in setting priorities and developing specifications.

IMPLICATIONS FOR LIBRARY
REFERENCE STAFFS

Acknowledge user acceptance of the online catalog, and plan accordingly. Cost management and service standards alone will favor the early implementation of computer catalogs in libraries.

The issue with online catalogs is not *whether* to adopt, but rather *what kind, when,* and *how.* Our survey suggests that the online catalog may affect the roles, tasks, and priorities of library staffs in many, immediate, and profound ways. Patron and staff needs will be best met if staff knowledge, experience, and perceptions are vigorously advocated from design through implementation and redesign.

Staff initiatives are required to define and deliver appropriate services to online catalog learners and users. Having a terminal at the information desk can greatly expedite teaching users while assisting them. Formerly, reference and information desk personnel often answered specific questions and sent the user off to the manual catalog. With a terminal at the inquiry desk, a staff member can formulate the reference question, demonstrate how to search, and help the user evaluate results. This may be done in the same or less time than formerly was required to understand and respond to a user's initial question.

Such considerations underscore the reality that the online catalog is something more and different than old wine in a new bottle. It is essential but by no means sufficient to have terminals at or near the manual catalog, so that users can use both. Where *else* to have them, and *why,* are concerns of vital importance to library staffs.

Library staffs should evaluate and recommend human-factor priorities for terminals and terminal areas. Physical features, e.g., space, lighting, terminal screen glare, table height, etc., lend themselves less well to user adaptation, compared with non-physical aspects. Human factor observation and design methods are well-established. The human factors literature should be reviewed and exploited intelligently before the online catalog terminals are selected and installed.

Extensive and intensive efforts must be mounted to make users aware of and informed about the online catalog's scope and content. Adequate means must be found to keep users well-informed about and constantly aware of what types of items are included in and excluded from the database, and any time limitation.

IMPLICATIONS FOR SYSTEM DESIGNERS

Features and aids can help users, but can also make the user interface too complex and wordy. When adding new software features or online help features, pay special attention to the way they manifest themselves in the interface, and make sure that the methods for accessing and controlling them are clear, concise, simple, and consistent with the existing interface.

Apparently there is no single aspect of the user's interaction with the online catalog that influences his or her satisfaction more than searching by subject. The users' stated preferences, their reported experience in "finding the correct subject terms," and our analysis of user satisfaction all point to two actions with the potential to improve subject searching:

1. Implement keyword searching for subjects (and for titles, although the users' interest in the latter is less marked).
2. Help them find the term(s) they want by permitting them to browse the subject index or thesaurus.

Users experience difficulties in remembering commands and controlling sessions, and to a lesser degree in using and understanding codes and abbreviations. This is a major problem area, but fortunately it can be addressed fairly easily by rationalizing command syntax, simplifying commands, speeding up menu displays, and the like.

The third-ranked request for system improvement is "ability to know if the book is available for my use." Providing circulation status information should be a high priority for systems without this facility.

The data show that a very small proportion of users (about 5%) use the online catalog to obtain and record the more technical details of bibliographic information. Most users are apparently satisfied with less-than-full bibliographic displays, and the time it takes the online catalog to display information they do not need may test their patience. Plan for relatively brief displays as a default, and offer more complete information as an option. Intermediate displays should include the title, subject headings, and call number to facilitate and improve subject searches.

Between 22 and 40 percent of all searches appear to require access to more than one index. If searches cannot be constructed across indexes with Boolean arguments, the user's task becomes very difficult. When this capability is present, it may not be well understood; clear explanation and examples are essential.

Response time is an important consideration in system design and operation, but it is the seventh-ranked problem area identified by users. Delays do not seem to play a predominant role in user satisfaction. Extended response times are probably unacceptable, but very short response times may not be necessary, especially if the resources needed to achieve them can be better used on other system improvements.

IMPLICATIONS FOR THE LIBRARY PROFESSION

Much of the data reported here reinforces the belief, articulated by Cochrane[1] and others, that subject searching is an important aspect of online catalog use, and that subject access must be improved. System designers can do much to help, but they can only work with the bibliographic data they have. It is up to the profession as a whole to improve standards for record creation that in turn help to improve subject-searching success.

There are two distinct areas for possible improvement. The first is to increase the amount of subject information in bibliographic records. Among the four highest user priorities for improvements of any type (systems, library services, databases) is "the ability to search a book's table of contents, summary, or index."

"Finding the correct subject term" is among the three most serious problems users experience with online catalog systems. The problem can be reduced by restricting the number of possible terms under which a user must search, either by rigorously controlling the vocabulary or by automatically linking the user's search terms with synonymous and related terms that appear in subject headings. The nature of this problem and proposals for its solution are being debated at length in the professional community at this moment, and we have nothing to add to that debate except this: whatever can be done to simplify subject access will be greatly appreciated by users of online catalogs.

NOTES

1. Pauline Atherton. *Books Are for Use.* Syracuse, New York: Syracuse University School of Information Studies. February 1978. (Available from ERIC, ED 156 131) and Pauline Atherton Cochrane. "Subject Access in the Online Catalog." *Research Libraries in OCLC,* No. 5, January 1982, pp. 1–7.

APPENDIX 1

User Questionnaire

Council on Library Resources

COMPUTER CATALOG STUDY

User Questionnaire

The library is conducting a study of its computer catalog to improve it. This questionnaire is a way to communicate your views. It should take you only about 15 minutes
to complete. Your responses are confidential. Please do not write your name anywhere
on the questionnaire. Thank you.

MARKING INSTRUCTIONS

- USE A NO. 2 PENCIL ONLY.

- FILL THE CIRCLES COMPLETELY.

- BE SURE TO ERASE CLEANLY ANY
  MARKS YOU WISH TO CHANGE.

- MAKE NO STRAY MARKS ON THIS
  QUESTIONNAIRE.

USE NO. 2 PENCIL ONLY

DO NOT WRITE IN THIS AREA

10844

NCS Trans-Optic 05-15301:321

PART 1: ABOUT YOUR MOST RECENT SEARCH

INSTRUCTIONS: Please answer these questions about the computer catalog search you just completed.

1. I came to this computer search with:
   (Mark ALL that apply)

   a. A complete author's name .... ○
   b. Part of an author's name .... ○
   c. A complete title .... ○
   d. Part of a title .... ○
   e. A topic word or words .... ○
   f. A subject heading or headings .... ○
   g. A complete call number .... ○
   h. Part of a call number .... ○

2. By searching this computer catalog I was trying to find:
   (Mark ALL that apply)

   a. A specific book, journal or magazine .... ○
   b. Books, journals or magazines on a topic or subject ..... ○
   c. Books by a specific author .... ○
   d. Information such as publisher, date, spelling
      of a name, etc. .... ○
   e. If a book that I know the library has is available
      for my use .... ○
   f. Another library that has a book, journal or
      magazine that I want .... ○

3. I searched for what I wanted by:
   (Mark ALL that apply)

   a. A complete author's name .... ○
   b. Part of an author's name .... ○
   c. A complete title .... ○
   d. Part of a title .... ○
   e. A topic word or words .... ○
   f. A subject heading or headings .... ○
   g. A complete call number .... ○
   h. Part of a call number .... ○

4. I need this information for:
   (Mark ALL that apply)

   a. Recreational uses .... ○
   b. Making or fixing something .... ○
   c. My work or job .... ○
   d. Personal interest .... ○
   e. A hobby .... ○
   f. Class or course reading .... ○
   g. A course paper or report .... ○
   h. A thesis or dissertation .... ○
   i. Writing for publication .... ○
   j. Teaching or planning a course .... ○
   k. Keeping up on a topic or subject .... ○

5. In this computer search I found:
   (Mark ONE only)

   a. More than I was looking for .... ○
   b. All that I was looking for .... ○
   c. Some of what I was looking for .... ○
   d. Nothing I was looking for .... ○

6. In relation to what I was looking for, this computer search was:
   (Mark ONE only)

   a. Very satisfactory .... ○
   b. Somewhat satisfactory .... ○
   c. Somewhat unsatisfactory .... ○
   d. Very unsatisfactory .... ○

7. I came across things of interest other than what I was looking for:

   a. YES .... ○
   b. NO .... ○

8. I got help in doing this computer catalog search from:
   (Mark ALL that apply)

   a. Printed material or signs .... ○
   b. Instructions on the terminal screen .... ○
   c. Library staff member .... ○
   d. Person nearby .... ○
   e. I did not get help .... ○

9. My overall or general attitude toward the computer catalog is:
(Mark **ONE** only)

a. Very favorable .... ○
b. Somewhat favorable .... ○
c. Somewhat unfavorable .... ○
d. Very unfavorable .... ○

10. Compared to the card, book, or microfiche catalog in this library, the computer catalog is:
(Mark **ONE** only)

a. Better .... ○
b. About the same .... ○
c. Worse .... ○
d. Can't decide .... ○

PART 2: YOUR EXPERIENCE WITH COMPUTER CATALOG FEATURES

INSTRUCTIONS: Mark the single column for each question that corresponds most closely to how you feel. If the statement does not apply to your experience at the computer catalog, mark the column, "Does Not Apply".

	STRONGLY AGREE	AGREE	NEITHER AGREE NOR DISAGREE	DISAGREE	STRONGLY DISAGREE	DOES NOT APPLY
11. A computer search by title is difficult	○	○	○	○	○	○
12. A computer search by author is easy	○	○	○	○	○	○
13. A computer search by subject is difficult	○	○	○	○	○	○
14. A computer search by call number is easy	○	○	○	○	○	○
15. A computer search by combined author/title is difficult	○	○	○	○	○	○
16. Remembering commands in the middle of the search is easy	○	○	○	○	○	○
17. Finding the correct subject term is difficult	○	○	○	○	○	○
18. Scanning through a long display (forward or backward) is easy	○	○	○	○	○	○
19. Increasing the result when too little is retrieved is difficult	○	○	○	○	○	○
20. Reducing the result when too much is retrieved is easy	○	○	○	○	○	○
21. Understanding explanations on the screen is difficult	○	○	○	○	○	○
22. Using codes or abbreviations for searching is easy	○	○	○	○	○	○
23. Abbreviations on the screen are easy to understand	○	○	○	○	○	○
24. Locating call numbers on the screen is difficult	○	○	○	○	○	○
25. Searching with a short form of a name or a word (truncation) is easy	○	○	○	○	○	○

	STRONGLY AGREE	AGREE	NEITHER AGREE NOR DISAGREE	DISAGREE	STRONGLY DISAGREE	DOES NOT APPLY
26. Using logical terms like AND, OR, NOT is difficult	○	○	○	○	○	○
27. Remembering the exact sequence or order of commands is easy	○	○	○	○	○	○
28. Understanding the initial instructions on the screen is difficult	○	○	○	○	○	○
29. Understanding the display for a single book, journal or magazine is easy	○	○	○	○	○	○
30. Understanding the display that shows more than a single book, journal or magazine is difficult	○	○	○	○	○	○
31. Interrupting or stopping the display of information is easy	○	○	○	○	○	○
32. Typing in exact spelling, initials, spaces and hyphens is difficult to do	○	○	○	○	○	○
33. Knowing what is included in the computer catalog is easy to remember	○	○	○	○	○	○
34. The order in which items are displayed is easy to understand	○	○	○	○	○	○
35. Displayed messages are too long	○	○	○	○	○	○

	STRONGLY AGREE	AGREE	NEITHER AGREE NOR DISAGREE	DISAGREE	STRONGLY DISAGREE	DOES NOT APPLY
36. Selecting from a list of choices takes too much time	O	O	O	O	O	O
37. Entering commands when I want to during the search process is difficult	O	O	O	O	O	O
38. The rate at which the computer responds is too slow	O	O	O	O	O	O
39. The availability of signs and brochures is adequate	O	O	O	O	O	O
40. Signs and brochures are not very useful	O	O	O	O	O	O
41. The staff advice is often not helpful	O	O	O	O	O	O
42. It is hard to find a free terminal	O	O	O	O	O	O

YOU ARE MORE THAN HALF - WAY DONE

PART 3: IMPROVING THE COMPUTER CATALOG

INSTRUCTIONS: Select the response or responses that best reflect your views about changes that should be made in the computer catalog.

43. When I use the computer catalog terminal:
(Mark YES or NO)

	YES	NO
a. The keyboard is confusing to use	O	O
b. There is too much glare on the screen	O	O
c. The letters and numbers are easy to read	O	O
d. The lighting around the terminal is too bright	O	O
e. There is enough writing space at the terminal	O	O
f. Nearby noise is distracting	O	O
g. The terminal table is too high or too low	O	O
h. The printer is easy to use	O	O

44. Select up to FOUR additional features you would like this computer catalog to have:

a. Providing step by step instructions .... O
b. Searching by any word or words in a title .... O
c. Searching by any word or words in a subject heading .... O
d. Limiting search results by date of publication .... O
e. Limiting search results by language .... O
f. Ability to search by journal title abbreviations .... O
g. Ability to change the order in which items are displayed .... O
h. Ability to view a list of words related to my search words .... O
i. Ability to search for illustrations and bibliographies .... O
j. Ability to search by call number .... O
k. Ability to print search results .... O
l. Ability to search a book's table of contents, summary or index .... O
m. Ability to know if a book is checked out .... O
n. Ability to tell where a book is located in the library .... O
o. None .... O

45. Select up to FOUR computer catalog service improvements you would like the library to make:

a. More terminals .... O
b. Terminals at locations other than near the card catalog .... O
c. Terminals at places other than library buildings .... O
d. A chart of commands posted at the terminal .... O
e. A manual or brochure at the terminal .... O
f. An instruction manual for purchase .... O
g. Training sessions .... O
h. Slide/tape/cassette training program .... O
i. None .... O

46. Select up to FOUR kinds of material you would like to see added to the computer catalog:

a. Dissertations .... O
b. Motion picture films .... O
c. Government publications .... O
d. Journal or magazine titles .... O
e. Maps .... O
f. Manuscripts .... O
g. Music scores .... O
h. Newspapers .... O
i. Phonograph records or tapes .... O
j. Technical reports .... O
k. More of the library's older books .... O
l. None .... O
m. Other .... O

47. BRIEFLY DESCRIBE ANY OTHER PROBLEMS WITH THIS COMPUTER CATALOG OR CHANGES YOU WOULD LIKE MADE TO IT: O

PART 4: ABOUT YOURSELF

INSTRUCTIONS: Your responses are confidential. Please do not write your name anywhere on this questionnaire.

48. I come to this library:

a. Daily .... ○
b. Weekly .... ○
c. Monthly .... ○
d. About four times a year .... ○
e. About once a year .... ○
f. Not before today .... ○

49. I use this computer catalog:

a. Every library visit .... ○
b. Almost every visit .... ○
c. Occasionally .... ○
d. Rarely .... ○
e. Not before today .... ○

50. I use this library's book, card or microfilm catalog:

a. Every visit .... ○
b. Almost every visit .... ○
c. Occasionally .... ○
d. Rarely .... ○
e. Never .... ○

51. I use a computer system other than the library's computer catalog:

a. Daily .... ○
b. Weekly .... ○
c. Monthly .... ○
d. About four times a year .... ○
e. About once a year .... ○
f. Never .... ○

52. I first heard about this computer catalog from: (Mark <u>ONE</u> only)

a. Noticing a terminal in the library .... ○
b. Library tour, orientation or demonstration .... ○
c. An article or written announcement .... ○
d. A course instructor .... ○
e. A friend or family member .... ○
f. Library staff .... ○

53. I learned how to use this computer catalog: (Mark <u>ALL</u> that apply)

a. From a friend or someone at a nearby terminal .... ○
b. Using printed instructions .... ○
c. Using instructions on the terminal screen .... ○
d. From the library staff .... ○
e. From a library course or orientation .... ○
f. From a slide/tape/cassette program .... ○
g. By myself without any help .... ○

54. My age group is:

a. 14 and under .... ○
b. 15 - 19 years .... ○
c. 20 - 24 years .... ○
d. 25 - 34 years .... ○
e. 35 - 44 years .... ○
f. 45 - 54 years .... ○
g. 55 - 64 years .... ○
h. 65 and over .... ○

55. I am:

a. Female .... ○
b. Male .... ○

56. Mark your current or highest educational level: (Mark <u>ONE</u> only)

a. Grade School or Elementary School .... ○
b. High School or Secondary School .... ○
c. Some College or University .... ○
d. College or University Graduate .... ○

If you <u>are not</u> completing this questionnaire at a college or university, please stop here. Thank you.

If you <u>are</u> completing this questionnaire at a college or university, please continue.

57. The category that best describes my academic area is: (Mark <u>ONE</u> only)

a. Arts and Humanities .... ○
b. Physical/Biological Sciences .... ○
c. Social Sciences .... ○
d. Business/Management .... ○
e. Education .... ○
f. Engineering .... ○
g. Medical/Health Sciences .... ○
h. Law .... ○
i. Major not declared .... ○
j. Interdisciplinary .... ○

58. The main focus of my academic work at the present time is:
(Mark **ALL** that apply)

a. Course Work .... ○
b. Teaching .... ○
c. Research .... ○

59. My present affiliation with this college or university is:

a. Freshman/Sophomore .... ○
b. Junior/Senior .... ○
c. Graduate - masters level .... ○
d. Graduate - doctoral level .... ○
e. Graduate - professional school .... ○
f. Faculty .... ○
g. Staff .... ○
h. Other .... ○

Thank you for participating in this study of the computer catalog. This completes the questionnaire. Please return it.

SUPPLEMENTARY QUESTIONNAIRE ITEMS

60. ○○○○○○○○○○○○○○○○○○
61. ○○○○○○○○○○○○○○○○○○
62. ○○○○○○○○○○○○○○○○○○
63. ○○○○○○○○○○○○○○○○○○
64. ○○○○○○○○○○○○○○○○○○

OFFICE USE ONLY

TERM I.D.	DATE			DATA COLL.	TERM LOC.	LIBRARY SYSTEM
	MO.	DAY	YR.			

VERIFIED:

BY: _____

DATE: _____

DO NOT WRITE IN THIS AREA

10844

APPENDIX 2

Non-User Questionnaire

Council on Library Resources

COMPUTER CATALOG STUDY

Questionnaire

The library has a computer catalog and not everyone has had a chance to use it yet. If you have <u>NEVER USED THE COMPUTER CATALOG</u> you can contribute to the quality of library services by completing this questionnaire. It takes about five minutes. Your responses are confidential. Please do not write your name anywhere on the questionnaire. Thank you.

MARKING INSTRUCTIONS

- USE A NO. 2 PENCIL ONLY.
- FILL THE CIRCLES COMPLETELY.
- BE SURE TO ERASE CLEANLY ANY MARKS YOU WISH TO CHANGE.
- MAKE NO STRAY MARKS ON THIS QUESTIONNAIRE.

DO NOT WRITE IN THIS AREA   10057

NCS Trans-Optic 05-15300:321

PART 1: WHAT YOU THINK ABOUT THE COMPUTER CATALOG

INSTRUCTIONS: Please mark the response that best describes how you view a computer catalog.

1. I have not used the computer catalog up to now because:
(Mark ALL that apply)

a. I do not like to use computers .... ○
b. I did not know there was a computer catalog .... ○

c. I do not know where it is .... ○
d. I have not had time to learn to use it .... ○

e. I have not taken training sessions on how to use it .... ○
f. There has not been any staff at the terminals to assist me in using it .... ○
g. The terminals were all in use when I wanted to use it .... ○
h. I have not needed to use any library catalog recently .... ○
i. The card catalog is easier to use .... ○
j. The card catalog contains more of the information I need .... ○
k. I am a visitor or infrequent user of this library .... ○

2. How much time do you think it takes to learn to use the computer catalog?

a. A day or more .... ○
b. Between 1/2 of a day and a day .... ○
c. Between an hour and 1/2 of a day .... ○
d. Between 30 minutes and an hour .... ○
e. Between 15 minutes and 30 minutes .... ○
f. 15 minutes or less .... ○

3. How difficult or easy do you think it would be to learn to use the computer catalog?

a. Very difficult .... ○
b. Somewhat difficult .... ○
c. Somewhat easy .... ○
d. Very easy .... ○

4. My overall or general attitude toward the computer catalog is:

a. Very favorable .... ○
b. Somewhat favorable .... ○
c. Somewhat unfavorable .... ○
d. Very unfavorable .... ○

5. How likely are you to use the computer catalog in the future?

a. Very likely .... ○
b. Somewhat likely .... ○
c. Somewhat unlikely .... ○
d. Very unlikely .... ○

6. Compared to the card, book, or microfiche catalog in this library the computer catalog is:
(Mark ONE only)

a. Better .... ○
b. About the same .... ○
c. Worse .... ○
d. Can't decide .... ○

PART 2: ABOUT YOURSELF

INSTRUCTIONS: Your responses are confidential. Please do not write your name anywhere on this questionnaire.

7. I come to this library:

a. Daily .... ○
b. Weekly .... ○
c. Monthly .... ○
d. About four times a year .... ○
e. About once a year .... ○
f. Not before today .... ○

8. I use this library's book, card or microfilm catalog:

a. Every visit .... ○
b. Almost every visit .... ○
c. Occasionally .... ○
d. Rarely .... ○
e. Not before today .... ○

9. I use a computer system other than the library's computer catalog:

a. Daily .... O
b. Weekly .... O
c. Monthly .... O
d. About four times a year .... O
e. About once a year .... O
f. Never .... O

10. My age group is:

a. 14 and under .... O
b. 15 - 19 years .... O
c. 20 - 24 years .... O
d. 25 - 34 years .... O
e. 35 - 44 years .... O
f. 45 - 54 years .... O
g. 55 - 64 years .... O
h. 65 and over .... O

11. I am:

a. Female .... O
b. Male .... O

12. Mark your current or highest educational level:
(Mark ONE only)

a. Grade School or Elementary School .... O
b. High School or Secondary School .... O
c. Some College or University .... O
d. College or University Graduate .... O

If you are not completing this questionnaire at a college or university, please stop here. Thank you.

If you are completing this questionnaire at a college or university, please continue.

13. The category that best describes my academic area is: (Mark ONE only)

a. Arts and Humanities .... O
b. Physical/Biological Sciences .... O
c. Social Sciences .... O
d. Business/Management .... O
e. Education .... O
f. Engineering .... O
g. Medical/Health Sciences .... O
h. Law .... O
i. Major not declared .... O
j. Interdisciplinary .... O

14. The main focus of my academic work at the present time is:
(Mark ALL that apply)

a. Course Work .... O
b. Teaching .... O
c. Research .... O

15. My present affiliation with this college or university is:

a. Freshman/Sophomore .... O
b. Junior/Senior .... O
c. Graduate - masters level .... O
d. Graduate - doctoral level .... O
e. Graduate - professional school .... O
f. Faculty .... O
g. Staff .... O
h. Other .... O

Thank you for participating in this study of the computer catalog. This completes the questionnaire. Please return it.

SUPPLEMENTARY QUESTIONNAIRE ITEMS

16. OOOOOOOOOOOOOOOOO
17. OOOOOOOOOOOOOOOOO
18. OOOOOOOOOOOOOOOOO
19. OOOOOOOOOOOOOOOOO

LIBRARY SYSTEM	LOC-ATION	DATA COLL.	DATE		
			MO.	DAY	YR.

TIME
| HR | MIN. |

VERIFIED:

BY: _____

DATE: __ _____

DO NOT WRITE IN THIS AREA

10057

APPENDIX 3

Survey Respondent Characteristics

$\mathbf{T}$HE response rates for both the user and non-user surveys averaged 59.6 percent and 52.2 percent, respectively (see Exhibit A, pages 200–201). The response rate is the percent of those who agreed to complete a questionnaire when asked. The response rates for completed user questionnaires ranged from a high of 93.9 percent at Syracuse University to a low of 29.4 percent at Mission/West Valley Community College. In all, the questionnaire response rates were quite good. For the non-user questionnaire, the response rate ranged from a high of 84.6 percent at Dartmouth College to a low of 24.1 percent at Syracuse University.

About 60 percent of the user data was collected at research libraries and 25 percent at public libraries as shown in Exhibit B, page 202. The non-user sample is more evenly distributed with about 40 percent of the data collected at research libraries, 25 percent from public libraries and 35 percent from the remaining types of libraries.

While the total number of responses is large it must be noted that about 75 percent of the responses to the questionnaire came from six library systems—Dallas Public, the Library of Congress, Northwestern University, Ohio State University, Syracuse University, and the University of California (nine campuses). Thus the study results are weighted to a smaller number of libraries—the majority of which are large academic libraries. The Dallas Public Library accounts for slightly more than half of all public library respondents and respondents from the Library of Congress make up 99 percent of the state and federal library respondents.

The user questionnaire, with a total of 59 questions, was relatively long and took 15 to 20 minutes to complete. Clearly Part II, "Your Experience with Online Catalog Features," required some patience and persistence on the part of the respondent and, as shown

EXHIBIT A   Questionnaire Response Rate

	USER QUESTIONNAIRE			NON-USER QUESTIONNAIRE		
	Approached	Completed N	Percent Completed %	Approached	Completed N	Percent Completed %
ARL Libraries (7)						
Dartmouth College	47	41	87.5	274	232	84.6
Northwestern University	928	616	66.4	511	276	54.6
Ohio State University	2,484	1,247	50.2	1,097	282	25.7
Stanford University	115	95	82.4	471	342	72.6
Syracuse University	1,425	1,339	93.9	1,220	294	24.1
University of California (9 campuses)*	3,357	1,259	37.5	*	*	*
University of Texas, Austin	?	104**	?	?	103**	?
ARL Libraries Subtotals	8,356	4,701	55.0	3,573	1,529	31.7
Other Academic Libraries (6)						
Claremont Colleges	103	49	47.5	84	54	64.1
Mankato State University	397	281	70.5	380	240	63.1
Ohio University, Athens	73	51	70.3	190	106	55.9
Stephen F. Austin State University	153	111	72.4	259	160	61.7
University of Akron	164	132	80.5	141	100	70.9
University of Texas, Dallas	46	37	80.9	148	104	70.3
Other Academic Libraries Subtotals	936	661	70.6	1,202	764	63.6

Community College Libraries (2)					
Mission/West Valley Colleges	527	155	29.4	304	228	75.0

Public Libraries (4)						
Dallas Public	1,493	1,081	72.4	428	299	69.9
Evanston Public	382	252	65.9	423	254	60.1
Iowa City Public	578	410	70.9	493	144	29.2
Pikes Peak Library District	677	304	44.9	663	379	57.2
Public Libraries Subtotals	3,130	2,047	65.4	2,007	1,076	53.6

State & Federal Libraries (2)						
Library of Congress	633	525	82.9	410	298	72.6
Ohio State Library	9	5	57.1	129	86	66.7
State and Federal Subtotals	642	530	82.6	539	384	71.2
Totals	13,591	8,094	59.6	7,625	3,981	52.2

*An online version of the User Questionnaire was used at the University of California. Non-user questionnaires were not solicited.
**Not included in computed completion rate.

EXHIBIT B   Sample Sizes, by Type of Library

Type of Library	USER SAMPLE		NON-USER SAMPLE	
	Number N	*Percent* %	*Number* N	*Percent* %
ARL Libraries	4,701	58	1,529	38
Other Academic Libraries	661	8	764	19
Community College Libraries	155	2	228	6
Public Libraries	2,047	25	1,076	27
State and Federal Libraries	530	7	384	10
Total	8,094	100	3,981	100

EXHIBIT C   Completion Rate of Parts of the Questionnaires

	QUESTION IN EACH PART WITH:	
	Largest Sample Size	*Smallest Sample Size*
User Questionnaires (N = 8,094)		
Part I (10 questions)	7,884	7,702
Part II (31 questions)	7,331	2,501
Part III (5 questions)	7,467	6,117
Part IV (12 questions)	7,447	4,751
Non-User Questionnaires (N = 3,981)		
Part I (6 questions)	3,916	3,618
Part II (9 questions)	3,931	2,394

in Exhibit C, there were some respondents who skipped some questions in this part—question sample size ranges from 2,501 to 7,331 out of a possible 7,884. Yet, the response rate improved considerably for the following two parts. Thus, while the length of the user questionnaire might have introduced some bias due to declining sample size for the later questions, this did not in fact occur.

The response rate for each item in the non-user questionnaire was uniformly quite high. This was no doubt due to the brief nature of the instrument. All completed questionnaires, even if some questions were skipped, were included in the data analysis. Null values, i.e., for questions skipped, were excluded from all analysis and calculations of percentages.

Due to the thorough preparation and pretesting of the data collection instruments, libraries installing public access online catalogs may wish to consider using the same questionnaires used in this study. Libraries wishing additional information about use of the questionnaires should contact the University of California, Library Plans and Policies, University Hall, Room 7, Berkeley, CA 94703.

APPENDIX 4

Responses by Type of Library for the User Questionnaire

LIBTYPE

	COUNT ROW PCT COL PCT	A.R.L. L IBS 1	OTHER AC ADEMIC 2	COMMUNIT Y COLLEG E 3	PUBLIC 4	STATE AN D FEDERA L 5	ROW TOTAL
RQUEST1							
RQ1A COMPLETE AUTHOR		2018 61.1 44.6	251 7.6 38.0	50 1.5 32.3	789 23.9 39.1	197 6.0 37.4	3305 41.9
RQ1B PART AUTHOR'S NAME		640 64.1 14.1	78 7.8 11.8	17 1.7 11.0	199 19.9 9.9	64 6.4 12.1	998 12.7
RQ1C COMPLETE TITLE		1831 59.1 40.5	276 8.9 41.8	52 1.7 33.5	777 25.1 38.5	162 5.2 30.7	3098 39.3
RQ1D PART TITLE		532 62.0 11.8	70 8.2 10.6	16 1.9 10.3	191 22.3 9.5	49 5.7 9.3	858 10.9
RQ1E TOPIC WORD OR WORDS		1255 55.4 27.7	239 10.6 36.2	37 1.6 23.9	513 22.6 25.4	221 9.8 41.9	2265 28.7
RQ1F SUBJECT HEADING		1878 53.6 41.5	264 7.5 40.0	103 2.9 66.5	976 27.9 48.4	282 8.1 53.5	3503 44.4
RQ1G COMPLETE CALL NUMBER		273 69.6 6.0	19 4.8 2.9	5 1.3 3.2	81 20.7 4.0	14 3.6 2.7	392 5.0
RQ1H PART CALL NUMBER		52 61.9 1.1	7 8.3 1.1	2 2.4 1.3	20 23.8 1.0	3 3.6 0.6	84 1.1
COLUMN TOTAL		4524 57.4	660 8.4	155 2.0	2018 25.6	527 6.7	7884 100.0

PERCENTS AND TOTALS BASED ON RESPONDENTS

7884 VALID CASES   210 MISSING CASES

LIBTYPE

	COUNT ROW PCT COL PCT	A.R.L. L IBS 1	OTHER AC ADEMIC 2	COMMUNIT Y COLLEG E 3	PUBLIC 4	STATE AN D FEDERA L 5	ROW TOTAL
RQUEST2							
RQ2A SPECIFIC BOOK ETC		2345 59.8 52.3	324 8.3 49.3	66 1.7 42.9	991 25.3 49.4	193 4.9 37.3	3919 50.1
RQ2B BOOKS ON TOPIC		2287 54.8 51.0	355 8.5 54.0	99 2.4 64.3	1080 25.9 53.9	355 8.5 68.7	4176 53.4
RQ2C BOOKS BY SPEC AUTHOR		1098 59.5 24.5	135 7.3 20.5	31 1.7 20.1	472 25.6 23.5	108 5.9 20.9	1844 23.6
RQ2D PUB-DATE-SPELLING		228 55.5 5.1	55 13.4 8.4	10 2.4 6.5	66 16.1 3.3	52 12.7 10.1	411 5.3
RQ2E IF BOOK IS AVAILABLE		786 60.1 17.5	90 6.9 13.7	28 2.1 18.2	381 29.1 19.0	23 1.8 4.4	1308 16.7
RQ2F OTHER LIBRARY W BOOK		313 54.3 7.0	104 18.1 15.8	9 1.6 5.8	140 24.3 7.0	10 1.7 1.9	576 7.4
COLUMN TOTAL		4483 57.4	657 8.4	154 2.0	2005 25.7	517 6.6	7816 100.0

PERCENTS AND TOTALS BASED ON RESPONDENTS

7816 VALID CASES   278 MISSING CASES

LIBTYPE

COUNT ROW PCT COL PCT	A.R.L. LIBS 1	OTHER AC ADEMIC 2	COMMUNITY COLLEGE 3	PUBLIC 4	STATE AN D FEDERA L 5	ROW TOTAL
RQUEST3						
RQ3A COMPLETE AUTHOR	1760 59.5 39.4	231 7.8 35.7	41 1.4 26.6	738 24.9 36.9	188 6.4 36.1	2958 38.0
RQ3B PART AUTHOR'S NAME	788 67.5 17.7	97 8.3 15.0	15 1.3 9.7	203 17.4 10.1	65 5.6 12.5	1168 15.0
RQ3C COMPLETE TITLE	1594 57.7 35.7	258 9.3 39.9	48 1.7 31.2	725 26.2 36.2	137 5.0 26.3	2762 35.5
RQ3D PART TITLE	694 62.7 15.6	105 9.5 16.2	20 1.8 13.0	231 20.9 11.5	56 5.1 10.7	1106 14.2
RQ3E TOPIC WORD OR WORDS	1246 53.6 27.9	238 10.2 36.8	37 1.6 24.0	573 24.6 28.6	232 10.0 44.5	2326 29.9
RQ3F SUBJECT HEADINGS	1798 53.3 40.3	240 7.1 37.1	103 3.1 66.9	944 28.0 47.2	290 8.6 55.7	3375 43.4
RQ3G COMPLETE CALL NUMBER	262 76.2 5.9	2 0.6 0.3	3 0.9 1.9	62 18.0 3.1	15 4.4 2.9	344 4.4
RQ3H PART CALL NUMBER	32 52.5 0.7	0 0.0 0.0	2 3.3 1.3	23 37.7 1.1	4 6.6 0.8	61 0.8
COLUMN TOTAL	4462 57.3	647 8.3	154 2.0	2001 25.7	521 6.7	7785 100.0

PERCENTS AND TOTALS BASED ON RESPONDENTS

7785 VALID CASES   309 MISSING CASES

LIBTYPE

COUNT ROW PCT COL PCT	A.R.L. LIBS 1	OTHER AC ADEMIC 2	COMMUNITY COLLEGE 3	PUBLIC 4	STATE AN D FEDERA L 5	ROW TOTAL
RQUEST4						
RQ4A RECREATIONAL USES	562 43.0 12.6	67 5.1 10.2	21 1.6 13.6	621 47.5 31.1	36 2.8 6.9	1307 16.8
RQ4B MAKE-FIX SOMETHING	82 33.3 1.8	9 3.7 1.4	7 2.8 4.5	144 58.5 7.2	4 1.6 0.8	246 3.2
RQ4C WORK OR JOB	663 50.2 14.8	91 6.9 13.8	8 0.6 5.2	338 25.6 17.0	221 16.7 42.3	1321 16.9
RQ4D PERSONAL INTEREST	1035 44.3 23.2	148 6.3 22.5	39 1.7 25.3	1009 43.2 50.6	103 4.4 19.7	2334 29.9
RQ4E HOBBY	270 44.9 6.0	27 4.5 4.1	13 2.2 8.4	271 45.0 13.6	21 3.5 4.0	602 7.7
RQ4F CLASS-COURSE READING	1473 65.8 33.0	251 11.2 38.1	87 3.9 56.5	346 15.5 17.4	81 3.6 15.5	2238 28.7
RQ4G COURSE PAPER-REPORT	2018 67.0 45.1	334 11.1 50.8	88 2.9 57.1	421 14.0 21.1	151 5.0 28.9	3012 38.6
RQ4H THESIS-DISSERTATION	524 69.4 11.7	59 7.8 9.0	11 1.5 7.1	78 10.3 3.9	83 11.0 15.9	755 9.7
COLUMN TOTAL	4470 57.3	658 8.4	154 2.0	1994 25.6	523 6.7	7799 100.0

PERCENTS AND TOTALS BASED ON RESPONDENTS

(CONTINUED)

```
               LIBTYPE

           COUNT   IA.R.L. L OTHER AC COMMUNIT PUBLIC   STATE AN
           ROW PCT IIBS      ADEMIC   Y COLLEG          D FEDERA    ROW
           COL PCT I                  E                 L           TOTAL
                   I    1   I    2   I    3   I    4   I    5   I
RQUEST4        --------I--------I--------I--------I--------I--------I
         RQ4I       I   335  I    46  I     3  I    66  I   110  I    560
   PUBLICATION      I  59.8  I   8.2  I   0.5  I  11.8  I  19.6  I    7.2
                   I   7.5  I   7.0  I   1.9  I   3.3  I  21.0  I
                   I--------I--------I--------I--------I--------I
         RQ4J       I   206  I    37  I     6  I    73  I    36  I    358
  TEACHING A COURSE I  57.5  I  10.3  I   1.7  I  20.4  I  10.1  I    4.6
                   I   4.6  I   5.6  I   3.9  I   3.7  I   6.9  I
                   I--------I--------I--------I--------I--------I
         RQ4K       I   597  I    96  I    19  I   302  I    93  I   1107
 KEEP UP ON TOPIC   I  53.9  I   8.7  I   1.7  I  27.3  I   8.4  I   14.2
                   I  13.4  I  14.6  I  12.3  I  15.1  I  17.8  I
                   I--------I--------I--------I--------I--------I
           COLUMN     4470      658      154     1994      523     7799
           TOTAL      57.3      8.4      2.0     25.6      6.7    100.0

PERCENTS AND TOTALS BASED ON RESPONDENTS

   7799 VALID CASES           295 MISSING CASES
```

```
               LIBTYPE
           COUNT   I
           ROW PCT IA.R.L. L OTHER AC COMMUNIT PUBLIC   STATE AN    ROW
           COL PCT IIBS      ADEMIC   Y COLLEG          D FEDERA    TOTAL
           TOT PCT I    1.I      2.I      3.I      4.I      5.I
RQ5        --------I--------I--------I--------I--------I--------I
            1.  I    655  I   114  I    30  I   386  I    95  I   1280
   MORE  THAN    I   51.2  I   8.9  I   2.3  I  30.2  I   7.4  I   16.6
                I   14.8  I  17.5  I  19.9  I  19.7  I  18.3  I
                I    8.5  I   1.5  I   0.4  I   5.0  I   1.2  I
               -I--------I--------I--------I--------I--------I
            2.  I   1162  I   198  I    42  I   621  I    99  I   2122
  ALL OR  MOST   I   54.8  I   9.3  I   2.0  I  29.3  I   4.7  I   27.5
                I   26.3  I  30.4  I  27.8  I  31.7  I  19.1  I
                I   15.1  I   2.6  I   0.5  I   8.1  I   1.3  I
               -I--------I--------I--------I--------I--------I
            3.  I   1776  I   264  I    62  I   668  I   280  I   3050
   SOME         I   58.2  I   8.7  I   2.0  I  21.9  I   9.2  I   39.6
                I   40.2  I  40.5  I  41.1  I  34.1  I  54.1  I
                I   23.1  I   3.4  I   0.8  I   8.7  I   3.6  I
               -I--------I--------I--------I--------I--------I
            4.  I    829  I    76  I    17  I   286  I    44  I   1252
   NOTHING      I   66.2  I   6.1  I   1.4  I  22.8  I   3.5  I   16.3
                I   18.7  I  11.7  I  11.3  I  14.6  I   8.5  I
                I   10.8  I   1.0  I   0.2  I   3.7  I   0.6  I
               -I--------I--------I--------I--------I--------I
           COLUMN    4422      652      151     1961      518     7704
           TOTAL      57.4      8.5      2.0     25.5      6.7    100.0

CHI SQUARE =   145.24255 WITH  12 DEGREES OF FREEDOM   SIGNIFICANCE =   0.0000
PEARSON'S R =-0.07877  SIGNIFICANCE =   0.0000

NUMBER OF MISSING OBSERVATIONS =      390
```

```
                    LIBTYPE
            COUNT  I
            ROW PCT IA.R.L. L OTHER AC COMMUNIT PUBLIC   STATE AN   ROW
            COL PCT IIBS     ADEMIC   Y COLLEG          D FEDERA  TOTAL
            TOT PCT I     1.I      2.I      3.I      4.I      5.I
RQ6         --------I--------I--------I--------I--------I--------I
            1. I     1928 I    345 I     77 I    979 I    258 I   3587
  VERY SATISFACTOR I  53.7 I    9.6 I    2.1 I   27.3 I    7.2 I   46.5
                 I   43.6 I   52.6 I   50.0 I   49.7 I   50.2 I
                 I   25.0 I    4.5 I    1.0 I   12.7 I    3.3 I
            -I--------I--------I--------I--------I--------I
            2. I     1499 I    212 I     60 I    626 I    193 I   2590
  SOMEWHAT SATISFA I  57.9 I    8.2 I    2.3 I   24.2 I    7.5 I   33.6
                 I   33.9 I   32.3 I   39.0 I   31.8 I   37.5 I
                 I   19.4 I    2.7 I    0.8 I    8.1 I    2.5 I
            -I--------I--------I--------I--------I--------I
            3. I      490 I     59 I     12 I    202 I     42 I    805
  SOMEWHAT UNSATIS I  60.9 I    7.3 I    1.5 I   25.1 I    5.2 I   10.4
                 I   11.1 I    9.0 I    7.8 I   10.3 I    8.2 I
                 I    6.3 I    0.8 I    0.2 I    2.6 I    0.5 I
            -I--------I--------I--------I--------I--------I
            4. I      508 I     40 I      5 I    162 I     21 I    736
  VERY UNSATISFACT I  69.0 I    5.4 I    0.7 I   22.0 I    2.9 I    9.5
                 I   11.5 I    6.1 I    3.2 I    8.2 I    4.1 I
                 I    6.6 I    0.5 I    0.1 I    2.1 I    0.3 I
            -I--------I--------I--------I--------I--------I
            COLUMN   4425     656     154    1969     514    7718
            TOTAL    57.3     8.5     2.0    25.5     6.7   100.0
```

CHI SQUARE =   84.01668 WITH 12 DEGREES OF FREEDOM SIGNIFICANCE = 0.0000
PEARSON'S R =-0.07807 SIGNIFICANCE = 0.0000

NUMBER OF MISSING OBSERVATIONS =   376

```
                    LIBTYPE
            COUNT  I
            ROW PCT IA.R.L. L OTHER AC COMMUNIT PUBLIC   STATE AN   ROW
            COL PCT IIBS     ADEMIC   Y COLLEG          D FEDERA  TOTAL
            TOT PCT I     1.I      2.I      3.I      4.I      5.I
RQ7         --------I--------I--------I--------I--------I--------I
            1. I     2032 I    341 I     78 I   1055 I    329 I   3835
  YES              I   53.0 I    8.9 I    2.0 I   27.5 I    8.6 I   49.8
                 I   46.0 I   52.1 I   51.0 I   53.8 I   63.8 I
                 I   26.4 I    4.4 I    1.0 I   13.7 I    4.3 I
            -I--------I--------I--------I--------I--------I
            2. I     2387 I    313 I     75 I    905 I    187 I   3867
  NO               I   61.7 I    8.1 I    1.9 I   23.4 I    4.8 I   50.2
                 I   54.0 I   47.9 I   49.0 I   46.2 I   36.2 I
                 I   31.0 I    4.1 I    1.0 I   11.8 I    2.4 I
            -I--------I--------I--------I--------I--------I
            COLUMN   4419     654     153    1960     516    7702
            TOTAL    57.4     8.5     2.0    25.4     6.7   100.0
```

CHI SQUARE =   80.20195 WITH   4 DEGREES OF FREEDOM SIGNIFICANCE = 0.0000
PEARSON'S R =-0.09554 SIGNIFICANCE = 0.0000

NUMBER OF MISSING OBSERVATIONS =   392

```
              LIBTYPE
         COUNT  IA.R.L. L OTHER AC COMMUNIT PUBLIC   STATE AN
         ROW PCT IIBS      ADEMIC   Y COLLEG          D FEDERA   ROW
         COL PCT I                  E                 L          TOTAL
              I    1    I    2    I    3    I    4    I    5    I
RQUEST8       --------I--------I--------I--------I--------I--------I
         RQ8A      I 1819   I  233   I   49   I  708   I  324   I  3133
PRINTED MATTER-SIGNS I 58.1   I  7.4   I  1.6   I 22.6   I 10.3   I  40.6
              I 41.2   I 35.5   I 32.0   I 35.9   I 62.4   I
              I--------I--------I--------I--------I--------I
         RQ8B      I 1456   I  226   I   79   I  528   I  175   I  2464
TERMINAL SCREEN INST I 59.1   I  9.2   I  3.2   I 21.4   I  7.1   I  32.0
              I 33.0   I 34.4   I 51.6   I 26.8   I 33.7   I
              I--------I--------I--------I--------I--------I
         RQ8C      I  516   I  218   I   48   I  668   I  260   I  1710
LIBRARY STAFF MEMBER I 30.2   I 12.7   I  2.8   I 39.1   I 15.2   I  22.2
              I 11.7   I 33.2   I 31.4   I 33.9   I 50.1   I
              I--------I--------I--------I--------I--------I
         RQ8D      I  196   I   26   I   10   I  165   I   37   I   434
PERSON NEARBY      I 45.2   I  6.0   I  2.3   I 38.0   I  8.5   I   5.6
              I  4.4   I  4.0   I  6.5   I  8.4   I  7.1   I
              I--------I--------I--------I--------I--------I
         RQ8E      I 1548   I  198   I   37   I  528   I   83   I  2394
I DID NOT GET HELP I 64.7   I  8.3   I  1.5   I 22.1   I  3.5   I  31.0
              I 35.1   I 30.1   I 24.2   I 26.8   I 16.0   I
              I--------I--------I--------I--------I--------I
         COLUMN   4412     657      153     1970      519     7711
         TOTAL    57.2     8.5      2.0     25.5      6.7    100.0

PERCENTS AND TOTALS BASED ON RESPONDENTS

   7711 VALID CASES        383 MISSING CASES
```

```
              LIBTYPE
         COUNT  I
         ROW PCT IA.R.L. L OTHER AC COMMUNIT PUBLIC   STATE AN   ROW
         COL PCT IIBS      ADEMIC   Y COLLEG          D FEDERA   TOTAL
         TOT PCT I   1. I    2. I    3. I    4. I    5. I
RQ9           --------I--------I--------I--------I--------I--------I
           1. I 2977   I  481   I  119   I 1194   I  403   I  5174
VERY FAVORABLE  I 57.5   I  9.3   I  2.3   I 23.1   I  7.8   I  67.0
              I 67.5   I 73.4   I 77.8   I 60.2   I 77.5   I
              I 38.6   I  6.2   I  1.5   I 15.5   I  5.2   I
           -I--------I--------I--------I--------I--------I
           2. I 1133   I  144   I   29   I  561   I   95   I  1962
SOMEWHAT FAVORAB I 57.7   I  7.3   I  1.5   I 28.6   I  4.8   I  25.4
              I 25.7   I 22.0   I 19.0   I 28.3   I 18.3   I
              I 14.7   I  1.9   I  0.4   I  7.3   I  1.2   I
           -I--------I--------I--------I--------I--------I
           3. I  206   I   25   I    5   I  151   I   19   I   406
SOMEWHAT UNFAVOR I 50.7   I  6.2   I  1.2   I 37.2   I  4.7   I   5.3
              I  4.7   I  3.8   I  3.3   I  7.6   I  3.7   I
              I  2.7   I  0.3   I  0.1   I  2.0   I  0.2   I
           -I--------I--------I--------I--------I--------I
           4. I   92   I    5   I    0   I   77   I    3   I   177
VERY  UNFAVORA  I 52.0   I  2.8   I  0.0   I 43.5   I  1.7   I   2.3
              I  2.1   I  0.8   I  0.0   I  3.9   I  0.6   I
              I  1.2   I  0.1   I  0.0   I  1.0   I  0.0   I
           -I--------I--------I--------I--------I--------I
         COLUMN   4408     655      153     1983      520     7719
         TOTAL    57.1     8.5      2.0     25.7      6.7    100.0

   1 OUT OF   20 ( 5.0%) OF THE VALID CELLS HAVE EXPECTED CELL FREQUENCY LESS THAN 5.0.
MINIMUM EXPECTED CELL FREQUENCY = 3.508
CHI SQUARE = 121.29240 WITH 12 DEGREES OF FREEDOM   SIGNIFICANCE = 0.0000
PEARSON'S R = 0.03602  SIGNIFICANCE = 0.0008

NUMBER OF MISSING OBSERVATIONS =      375
```

```
                 LIBTYPE
          COUNT  I
          ROW PCT IA.R.L. L OTHER AC COMMUNIT PUBLIC   STATE AN   ROW
          COL PCT IIBS      ADEMIC   Y COLLEG          D FEDERA   TOTAL
          TOT PCT I    1. I    2. I    3. I    4. I    5. I
RQ10      --------I--------I--------I--------I--------I--------I
            1. I   3032 I    502 I    133 I   1247 I    391 I    5305
 BETTER        I   57.2 I    9.5 I    2.5 I   23.5 I    7.4 I    74.5
               I   74.0 I   81.6 I   91.1 I   69.5 I   84.1 I
               I   42.6 I    7.1 I    1.9 I   17.5 I    5.5 I
          -I--------I--------I--------I--------I--------I
            2. I    702 I     95 I     11 I    315 I     54 I    1177
 EQUAL         I   59.6 I    8.1 I    0.9 I   26.8 I    4.6 I    16.5
               I   17.1 I   15.4 I    7.5 I   17.5 I   11.6 I
               I    9.9 I    1.3 I    0.2 I    4.4 I    0.8 I
          -I--------I--------I--------I--------I--------I
            3. I    365 I     18 I      2 I    233 I     20 I     638
 WORSE         I   57.2 I    2.8 I    0.3 I   36.5 I    3.1 I     9.0
               I    8.9 I    2.9 I    1.4 I   13.0 I    4.3 I
               I    5.1 I    0.3 I    0.0 I    3.3 I    0.3 I
          -I--------I--------I--------I--------I--------I
        COLUMN    4099      615      146     1795      465     7120
        TOTAL     57.6      8.6      2.1     25.2      6.5    100.0

CHI SQUARE =    115.99091 WITH   8 DEGREES OF FREEDOM   SIGNIFICANCE =  0.0000
PEARSON'S R = 0.01070   SIGNIFICANCE =   0.1833

NUMBER OF MISSING OBSERVATIONS =      974
```

```
                 LIBTYPE
          COUNT  I
          ROW PCT IA.R.L. L OTHER AC COMMUNIT PUBLIC   STATE AN   ROW
          COL PCT IIBS      ADEMIC   Y COLLEG          D FEDERA   TOTAL
          TOT PCT I    1. I    2. I    3. I    4. I    5. I
RQ11      --------I--------I--------I--------I--------I--------I
           -2. I   1442 I    187 I     42 I    470 I    150 I    2291
STRONGLY DISAGRE   I   62.9 I    8.2 I    1.8 I   20.5 I    6.5 I    32.6
               I   35.0 I   31.0 I   31.8 I   26.6 I   36.1 I
               I   20.5 I    2.7 I    0.6 I    6.7 I    2.1 I
          -I--------I--------I--------I--------I--------I
           -1. I   1661 I    279 I     62 I    794 I    156 I    2952
DISAGREE       I   56.3 I    9.5 I    2.1 I   26.9 I    5.3 I    42.0
               I   40.4 I   46.3 I   47.0 I   44.9 I   37.6 I
               I   23.6 I    4.0 I    0.9 I   11.3 I    2.2 I
          -I--------I--------I--------I--------I--------I
            0. I    494 I     77 I     17 I    250 I     51 I     889
NEITHER A OR D     I   55.6 I    8.7 I    1.9 I   28.1 I    5.7 I    12.6
               I   12.0 I   12.8 I   12.9 I   14.1 I   12.3 I
               I    7.0 I    1.1 I    0.2 I    3.6 I    0.7 I
          -I--------I--------I--------I--------I--------I
            1. I    405 I     49 I     10 I    191 I     42 I     697
AGREE          I   58.1 I    7.0 I    1.4 I   27.4 I    6.0 I     9.9
               I    9.8 I    8.1 I    7.6 I   10.8 I   10.1 I
               I    5.8 I    0.7 I    0.1 I    2.7 I    0.6 I
          -I--------I--------I--------I--------I--------I
            2. I    113 I     11 I      1 I     64 I     16 I     205
STRONGLY AGREE     I   55.1 I    5.4 I    0.5 I   31.2 I    7.8 I     2.9
               I    2.7 I    1.8 I    0.8 I    3.6 I    3.9 I
               I    1.6 I    0.2 I    0.0 I    0.9 I    0.2 I
          -I--------I--------I--------I--------I--------I
        COLUMN    4115      603      132     1769      415     7034
        TOTAL     58.5      8.6      1.9     25.1      5.9    100.0

    1 OUT OF    25 (  4.0%) OF THE VALID CELLS HAVE EXPECTED CELL FREQUENCY LESS THAN 5.0.
MINIMUM EXPECTED CELL FREQUENCY =   3.847
CHI SQUARE =     58.65092 WITH  16 DEGREES OF FREEDOM   SIGNIFICANCE =  0.0000
PEARSON'S R = 0.04964   SIGNIFICANCE =   0.0000

NUMBER OF MISSING OBSERVATIONS =     1060
```

```
                     LIBTYPE
           COUNT   I
           ROW PCT IA.R.L. L OTHER AC COMMUNIT PUBLIC   STATE AN   ROW
           COL PCT IIBS      ADEMIC   Y COLLEG          D FEDERA   TOTAL
           TOT PCT I     1.I      2.I      3.I      4.I      5.I
RQ12       --------I--------I--------I--------I--------I--------I
        -2. I   106  I    15  I     4  I    58  I     9  I   192
STRONGLY DISAGRE I  55.2  I   7.8  I   2.1  I  30.2  I   4.7  I   2.7
                 I   2.5  I   2.5  I   2.9  I   3.3  I   2.2  I
                 I   1.5  I   0.2  I   0.1  I   0.8  I   0.1  I
        -I--------I--------I--------I--------I--------I
        -1. I   287  I    36  I     7  I   134  I    15  I   479
DISAGREE         I  59.9  I   7.5  I   1.5  I  28.0  I   3.1  I   6.8
                 I   6.9  I   5.9  I   5.0  I   7.6  I   3.6  I
                 I   4.0  I   0.5  I   0.1  I   1.9  I   0.2  I
        -I--------I--------I--------I--------I--------I
         0. I   389  I    50  I    16  I   178  I    48  I   681
NEITHER A OR D   I  57.1  I   7.3  I   2.3  I  26.1  I   7.0  I   9.6
                 I   9.4  I   8.3  I  11.4  I  10.1  I  11.6  I
                 I   5.5  I   0.7  I   0.2  I   2.5  I   0.7  I
        -I--------I--------I--------I--------I--------I
         1. I  1948  I   314  I    68  I   874  I   190  I  3394
AGREE            I  57.4  I   9.3  I   2.0  I  25.8  I   5.6  I  47.9
                 I  46.9  I  51.8  I  48.6  I  49.4  I  46.0  I
                 I  27.5  I   4.4  I   1.0  I  12.3  I   2.7  I
        -I--------I--------I--------I--------I--------I
         2. I  1427  I   191  I    45  I   527  I   151  I  2341
STRONGLY AGREE   I  61.0  I   8.2  I   1.9  I  22.5  I   6.5  I  33.0
                 I  34.3  I  31.5  I  32.1  I  29.8  I  36.6  I
                 I  20.1  I   2.7  I   0.6  I   7.4  I   2.1  I
        -I--------I--------I--------I--------I--------I
          COLUMN    4157     606     140    1771     413    7087
          TOTAL     58.7     8.6     2.0    25.0     5.8   100.0
```

1 OUT OF   25 (4.0%) OF THE VALID CELLS HAVE EXPECTED CELL FREQUENCY LESS THAN 5.0.
MINIMUM EXPECTED CELL FREQUENCY =   3.793
CHI SQUARE =   29.97052 WITH 16 DEGREES OF FREEDOM   SIGNIFICANCE =   0.0182
PEARSON'S R =-0.02045 SIGNIFICANCE =   0.0426

NUMBER OF MISSING OBSERVATIONS =   1007

```
                     LIBTYPE
           COUNT   I
           ROW PCT IA.R.L. L OTHER AC COMMUNIT PUBLIC   STATE AN   ROW
           COL PCT IIBS      ADEMIC   Y COLLEG          D FEDERA   TOTAL
           TOT PCT I     1.I      2.I      3.I      4.I      5.I
RQ13       --------I--------I--------I--------I--------I--------I
        -2. I   823  I   115  I    47  I   373  I   103  I  1461
STRONGLY DISAGRE I  56.3  I   7.9  I   3.2  I  25.5  I   7.0  I  21.3
                 I  20.6  I  26.7  I  34.3  I  20.5  I  22.0  I
                 I  12.0  I   1.7  I   0.7  I   5.4  I   1.5  I
        -I--------I--------I--------I--------I--------I
        -1. I  1222  I   183  I    52  I   633  I   167  I  2257
DISAGREE         I  54.1  I   8.1  I   2.3  I  28.0  I   7.4  I  32.9
                 I  30.5  I  42.5  I  38.0  I  34.8  I  35.6  I
                 I  17.8  I   2.7  I   0.8  I   9.2  I   2.4  I
        -I--------I--------I--------I--------I--------I
         0. I   615  I    50  I    18  I   251  I    78  I  1012
NEITHER A OR D   I  60.8  I   4.9  I   1.8  I  24.8  I   7.7  I  14.8
                 I  15.4  I  11.6  I  13.1  I  13.8  I  16.6  I
                 I   9.0  I   0.7  I   0.3  I   3.7  I   1.1  I
        -I--------I--------I--------I--------I--------I
         1. I   998  I    72  I    19  I   376  I    89  I  1554
AGREE            I  64.2  I   4.6  I   1.2  I  24.2  I   5.7  I  22.7
                 I  24.9  I  16.7  I  13.9  I  20.7  I  19.0  I
                 I  14.5  I   1.0  I   0.3  I   5.5  I   1.3  I
        -I--------I--------I--------I--------I--------I
         2. I   345  I    11  I     1  I   187  I    32  I   576
STRONGLY AGREE   I  59.9  I   1.9  I   0.2  I  32.5  I   5.6  I   8.4
                 I   8.6  I   2.6  I   0.7  I  10.3  I   6.8  I
                 I   5.0  I   0.2  I   0.0  I   2.7  I   0.5  I
        -I--------I--------I--------I--------I--------I
          COLUMN    4003     431     137    1820     469    6860
          TOTAL     58.4     6.3     2.0    26.5     6.8   100.0
```

CHI SQUARE =   110.67963 WITH 16 DEGREES OF FREEDOM   SIGNIFICANCE =   0.0000
PEARSON'S R =-0.03345 SIGNIFICANCE =   0.0028

NUMBER OF MISSING OBSERVATIONS =   1234

```
                LIBTYPE
        COUNT   I
        ROW PCT IA.R.L. L OTHER AC COMMUNIT PUBLIC   STATE AN   ROW
        COL PCT IIBS      ADEMIC   Y COLLEG          D FEDERA   TOTAL
        TOT PCT I    1.I      2.I      3.I      4.I      5.I
RQ14    --------I--------I--------I--------I--------I--------I
            -2. I    105  I     10  I      5  I     62  I     17  I   199
STRONGLY DISAGRE I  52.8  I    5.0  I    2.5  I   31.2  I    8.5  I   5.3
             I    4.5  I   14.1  I    6.2  I    5.9  I    7.2  I
             I    2.8  I    0.3  I    0.1  I    1.6  I    0.4  I
        -I--------I--------I--------I--------I--------I
            -1. I    194  I      6  I      8  I    142  I     19  I   369
DISAGREE     I   52.6  I    1.6  I    2.2  I   38.5  I    5.1  I   9.7
             I    8.3  I    8.5  I    9.9  I   13.5  I    8.1  I
             I    5.1  I    0.2  I    0.2  I    3.7  I    0.5  I
        -I--------I--------I--------I--------I--------I
             0. I    499  I     29  I     39  I    320  I     69  I   956
NEITHER A OR D   I   52.2  I    3.0  I    4.1  I   33.5  I    7.2  I   25.2
             I   21.3  I   40.8  I   48.1  I   30.4  I   29.4  I
             I   13.2  I    0.8  I    1.0  I    8.4  I    1.8  I
        -I--------I--------I--------I--------I--------I
             1. I    839  I     19  I     15  I    337  I     77  I   1287
AGREE        I   65.2  I    1.5  I    1.2  I   26.2  I    6.0  I   34.0
             I   35.7  I   26.8  I   18.5  I   32.0  I   32.8  I
             I   22.1  I    0.5  I    0.4  I    8.9  I    2.0  I
        -I--------I--------I--------I--------I--------I
             2. I    711  I      7  I     14  I    192  I     53  I   977
STRONGLY AGREE   I   72.8  I    0.7  I    1.4  I   19.7  I    5.4  I   25.8
             I   30.3  I    9.9  I   17.3  I   18.2  I   22.6  I
             I   18.8  I    0.2  I    0.4  I    5.1  I    1.4  I
        -I--------I--------I--------I--------I--------I
        COLUMN     2348       71       81      1053      235      3788
        TOTAL      62.0      1.9      2.1      27.8      6.2     100.0
```

2 OUT OF   25 (8.0%) OF THE VALID CELLS HAVE EXPECTED CELL FREQUENCY LESS THAN 5.0.
MINIMUM EXPECTED CELL FREQUENCY = 3.730
CHI SQUARE =   150.41559 WITH 16 DEGREES OF FREEDOM   SIGNIFICANCE = 0.0
PEARSON'S R =-0.13829 SIGNIFICANCE = 0.0000

NUMBER OF MISSING OBSERVATIONS =   4306

```
                LIBTYPE
        COUNT   I
        ROW PCT IA.R.L. L OTHER AC COMMUNIT PUBLIC   STATE AN   ROW
        COL PCT IIBS      ADEMIC   Y COLLEG          D FEDERA   TOTAL
        TOT PCT I    1.I      2.I      3.I      4.I      5.I
RQ15    --------I--------I--------I--------I--------I--------I
            -2. I   1142  I    142  I     22  I    166  I     93  I   1565
STRONGLY DISAGRE I   73.0  I    9.1  I    1.4  I   10.6  I    5.9  I   32.3
             I   35.7  I   30.7  I   20.4  I   22.1  I   28.7  I
             I   23.6  I    2.9  I    0.5  I    3.4  I    1.9  I
        -I--------I--------I--------I--------I--------I
            -1. I   1117  I    158  I     32  I    327  I    118  I   1752
DISAGREE     I   63.8  I    9.0  I    1.8  I   18.7  I    6.7  I   36.2
             I   34.9  I   34.1  I   29.6  I   43.5  I   36.4  I
             I   23.0  I    3.3  I    0.7  I    6.7  I    2.4  I
        -I--------I--------I--------I--------I--------I
             0. I    564  I    108  I     42  I    150  I     71  I   935
NEITHER A OR D   I   60.3  I   11.6  I    4.5  I   16.0  I    7.6  I   19.3
             I   17.6  I   23.3  I   38.9  I   20.0  I   21.9  I
             I   11.6  I    2.2  I    0.9  I    3.1  I    1.5  I
        -I--------I--------I--------I--------I--------I
             1. I    282  I     43  I      8  I     83  I     26  I   442
AGREE        I   63.8  I    9.7  I    1.8  I   18.8  I    5.9  I   9.1
             I    8.8  I    9.3  I    7.4  I   11.1  I    8.0  I
             I    5.8  I    0.9  I    0.2  I    1.7  I    0.5  I
        -I--------I--------I--------I--------I--------I
             2. I     95  I     12  I      4  I     25  I     16  I   152
STRONGLY AGREE   I   62.5  I    7.9  I    2.6  I   16.4  I   10.5  I   3.1
             I    3.0  I    2.6  I    3.7  I    3.3  I    4.9  I
             I    2.0  I    0.2  I    0.1  I    0.5  I    0.3  I
        -I--------I--------I--------I--------I--------I
        COLUMN     3200      463      108      751      324      4846
        TOTAL      66.0      9.6      2.2     15.5      6.7     100.0
```

1 OUT OF   25 (4.0%) OF THE VALID CELLS HAVE EXPECTED CELL FREQUENCY LESS THAN 5.0.
MINIMUM EXPECTED CELL FREQUENCY = 3.388
CHI SQUARE =   96.32101 WITH 16 DEGREES OF FREEDOM   SIGNIFICANCE = 0.0000
PEARSON'S R = 0.07753 SIGNIFICANCE = 0.0000

NUMBER OF MISSING OBSERVATIONS =   3248

```
              LIBTYPE
         COUNT  I
         ROW PCT IA.R.L. L OTHER AC COMMUNIT PUBLIC   STATE AN    ROW
         COL PCT IIBS     ADEMIC   Y COLLEG           D FEDERA   TOTAL
         TOT PCT I    1. I    2. I    3. I    4. I    5. I
RQ16     --------I--------I--------I--------I--------I--------I
            -2. I    165 I     20 I      4 I     50 I     20 I     259
STRONGLY DISAGRE I   63.7 I    7.7 I    1.5 I   19.3 I    7.7 I     3.6
                 I    4.0 I    3.2 I    2.8 I    2.8 I    4.1 I
                 I    2.3 I    0.3 I    0.1 I    0.7 I    0.3 I
         -I--------I--------I--------I--------I--------I
            -1. I    682 I    108 I     17 I    255 I    129 I    1191
DISAGREE         I   57.3 I    9.1 I    1.4 I   21.4 I   10.8 I    16.8
                 I   16.7 I   17.2 I   12.0 I   14.5 I   26.3 I
                 I    9.6 I    1.5 I    0.2 I    3.6 I    1.8 I
         -I--------I--------I--------I--------I--------I
             0. I    736 I    123 I     29 I    320 I     93 I    1301
NEITHER A OR D   I   56.6 I    9.5 I    2.2 I   24.6 I    7.1 I    18.3
                 I   18.0 I   19.6 I   20.4 I   18.2 I   19.0 I
                 I   10.4 I    1.7 I    0.4 I    4.5 I    1.3 I
         -I--------I--------I--------I--------I--------I
             1. I   1793 I    289 I     60 I    781 I    189 I    3112
AGREE            I   57.6 I    9.3 I    1.9 I   25.1 I    6.1 I    43.8
                 I   43.9 I   46.1 I   42.3 I   44.3 I   38.6 I
                 I   25.3 I    4.1 I    0.8 I   11.0 I    2.7 I
         -I--------I--------I--------I--------I--------I
             2. I    704 I     87 I     32 I    355 I     59 I    1237
STRONGLY AGREE   I   56.9 I    7.0 I    2.6 I   28.7 I    4.8 I    17.4
                 I   17.3 I   13.9 I   22.5 I   20.2 I   12.0 I
                 I    9.9 I    1.2 I    0.5 I    5.0 I    0.8 I
         -I--------I--------I--------I--------I--------I
          COLUMN   4080     627     142    1761     490    7100
          TOTAL    57.5     8.8     2.0    24.8     6.9   100.0

CHI SQUARE =    67.70325 WITH  16 DEGREES OF FREEDOM   SIGNIFICANCE =   0.0000
PEARSON'S R = 0.00182  SIGNIFICANCE =   0.4392

NUMBER OF MISSING OBSERVATIONS =     994
```

```
              LIBTYPE
         COUNT  I
         ROW PCT IA.R.L. L OTHER AC COMMUNIT PUBLIC   STATE AN    ROW
         COL PCT IIBS     ADEMIC   Y COLLEG           D FEDERA   TOTAL
         TOT PCT I    1. I    2. I    3. I    4. I    5. I
RQ17     --------I--------I--------I--------I--------I--------I
            -2. I    295 I     36 I     17 I    170 I     55 I     573
STRONGLY DISAGRE I   51.5 I    6.3 I    3.0 I   29.7 I    9.6 I     8.5
                 I    7.4 I    8.4 I   12.2 I    9.5 I   11.8 I
                 I    4.4 I    0.5 I    0.3 I    2.5 I    0.8 I
         -I--------I--------I--------I--------I--------I
            -1. I   1052 I    161 I     42 I    574 I    165 I    1994
DISAGREE         I   52.8 I    8.1 I    2.1 I   28.8 I    8.3 I    29.4
                 I   26.6 I   37.4 I   30.2 I   32.2 I   35.4 I
                 I   15.5 I    2.4 I    0.6 I    8.5 I    2.4 I
         -I--------I--------I--------I--------I--------I
             0. I    786 I     71 I     35 I    328 I     88 I    1308
NEITHER A OR D   I   60.1 I    5.4 I    2.7 I   25.1 I    6.7 I    19.3
                 I   19.8 I   16.5 I   25.2 I   18.4 I   18.9 I
                 I   11.6 I    1.0 I    0.5 I    4.8 I    1.3 I
         -I--------I--------I--------I--------I--------I
             1. I   1341 I    138 I     38 I    508 I    123 I    2148
AGREE            I   62.4 I    6.4 I    1.8 I   23.6 I    5.7 I    31.7
                 I   33.9 I   32.1 I   27.3 I   28.5 I   26.4 I
                 I   19.8 I    2.0 I    0.6 I    7.5 I    1.8 I
         -I--------I--------I--------I--------I--------I
             2. I    487 I     24 I      7 I    203 I     35 I     756
STRONGLY AGREE   I   64.4 I    3.2 I    0.9 I   26.9 I    4.6 I    11.2
                 I   12.3 I    5.6 I    5.0 I   11.4 I    7.5 I
                 I    7.2 I    0.4 I    0.1 I    3.0 I    0.5 I
         -I--------I--------I--------I--------I--------I
          COLUMN   3961     430     139    1783     466    6779
          TOTAL    58.4     6.3     2.1    26.3     6.9   100.0

CHI SQUARE =    95.65399 WITH  16 DEGREES OF FREEDOM   SIGNIFICANCE =   0.0000
PEARSON'S R =-0.08604  SIGNIFICANCE =   0.0000

NUMBER OF MISSING OBSERVATIONS =    1315
```

```
                  LIBTYPE
          COUNT  I
          ROW PCT IA.R.L. L OTHER AC COMMUNIT PUBLIC   STATE AN   ROW
          COL PCT I IBS      ADEMIC   Y COLLEG          D FEDERA   TOTAL
          TOT PCT I     1. I     2. I     3. I     4. I     5. I
RQ18      --------I--------I--------I--------I--------I--------I
              -2. I   263  I    28  I     5  I    98  I    36  I    430
STRONGLY DISAGRE I   61.2  I   6.5  I   1.2  I  22.8  I   8.4  I    6.2
                 I    6.5  I   4.9  I   3.8  I   5.6  I   7.7  I
                 I    3.8  I   0.4  I   0.1  I   1.4  I   0.5  I
          -I--------I--------I--------I--------I--------I
              -1. I   910  I   132  I    15  I   344  I   143  I   1544
DISAGREE         I   58.9  I   8.5  I   1.0  I  22.3  I   9.3  I   22.2
                 I   22.6  I  23.0  I  11.3  I  19.5  I  30.7  I
                 I   13.1  I   1.9  I   0.2  I   4.9  I   2.1  I
          -I--------I--------I--------I--------I--------I
               0. I   792  I   114  I    28  I   298  I    85  I   1317
NEITHER A OR D   I   60.1  I   8.7  I   2.1  I  22.6  I   6.5  I   18.9
                 I   19.6  I  19.9  I  21.1  I  16.9  I  18.2  I
                 I   11.4  I   1.6  I   0.4  I   4.3  I   1.2  I
          -I--------I--------I--------I--------I--------I
               1. I  1605  I   252  I    65  I   767  I   161  I   2850
AGREE            I   56.3  I   8.8  I   2.3  I  26.9  I   5.6  I   40.9
                 I   39.8  I  43.9  I  48.9  I  43.6  I  34.5  I
                 I   23.0  I   3.6  I   0.9  I  11.0  I   2.3  I
          -I--------I--------I--------I--------I--------I
               2. I   461  I    48  I    20  I   253  I    41  I    823
STRONGLY AGREE   I   56.0  I   5.8  I   2.4  I  30.7  I   5.0  I   11.8
                 I   11.4  I   8.4  I  15.0  I  14.4  I   8.8  I
                 I    6.6  I   0.7  I   0.3  I   3.6  I   0.6  I
          -I--------I--------I--------I--------I--------I
          COLUMN    4031      574      133     1760      466     6964
          TOTAL     57.9      8.2      1.9     25.3      6.7    100.0

CHI SQUARE =    73.25720 WITH  16 DEGREES OF FREEDOM   SIGNIFICANCE =   0.0000
PEARSON'S R = 0.02010   SIGNIFICANCE =   0.0467

NUMBER OF MISSING OBSERVATIONS =     1130
```

```
                  LIBTYPE
          COUNT  I
          ROW PCT IA.R.L. L OTHER AC COMMUNIT PUBLIC   STATE AN   ROW
          COL PCT I IBS      ADEMIC   Y COLLEG          D FEDERA   TOTAL
          TOT PCT I     1. I     2. I     3. I     4. I     5. I
RQ19      --------I--------I--------I--------I--------I--------I
              -2. I    86  I    25  I     7  I    20  I    19  I    157
STRONGLY DISAGRE I   54.8  I  15.9  I   4.5  I  12.7  I  12.1  I    5.7
                 I    6.0  I   6.9  I   5.9  I   4.6  I   4.9  I
                 I    3.1  I   0.9  I   0.3  I   0.7  I   0.7  I
          -I--------I--------I--------I--------I--------I
              -1. I   255  I    68  I    35  I    93  I    93  I    544
DISAGREE         I   46.9  I  12.5  I   6.4  I  17.1  I  17.1  I   19.9
                 I   17.8  I  18.7  I  29.4  I  21.2  I  24.2  I
                 I    9.3  I   2.5  I   1.3  I   3.4  I   3.4  I
          -I--------I--------I--------I--------I--------I
               0. I   384  I   127  I    44  I   115  I   107  I    777
NEITHER A OR D   I   49.4  I  16.3  I   5.7  I  14.8  I  13.8  I   28.4
                 I   26.8  I  34.9  I  37.0  I  26.3  I  27.9  I
                 I   14.0  I   4.6  I   1.6  I   4.2  I   3.9  I
          -I--------I--------I--------I--------I--------I
               1. I   571  I   123  I    28  I   165  I   140  I   1027
AGREE            I   55.6  I  12.0  I   2.7  I  16.1  I  13.6  I   37.5
                 I   39.8  I  33.8  I  23.5  I  37.7  I  36.5  I
                 I   20.9  I   4.5  I   1.0  I   6.0  I   5.1  I
          -I--------I--------I--------I--------I--------I
               2. I   137  I    21  I     5  I    45  I    25  I    233
STRONGLY AGREE   I   58.8  I   9.0  I   2.1  I  19.3  I  10.7  I    8.5
                 I    9.6  I   5.8  I   4.2  I  10.3  I   6.5  I
                 I    5.0  I   0.8  I   0.2  I   1.6  I   0.9  I
          -I--------I--------I--------I--------I--------I
          COLUMN    1433      364      119      438      384     2738
          TOTAL     52.3     13.3      4.3     16.0     14.0    100.0

CHI SQUARE =    46.68639 WITH  16 DEGREES OF FREEDOM   SIGNIFICANCE =   0.0001
PEARSON'S R =-0.03920   SIGNIFICANCE =   0.0201

NUMBER OF MISSING OBSERVATIONS =     5356
```

```
                   LIBTYPE
          COUNT  I
          ROW PCT IA.R.L. L OTHER AC COMMUNIT PUBLIC    STATE AN   ROW
          COL PCT IIBS      ADEMIC   Y COLLEG           D FEDERA   TOTAL
          TOT PCT I    1.I      2.I      3.I      4.I      5.I
RQ20      --------I--------I--------I--------I--------I--------I
             -2.  I   219  I    17  I     8  I    66  I    19  I    329
STRONGLY DISAGRE  I  66.6  I   5.2  I   2.4  I  20.1  I   5.8  I    5.6
                  I   6.2  I   3.4  I   7.0  I   4.7  I   5.0  I
                  I   3.7  I   0.3  I   0.1  I   1.1  I   0.3  I
                 -I--------I--------I--------I--------I--------I
             -1.  I   778  I   106  I     8  I   262  I    91  I   1245
DISAGREE          I  62.5  I   8.5  I   0.6  I  21.0  I   7.3  I   21.0
                  I  22.0  I  21.4  I   7.0  I  18.8  I  23.8  I
                  I  13.1  I   1.8  I   0.1  I   4.4  I   1.5  I
                 -I--------I--------I--------I--------I--------I
              0.  I  1038  I   150  I    43  I   506  I   110  I   1847
NEITHER A OR D    I  56.2  I   8.1  I   2.3  I  27.4  I   6.0  I   31.2
                  I  29.3  I  30.2  I  37.4  I  36.3  I  28.8  I
                  I  17.5  I   2.5  I   0.7  I   8.5  I   1.9  I
                 -I--------I--------I--------I--------I--------I
              1.  I  1172  I   185  I    44  I   450  I   132  I   1983
AGREE             I  59.1  I   9.3  I   2.2  I  22.7  I   6.7  I   33.5
                  I  33.1  I  37.3  I  38.3  I  32.3  I  34.6  I
                  I  19.8  I   3.1  I   0.7  I   7.6  I   2.2  I
                 -I--------I--------I--------I--------I--------I
              2.  I   333  I    38  I    12  I   109  I    30  I    522
STRONGLY AGREE    I  63.8  I   7.3  I   2.3  I  20.9  I   5.7  I    8.8
                  I   9.4  I   7.7  I  10.4  I   7.8  I   7.9  I
                  I   5.6  I   0.6  I   0.2  I   1.8  I   0.5  I
                 -I--------I--------I--------I--------I--------I
          COLUMN     3540     496      115     1393     382      5926
          TOTAL      59.7     8.4      1.9     23.5     6.4     100.0
```

CHI SQUARE =   52.23062 WITH 16 DEGREES OF FREEDOM SIGNIFICANCE = 0.0000
PEARSON'S R = 0.00698 SIGNIFICANCE = 0.2955

NUMBER OF MISSING OBSERVATIONS =   2168

```
                   LIBTYPE
          COUNT  I
          ROW PCT IA.R.L. L OTHER AC COMMUNIT PUBLIC    STATE AN   ROW
          COL PCT IIBS      ADEMIC   Y COLLEG           D FEDERA   TOTAL
          TOT PCT I    1.I      2.I      3.I      4.I      5.I
RQ21      --------I--------I--------I--------I--------I--------I
             -2.  I  1180  I   118  I    56  I   407  I    88  I   1849
STRONGLY DISAGRE  I  63.8  I   6.4  I   3.0  I  22.0  I   4.8  I   25.2
                  I  28.2  I  18.4  I  38.1  I  21.9  I  17.8  I
                  I  16.1  I   1.6  I   0.8  I   5.6  I   1.2  I
                 -I--------I--------I--------I--------I--------I
             -1.  I  2069  I   348  I    71  I   934  I   224  I   3646
DISAGREE          I  56.7  I   9.5  I   1.9  I  25.6  I   6.1  I   49.7
                  I  49.4  I  54.2  I  48.3  I  50.2  I  45.4  I
                  I  28.2  I   4.7  I   1.0  I  12.7  I   3.1  I
                 -I--------I--------I--------I--------I--------I
              0.  I   416  I    72  I    14  I   211  I    66  I    779
NEITHER A OR D    I  53.4  I   9.2  I   1.8  I  27.1  I   8.5  I   10.6
                  I   9.9  I  11.2  I   9.5  I  11.4  I  13.4  I
                  I   5.7  I   1.0  I   0.2  I   2.9  I   0.9  I
                 -I--------I--------I--------I--------I--------I
              1.  I   398  I    90  I     6  I   244  I    89  I    827
AGREE             I  48.1  I  10.9  I   0.7  I  29.5  I  10.8  I   11.3
                  I   9.5  I  14.0  I   4.1  I  13.1  I  18.1  I
                  I   5.4  I   1.2  I   0.1  I   3.3  I   1.2  I
                 -I--------I--------I--------I--------I--------I
              2.  I   127  I    14  I     0  I    63  I    26  I    230
STRONGLY AGREE    I  55.2  I   6.1  I   0.0  I  27.4  I  11.3  I    3.1
                  I   3.0  I   2.2  I   0.0  I   3.4  I   5.3  I
                  I   1.7  I   0.2  I   0.0  I   0.9  I   0.4  I
                 -I--------I--------I--------I--------I--------I
          COLUMN     4190     642      147     1859     493      7331
          TOTAL      57.2     8.8      2.0     25.4     6.7     100.0
```

   1 OUT OF   25 (4.0%) OF THE VALID CELLS HAVE EXPECTED CELL FREQUENCY LESS THAN 5.0.
MINIMUM EXPECTED CELL FREQUENCY =   4.612
CHI SQUARE =   128.79872 WITH 16 DEGREES OF FREEDOM   SIGNIFICANCE = 0.0000
PEARSON'S R = 0.09135 SIGNIFICANCE = 0.0000

NUMBER OF MISSING OBSERVATIONS =   763

```
               LIBTYPE
       COUNT  I
       ROW PCT IA.R.L. L OTHER AC COMMUNIT PUBLIC   STATE AN   ROW
       COL PCT IIBS      ADEMIC  Y COLLEG          D FEDERA  TOTAL
       TOT PCT I    1. I     2. I     3. I     4. I     5. I
RQ22   --------I--------I--------I--------I--------I--------I
        -2.  I    103 I     14 I      6 I     85 I     15 I    223
STRONGLY DISAGRE I   46.2 I    6.3 I    2.7 I   38.1 I    6.7 I    3.3
             I    2.6 I    2.3 I    4.5 I    5.7 I    3.1 I
             I    1.5 I    0.2 I    0.1 I    1.3 I    0.2 I
        -I--------I--------I--------I--------I--------I
        -1.  I    470 I     76 I     10 I    310 I     69 I    935
DISAGREE     I   50.3 I    8.1 I    1.1 I   33.2 I    7.4 I   14.0
             I   11.8 I   12.3 I    7.6 I   20.9 I   14.4 I
             I    7.0 I    1.1 I    0.1 I    4.6 I    1.0 I
        -I--------I--------I--------I--------I--------I
        0.   I    717 I    133 I     27 I    326 I     71 I   1274
NEITHER A OR D I   56.3 I   10.4 I    2.1 I   25.6 I    5.6 I   19.0
             I   18.0 I   21.6 I   20.5 I   22.0 I   14.8 I
             I   10.7 I    2.0 I    0.4 I    4.9 I    1.1 I
        -I--------I--------I--------I--------I--------I
        1.   I   2007 I    320 I     61 I    595 I    253 I   3236
AGREE        I   62.0 I    9.9 I    1.9 I   18.4 I    7.8 I   48.3
             I   50.4 I   51.9 I   46.2 I   40.1 I   52.8 I
             I   30.0 I    4.8 I    0.9 I    8.9 I    3.8 I
        -I--------I--------I--------I--------I--------I
        2.   I    686 I     74 I     28 I    167 I     71 I   1026
STRONGLY AGREE I   66.9 I    7.2 I    2.7 I   16.3 I    6.9 I   15.3
             I   17.2 I   12.0 I   21.2 I   11.3 I   14.8 I
             I   10.2 I    1.1 I    0.4 I    2.5 I    1.1 I
        -I--------I--------I--------I--------I--------I
       COLUMN   3983     617      132     1483      479     6694
       TOTAL    59.5      9.2      2.0     22.2      7.2    100.0
```

1 OUT OF   25 (4.0%) OF THE VALID CELLS HAVE EXPECTED CELL FREQUENCY LESS THAN 5.0.
MINIMUM EXPECTED CELL FREQUENCY =   4.397
CHI SQUARE =   181.04729 WITH 16 DEGREES OF FREEDOM   SIGNIFICANCE =   0.0
PEARSON'S R =-0.11525 SIGNIFICANCE =   0.0000

NUMBER OF MISSING OBSERVATIONS =   1400

```
               LIBTYPE
       COUNT  I
       ROW PCT IA.R.L. L OTHER AC COMMUNIT PUBLIC   STATE AN   ROW
       COL PCT IIBS      ADEMIC  Y COLLEG          D FEDERA  TOTAL
       TOT PCT I    1. I     2. I     3. I     4. I     5. I
RQ23   --------I--------I--------I--------I--------I--------I
        -2.  I    122 I     21 I      3 I     70 I     25 I    241
STRONGLY DISAGRE I   50.6 I    8.7 I    1.2 I   29.0 I   10.4 I    3.3
             I    2.9 I    3.3 I    2.1 I    3.9 I    5.1 I
             I    1.7 I    0.3 I    0.0 I    1.0 I    0.3 I
        -I--------I--------I--------I--------I--------I
        -1.  I    484 I     95 I     11 I    315 I     84 I    989
DISAGREE     I   48.9 I    9.6 I    1.1 I   31.9 I    8.5 I   13.7
             I   11.7 I   14.9 I    7.7 I   17.4 I   17.3 I
             I    6.7 I    1.3 I    0.2 I    4.4 I    1.2 I
        -I--------I--------I--------I--------I--------I
        0.   I    665 I    122 I     26 I    344 I     85 I   1242
NEITHER A OR D I   53.5 I    9.8 I    2.1 I   27.7 I    6.8 I   17.2
             I   16.1 I   19.2 I   18.3 I   19.0 I   17.5 I
             I    9.2 I    1.7 I    0.4 I    4.8 I    1.2 I
        -I--------I--------I--------I--------I--------I
        1.   I   2196 I    332 I     75 I    867 I    239 I   3709
AGREE        I   59.2 I    9.0 I    2.0 I   23.4 I    6.4 I   51.4
             I   53.1 I   52.2 I   52.8 I   47.8 I   49.2 I
             I   30.4 I    4.6 I    1.0 I   12.0 I    3.3 I
        -I--------I--------I--------I--------I--------I
        2.   I    670 I     66 I     27 I    216 I     53 I   1032
STRONGLY AGREE I   64.9 I    6.4 I    2.6 I   20.9 I    5.1 I   14.3
             I   16.2 I   10.4 I   19.0 I   11.9 I   10.9 I
             I    9.3 I    0.9 I    0.4 I    3.0 I    0.7 I
        -I--------I--------I--------I--------I--------I
       COLUMN   4137     636      142     1812      486     7213
       TOTAL    57.4      8.8      2.0     25.1      6.7    100.0
```

1 OUT OF   25 (4.0%) OF THE VALID CELLS HAVE EXPECTED CELL FREQUENCY LESS THAN 5.0.
MINIMUM EXPECTED CELL FREQUENCY =   4.744
CHI SQUARE =   93.51187 WITH 16 DEGREES OF FREEDOM   SIGNIFICANCE =   0.0000
PEARSON'S R =-0.09597 SIGNIFICANCE =   0.0000

NUMBER OF MISSING OBSERVATIONS =   881

```
                 LIBTYPE
          COUNT  I
          ROW PCT IA.R.L. L OTHER AC COMMUNIT PUBLIC   STATE AN   ROW
          COL PCT IIBS      ADEMIC   Y COLLEG          D FEDERA   TOTAL
          TOT PCT I     1.I      2.I      3.I      4.I      5.I
RQ24      --------I--------I--------I--------I--------I--------I
            -2.   I  1130  I   116  I    40  I   377  I   100  I   1763
STRONGLY DISAGRE  I  64.1  I   6.6  I   2.3  I  21.4  I   5.7  I   25.5
                  I  28.0  I  20.3  I  29.4  I  21.9  I  22.5  I
                  I  16.4  I   1.7  I   0.6  I   5.5  I   1.4  I
                 -I--------I--------I--------I--------I--------I
            -1.   I  1883  I   302  I    69  I   856  I   202  I   3312
DISAGREE          I  56.9  I   9.1  I   2.1  I  25.8  I   6.1  I   48.0
                  I  46.7  I  52.9  I  50.7  I  49.7  I  45.4  I
                  I  27.3  I   4.4  I   1.0  I  12.4  I   2.9  I
                 -I--------I--------I--------I--------I--------I
             0.   I   464  I    77  I    19  I   240  I    75  I    875
NEITHER A OR D    I  53.0  I   8.8  I   2.2  I  27.4  I   8.6  I   12.7
                  I  11.5  I  13.5  I  14.0  I  13.9  I  16.9  I
                  I   6.7  I   1.1  I   0.3  I   3.5  I   1.1  I
                 -I--------I--------I--------I--------I--------I
             1.   I   415  I    61  I     7  I   200  I    53  I    736
AGREE             I  56.4  I   8.3  I   1.0  I  27.2  I   7.2  I   10.7
                  I  10.3  I  10.7  I   5.1  I  11.6  I  11.9  I
                  I   6.0  I   0.9  I   0.1  I   2.9  I   0.8  I
                 -I--------I--------I--------I--------I--------I
             2.   I   137  I    15  I     1  I    51  I    15  I    219
STRONGLY AGREE    I  62.6  I   6.8  I   0.5  I  23.3  I   6.8  I    3.2
                  I   3.4  I   2.6  I   0.7  I   3.0  I   3.4  I
                  I   2.0  I   0.2  I   0.0  I   0.7  I   0.2  I
                 -I--------I--------I--------I--------I--------I
          COLUMN    4029      571      136     1724      445     6905
          TOTAL     58.3      8.3      2.0     25.0      6.4    100.0
```

1 OUT OF   25 (4.0%) OF THE VALID CELLS HAVE EXPECTED CELL FREQUENCY LESS THAN 5.0.
MINIMUM EXPECTED CELL FREQUENCY =   4.313
CHI SQUARE =   57.06093 WITH 16 DEGREES OF FREEDOM   SIGNIFICANCE =   0.0000
PEARSON'S R = 0.04500 SIGNIFICANCE =   0.0001

NUMBER OF MISSING OBSERVATIONS =   1189

```
                 LIBTYPE
          COUNT  I
          ROW PCT IA.R.L. L OTHER AC COMMUNIT PUBLIC   STATE AN   ROW
          COL PCT IIBS      ADEMIC   Y COLLEG          D FEDERA   TOTAL
          TOT PCT I     1.I      2.I      3.I      4.I      5.I
RQ25      --------I--------I--------I--------I--------I--------I
            -2.   I   223  I    18  I     6  I    71  I    15  I    333
STRONGLY DISAGRE  I  67.0  I   5.4  I   1.8  I  21.3  I   4.5  I    6.0
                  I   6.4  I   3.5  I   5.6  I   6.7  I   4.3  I
                  I   4.0  I   0.3  I   0.1  I   1.3  I   0.3  I
                 -I--------I--------I--------I--------I--------I
            -1.   I   742  I   115  I    23  I   254  I    63  I   1197
DISAGREE          I  62.0  I   9.6  I   1.9  I  21.2  I   5.3  I   21.7
                  I  21.3  I  22.3  I  21.3  I  23.9  I  18.1  I
                  I  13.4  I   2.1  I   0.4  I   4.6  I   1.1  I
                 -I--------I--------I--------I--------I--------I
             0.   I  1035  I   152  I    31  I   272  I   112  I   1602
NEITHER A OR D    I  64.6  I   9.5  I   1.9  I  17.0  I   7.0  I   29.0
                  I  29.7  I  29.5  I  28.7  I  25.6  I  32.2  I
                  I  18.7  I   2.8  I   0.6  I   4.9  I   2.0  I
                 -I--------I--------I--------I--------I--------I
             1.   I  1135  I   187  I    35  I   368  I   133  I   1858
AGREE             I  61.1  I  10.1  I   1.9  I  19.8  I   7.2  I   33.7
                  I  32.6  I  36.2  I  32.4  I  34.6  I  38.2  I
                  I  20.6  I   3.4  I   0.6  I   6.7  I   2.4  I
                 -I--------I--------I--------I--------I--------I
             2.   I   350  I    44  I    13  I    99  I    25  I    531
STRONGLY AGREE    I  65.9  I   8.3  I   2.4  I  18.6  I   4.7  I    9.6
                  I  10.0  I   8.5  I  12.0  I   9.3  I   7.2  I
                  I   6.3  I   0.8  I   0.2  I   1.8  I   0.5  I
                 -I--------I--------I--------I--------I--------I
          COLUMN    3485      516      108     1064      348     5521
          TOTAL     63.1      9.3      2.0     19.3      6.3    100.0
```

CHI SQUARE =   28.63750 WITH 16 DEGREES OF FREEDOM   SIGNIFICANCE =   0.0265
PEARSON'S R = 0.00340 SIGNIFICANCE =   0.4004

NUMBER OF MISSING OBSERVATIONS =   2573

```
                    LIBTYPE
            COUNT  I
            ROW PCT IA.R.L. L OTHER AC STATE AN  ROW
            COL PCT IIBS      ADEMIC  D FEDERA  TOTAL
            TOT PCT I     1.I      2.I      5.I
RQ26        --------I--------I--------I--------I
            -2.  I    326 I     36 I     50 I    412
  STRONGLY DISAGRE I   79.1 I    8.7 I   12.1 I   16.5
            I   17.8 I   11.4 I   14.0 I
            I   13.0 I    1.4 I    2.0 I
            -I--------I--------I--------I
            -1.  I    566 I    136 I    143 I    845
  DISAGREE  I   67.0 I   16.1 I   16.9 I   33.8
            I   30.9 I   43.0 I   40.2 I
            I   22.6 I    5.4 I    5.7 I
            -I--------I--------I--------I
             0.  I    535 I     75 I    108 I    718
  NEITHER A OR D  I   74.5 I   10.4 I   15.0 I   28.7
            I   29.3 I   23.7 I   30.3 I
            I   21.4 I    3.0 I    4.3 I
            -I--------I--------I--------I
             1.  I    284 I     64 I     42 I    390
  AGREE     I   72.8 I   16.4 I   10.8 I   15.6
            I   15.5 I   20.3 I   11.8 I
            I   11.4 I    2.6 I    1.7 I
            -I--------I--------I--------I
             2.  I    118 I      5 I     13 I    136
  STRONGLY AGREE  I   86.8 I    3.7 I    9.6 I    5.4
            I    6.5 I    1.6 I    3.7 I
            I    4.7 I    0.2 I    0.5 I
            -I--------I--------I--------I
          COLUMN    1829      316      356     2501
          TOTAL     73.1     12.6     14.2    100.0
```

CHI SQUARE =   50.03474 WITH   8 DEGREES OF FREEDOM   SIGNIFICANCE =   0.0000
PEARSON'S R =-0.03503 SIGNIFICANCE =   0.0399

NUMBER OF MISSING OBSERVATIONS =   5593

```
                    LIBTYPE
            COUNT  I
            ROW PCT IA.R.L. L OTHER AC COMMUNIT PUBLIC   STATE AN  ROW
            COL PCT IIBS      ADEMIC   Y COLLEG           D FEDERA  TOTAL
            TOT PCT I     1.I      2.I      3.I      4.I      5.I
RQ27        --------I--------I--------I--------I--------I--------I
            -2.  I     95 I      4 I      3 I     34 I     15 I    151
  STRONGLY DISAGRE I   62.9 I    2.6 I    2.0 I   22.5 I    9.9 I    2.2
            I    2.4 I    0.6 I    2.1 I    1.9 I    3.1 I
            I    1.4 I    0.1 I    0.0 I    0.5 I    0.2 I
            -I--------I--------I--------I--------I--------I
            -1.  I    643 I    134 I     15 I    276 I    114 I   1182
  DISAGREE  I   54.4 I   11.3 I    1.3 I   23.4 I    9.6 I   17.1
            I   16.4 I   21.6 I   10.4 I   15.7 I   23.8 I
            I    9.3 I    1.9 I    0.2 I    4.0 I    1.6 I
            -I--------I--------I--------I--------I--------I
             0.  I    815 I    141 I     29 I    327 I     91 I   1403
  NEITHER A OR D  I   58.1 I   10.0 I    2.1 I   23.3 I    6.5 I   20.3
            I   20.7 I   22.8 I   20.1 I   18.6 I   19.0 I
            I   11.8 I    2.0 I    0.4 I    4.7 I    1.3 I
            -I--------I--------I--------I--------I--------I
             1.  I   1903 I    304 I     81 I    896 I    219 I   3403
  AGREE     I   55.9 I    8.9 I    2.4 I   26.3 I    6.4 I   49.1
            I   48.4 I   49.1 I   56.3 I   51.1 I   45.7 I
            I   27.5 I    4.4 I    1.2 I   12.9 I    3.2 I
            -I--------I--------I--------I--------I--------I
             2.  I    473 I     36 I     16 I    221 I     40 I    786
  STRONGLY AGREE  I   60.2 I    4.6 I    2.0 I   28.1 I    5.1 I   11.4
            I   12.0 I    5.8 I   11.1 I   12.6 I    8.4 I
            I    6.8 I    0.5 I    0.2 I    3.2 I    0.6 I
            -I--------I--------I--------I--------I--------I
          COLUMN    3929      619      144     1754      479     6925
          TOTAL     56.7      8.9      2.1     25.3      6.9    100.0
```

    1 OUT OF   25 (4.0%) OF THE VALID CELLS HAVE EXPECTED CELL FREQUENCY LESS THAN 5.0.
MINIMUM EXPECTED CELL FREQUENCY =   3.140
CHI SQUARE =   71.13995 WITH 16 DEGREES OF FREEDOM   SIGNIFICANCE =   0.0000
PEARSON'S R =-0.00558 SIGNIFICANCE =   0.3213

NUMBER OF MISSING OBSERVATIONS =   1169

```
                    LIBTYPE
          COUNT   I
          ROW PCT IA.R.L. L OTHER AC COMMUNIT PUBLIC    STATE AN   ROW
          COL PCT IIBS      ADEMIC   Y COLLEG           D FEDERA   TOTAL
          TOT PCT I     1.I      2.I      3.I      4.I      5.I
RQ28      --------I--------I--------I--------I--------I--------I
               -2. I   528   I    58   I    34   I   310   I    50   I    980
STRONGLY DISAGRE I  53.9   I   5.9   I   3.5   I  31.6   I   5.1   I   22.1
                 I  32.8   I  13.5   I  23.9   I  17.3   I  10.6   I
                 I  11.9   I   1.3   I   0.8   I   7.0   I   1.1   I
                 -I--------I--------I--------I--------I--------I
               -1. I   737   I   277   I    78   I   923   I   236   I   2251
DISAGREE         I  32.7   I  12.3   I   3.5   I  41.0   I  10.5   I   50.7
                 I  45.8   I  64.4   I  54.9   I  51.6   I  50.2   I
                 I  16.6   I   6.2   I   1.8   I  20.8   I   5.3   I
                 -I--------I--------I--------I--------I--------I
                0. I   166   I    44   I    15   I   223   I    84   I    532
NEITHER A OR D   I  31.2   I   8.3   I   2.8   I  41.9   I  15.8   I   12.0
                 I  10.3   I  10.2   I  10.6   I  12.5   I  17.9   I
                 I   3.7   I   1.0   I   0.3   I   5.0   I   1.9   I
                 -I--------I--------I--------I--------I--------I
                1. I   127   I    49   I    12   I   255   I    79   I    522
AGREE            I  24.3   I   9.4   I   2.3   I  48.9   I  15.1   I   11.8
                 I   7.9   I  11.4   I   8.5   I  14.2   I  16.8   I
                 I   2.9   I   1.1   I   0.3   I   5.7   I   1.8   I
                 -I--------I--------I--------I--------I--------I
                2. I    50   I     2   I     3   I    79   I    21   I    155
STRONGLY AGREE   I  32.3   I   1.3   I   1.9   I  51.0   I  13.5   I    3.5
                 I   3.1   I   0.5   I   2.1   I   4.4   I   4.5   I
                 I   1.1   I   0.0   I   0.1   I   1.8   I   0.5   I
                 -I--------I--------I--------I--------I--------I
          COLUMN    1608      430       142      1790       470      4440
          TOTAL     36.2      9.7       3.2      40.3      10.6     100.0
```

1 OUT OF   25 (4.0%) OF THE VALID CELLS HAVE EXPECTED CELL FREQUENCY LESS THAN 5.0.
MINIMUM EXPECTED CELL FREQUENCY = 4.957
CHI SQUARE =   248.12369 WITH 16 DEGREES OF FREEDOM   SIGNIFICANCE = 0.0
PEARSON'S R = 0.17348 SIGNIFICANCE = 0.0000

NUMBER OF MISSING OBSERVATIONS =   3654

```
                    LIBTYPE
          COUNT   I
          ROW PCT IA.R.L. L OTHER AC COMMUNIT PUBLIC    STATE AN   ROW
          COL PCT IIBS      ADEMIC   Y COLLEG           D FEDERA   TOTAL
          TOT PCT I     1.I      2.I      3.I      4.I      5.I
RQ29      --------I--------I--------I--------I--------I--------I
               -2. I    65   I     6   I     1   I    36   I     7   I    115
STRONGLY DISAGRE I  56.5   I   5.2   I   0.9   I  31.3   I   6.1   I    1.6
                 I   1.6   I   1.0   I   0.7   I   2.1   I   1.5   I
                 I   0.9   I   0.1   I   0.0   I   0.5   I   0.1   I
                 -I--------I--------I--------I--------I--------I
               -1. I   296   I    56   I     4   I   148   I    31   I    535
DISAGREE         I  55.3   I  10.5   I   0.7   I  27.7   I   5.8   I    7.7
                 I   7.4   I   9.2   I   3.0   I   8.4   I   6.7   I
                 I   4.2   I   0.8   I   0.1   I   2.1   I   0.4   I
                 -I--------I--------I--------I--------I--------I
                0. I   437   I    66   I    20   I   219   I    41   I    783
NEITHER A OR D   I  55.8   I   8.4   I   2.6   I  28.0   I   5.2   I   11.2
                 I  10.9   I  10.9   I  14.9   I  12.5   I   8.8   I
                 I   6.3   I   0.9   I   0.3   I   3.1   I   0.6   I
                 -I--------I--------I--------I--------I--------I
                1. I  2340   I   384   I    84   I  1055   I   276   I   4139
AGREE            I  56.5   I   9.3   I   2.0   I  25.5   I   6.7   I   59.2
                 I  58.2   I  63.2   I  62.7   I  60.1   I  59.2   I
                 I  33.5   I   5.5   I   1.2   I  15.1   I   4.0   I
                 -I--------I--------I--------I--------I--------I
                2. I   884   I    96   I    25   I   298   I   111   I   1414
STRONGLY AGREE   I  62.5   I   6.8   I   1.8   I  21.1   I   7.9   I   20.2
                 I  22.0   I  15.8   I  18.7   I  17.0   I  23.8   I
                 I  12.7   I   1.4   I   0.4   I   4.3   I   1.6   I
                 -I--------I--------I--------I--------I--------I
          COLUMN    4022      608       134      1756       466      6986
          TOTAL     57.6      8.7       1.9      25.1       6.7     100.0
```

1 OUT OF   25 (4.0%) OF THE VALID CELLS HAVE EXPECTED CELL FREQUENCY LESS THAN 5.0.
MINIMUM EXPECTED CELL FREQUENCY = 2.206
CHI SQUARE =   46.48723 WITH 16 DEGREES OF FREEDOM   SIGNIFICANCE = 0.0001
PEARSON'S R =-0.02679 SIGNIFICANCE = 0.0126

NUMBER OF MISSING OBSERVATIONS =   1108

```
                   LIBTYPE
          COUNT  I
          ROW PCT IA.R.L. L OTHER AC COMMUNIT PUBLIC   STATE AN   ROW
          COL PCT IIBS      ADEMIC   Y COLLEG          D FEDERA  TOTAL
          TOT PCT I    1.I      2.I      3.I      4.I      5.I
RQ30      --------I--------I--------I--------I--------I--------I
             -2. I    791 I     89 I     34 I    302 I    108 I   1324
STRONGLY DISAGRE I   59.7 I    6.7 I    2.6 I   22.8 I    8.2 I   19.2
                 I   19.8 I   14.9 I   23.9 I   17.7 I   22.8 I
                 I   11.4 I    1.3 I    0.5 I    4.4 I    1.6 I
          -------I--------I--------I--------I--------I--------I
             -1. I   2166 I    319 I     81 I    913 I    267 I   3746
DISAGREE         I   57.8 I    8.5 I    2.2 I   24.4 I    7.1 I   54.2
                 I   54.3 I   53.4 I   57.0 I   53.4 I   56.3 I
                 I   31.3 I    4.6 I    1.2 I   13.2 I    3.9 I
          -------I--------I--------I--------I--------I--------I
              0. I    604 I    112 I     19 I    265 I     55 I   1055
NEITHER A OR D   I   57.3 I   10.6 I    1.8 I   25.1 I    5.2 I   15.3
                 I   15.1 I   18.8 I   13.4 I   15.5 I   11.6 I
                 I    8.7 I    1.6 I    0.3 I    3.8 I    0.8 I
          -------I--------I--------I--------I--------I--------I
              1. I    345 I     74 I      6 I    186 I     37 I    648
AGREE            I   53.2 I   11.4 I    0.9 I   28.7 I    5.7 I    9.4
                 I    8.7 I   12.4 I    4.2 I   10.9 I    7.8 I
                 I    5.0 I    1.1 I    0.1 I    2.7 I    0.5 I
          -------I--------I--------I--------I--------I--------I
              2. I     81 I      3 I      2 I     45 I      7 I    138
STRONGLY AGREE   I   58.7 I    2.2 I    1.4 I   32.6 I    5.1 I    2.0
                 I    2.0 I    0.5 I    1.4 I    2.6 I    1.5 I
                 I    1.2 I    0.0 I    0.0 I    0.7 I    0.1 I
          -------I--------I--------I--------I--------I--------I
          COLUMN    3987      597      142     1711      474      6911
          TOTAL     57.7      8.6      2.1     24.8      6.9     100.0
```

```
    1 OUT OF    25 (  4.0%) OF THE VALID CELLS HAVE EXPECTED CELL FREQUENCY LESS THAN 5.0.
MINIMUM EXPECTED CELL FREQUENCY =  2.835
CHI SQUARE =   52.23840 WITH 16 DEGREES OF FREEDOM   SIGNIFICANCE =  0.0000
PEARSON'S R = 0.01214  SIGNIFICANCE =  0.1564

NUMBER OF MISSING OBSERVATIONS =    1183
```

```
                   LIBTYPE
          COUNT  I
          ROW PCT IA.R.L. L OTHER AC COMMUNIT PUBLIC   STATE AN   ROW
          COL PCT IIBS      ADEMIC   Y COLLEG          D FEDERA  TOTAL
          TOT PCT I    1.I      2.I      3.I      4.I      5.I
RQ31      --------I--------I--------I--------I--------I--------I
             -2. I    232 I     19 I     14 I     24 I     18 I    307
STRONGLY DISAGRE I   75.6 I    6.2 I    4.6 I    7.8 I    5.9 I    6.0
                 I    6.4 I    3.6 I   12.5 I    5.2 I    4.2 I
                 I    4.5 I    0.4 I    0.3 I    0.5 I    0.3 I
          -------I--------I--------I--------I--------I--------I
             -1. I    680 I    123 I     18 I     81 I     87 I    989
DISAGREE         I   68.8 I   12.4 I    1.8 I    8.2 I    8.8 I   19.2
                 I   18.8 I   23.3 I   16.1 I   17.5 I   20.3 I
                 I   13.2 I    2.4 I    0.3 I    1.6 I    1.7 I
          -------I--------I--------I--------I--------I--------I
              0. I    697 I    106 I     23 I     69 I     78 I    973
NEITHER A OR D   I   71.6 I   10.9 I    2.4 I    7.1 I    8.0 I   18.9
                 I   19.3 I   20.1 I   20.5 I   14.9 I   18.2 I
                 I   13.5 I    2.1 I    0.4 I    1.3 I    1.5 I
          -------I--------I--------I--------I--------I--------I
              1. I   1502 I    237 I     44 I    218 I    206 I   2207
AGREE            I   68.1 I   10.7 I    2.0 I    9.9 I    9.3 I   42.9
                 I   41.5 I   44.9 I   39.3 I   47.1 I   48.0 I
                 I   29.2 I    4.6 I    0.9 I    4.2 I    4.0 I
          -------I--------I--------I--------I--------I--------I
              2. I    507 I     43 I     13 I     71 I     40 I    674
STRONGLY AGREE   I   75.2 I    6.4 I    1.9 I   10.5 I    5.9 I   13.1
                 I   14.0 I    8.1 I   11.6 I   15.3 I    9.3 I
                 I    9.8 I    0.8 I    0.3 I    1.4 I    0.8 I
          -------I--------I--------I--------I--------I--------I
          COLUMN    3618      528      112      463      429      5150
          TOTAL     70.3     10.3      2.2      9.0      8.3     100.0
```

```
CHI SQUARE =   54.01665 WITH 16 DEGREES OF FREEDOM   SIGNIFICANCE =  0.0000
PEARSON'S R = 0.01220  SIGNIFICANCE =  0.1906

NUMBER OF MISSING OBSERVATIONS =    2944
```

```
                    LIBTYPE
           COUNT  I
           ROW PCT IA.R.L. L OTHER AC COMMUNIT PUBLIC    STATE AN    ROW
           COL PCT IIBS      ADEMIC   Y COLLEG          D FEDERA   TOTAL
           TOT PCT I    1. I     2. I     3. I     4. I     5. I
RQ32       --------I--------I--------I--------I--------I--------I
             -2. I    792 I     87 I     34 I    188 I     81 I    1182
STRONGLY DISAGRE I   67.0 I    7.4 I    2.9 I   15.9 I    6.9 I    18.0
                 I   19.3 I   14.0 I   24.1 I   15.4 I   16.5 I
                 I   12.1 I    1.3 I    0.5 I    2.9 I    1.2 I
           - I--------I--------I--------I--------I--------I
             -1. I   1796 I    318 I     55 I    513 I    272 I    2954
DISAGREE         I   60.8 I   10.8 I    1.9 I   17.4 I    9.2 I    45.0
                 I   43.8 I   51.2 I   39.0 I   41.9 I   55.5 I
                 I   27.3 I    4.8 I    0.8 I    7.8 I    4.1 I
           - I--------I--------I--------I--------I--------I
              0. I    636 I     90 I     22 I    165 I     67 I     980
NEITHER A OR D   I   64.9 I    9.2 I    2.2 I   16.8 I    6.8 I    14.9
                 I   15.5 I   14.5 I   15.6 I   13.5 I   13.7 I
                 I    9.7 I    1.4 I    0.3 I    2.5 I    1.0 I
           - I--------I--------I--------I--------I--------I
              1. I    708 I    107 I     23 I    296 I     57 I    1191
AGREE            I   59.4 I    9.0 I    1.9 I   24.9 I    4.8 I    18.1
                 I   17.3 I   17.2 I   16.3 I   24.2 I   11.6 I
                 I   10.8 I    1.6 I    0.4 I    4.5 I    0.9 I
           - I--------I--------I--------I--------I--------I
              2. I    164 I     19 I      7 I     61 I     13 I     264
STRONGLY AGREE   I   62.1 I    7.2 I    2.7 I   23.1 I    4.9 I     4.0
                 I    4.0 I    3.1 I    5.0 I    5.0 I    2.7 I
                 I    2.5 I    0.3 I    0.1 I    0.9 I    0.2 I
           - I--------I--------I--------I--------I--------I
           COLUMN   4096      621      141     1223      490      6571
           TOTAL    62.3      9.5      2.1     18.6      7.5     100.0
CHI SQUARE =     88.64006 WITH 16 DEGREES OF FREEDOM   SIGNIFICANCE =  0.0000
PEARSON'S R = 0.02328  SIGNIFICANCE =   0.0296

NUMBER OF MISSING OBSERVATIONS =     1523
```

```
                    LIBTYPE
           COUNT  I
           ROW PCT IA.R.L. L OTHER AC COMMUNIT PUBLIC    STATE AN    ROW
           COL PCT IIBS      ADEMIC   Y COLLEG          D FEDERA   TOTAL
           TOT PCT I    1. I     2. I     3. I     4. I     5. I
RQ33       --------I--------I--------I--------I--------I--------I
             -2. I    284 I     30 I     10 I    108 I     32 I     464
STRONGLY DISAGRE I   61.2 I    6.5 I    2.2 I   23.3 I    6.9 I     6.9
                 I    7.3 I    5.1 I    7.5 I    6.4 I    6.9 I
                 I    4.2 I    0.4 I    0.1 I    1.6 I    0.5 I
           - I--------I--------I--------I--------I--------I
             -1. I   1144 I    208 I     38 I    446 I    168 I    2004
DISAGREE         I   57.1 I   10.4 I    1.9 I   22.3 I    8.4 I    29.8
                 I   29.5 I   35.5 I   28.4 I   26.6 I   36.4 I
                 I   17.0 I    3.1 I    0.6 I    6.6 I    2.5 I
           - I--------I--------I--------I--------I--------I
              0. I   1087 I    182 I     37 I    462 I    108 I    1876
NEITHER A OR D   I   57.9 I    9.7 I    2.0 I   24.6 I    5.8 I    27.9
                 I   28.0 I   31.1 I   27.6 I   27.6 I   23.4 I
                 I   16.1 I    2.7 I    0.5 I    6.9 I    1.6 I
           - I--------I--------I--------I--------I--------I
              1. I   1096 I    149 I     42 I    540 I    129 I    1956
AGREE            I   56.0 I    7.6 I    2.1 I   27.6 I    6.6 I    29.0
                 I   28.3 I   25.4 I   31.3 I   32.2 I   27.9 I
                 I   16.3 I    2.2 I    0.6 I    8.0 I    1.9 I
           - I--------I--------I--------I--------I--------I
              2. I    265 I     17 I      7 I    120 I     25 I     434
STRONGLY AGREE   I   61.1 I    3.9 I    1.6 I   27.6 I    5.8 I     6.4
                 I    6.8 I    2.9 I    5.2 I    7.2 I    5.4 I
                 I    3.9 I    0.3 I    0.1 I    1.8 I    0.4 I
           - I--------I--------I--------I--------I--------I
           COLUMN   3876      586      134     1676      462      6734
           TOTAL    57.6      8.7      2.0     24.9      6.9     100.0
CHI SQUARE =     53.31171 WITH 16 DEGREES OF FREEDOM   SIGNIFICANCE =  0.0000
PEARSON'S R = 0.01678  SIGNIFICANCE =   0.0842

NUMBER OF MISSING OBSERVATIONS =     1360
```

```
                  LIBTYPE
         COUNT  I
         ROW PCT IA.R.L. L OTHER AC COMMUNIT PUBLIC   STATE AN   ROW
         COL PCT IIBS      ADEMIC   Y COLLEG          D FEDERA   TOTAL
         TOT PCT I    1.I      2.I      3.I      4.I      5.I
RQ34            --------I--------I--------I--------I--------I--------I
           -2.  I   108  I    11  I     3  I    49  I    17  I    188
STRONGLY DISAGRE I  57.4  I   5.9  I   1.6  I  26.1  I   9.0  I    2.6
                 I   2.6  I   1.8  I   2.1  I   2.7  I   3.5  I
                 I   1.5  I   0.2  I   0.0  I   0.7  I   0.2  I
                -I--------I--------I--------I--------I--------I
           -1.  I   401  I    57  I     8  I   186  I    50  I    702
DISAGREE         I  57.1  I   8.1  I   1.1  I  26.5  I   7.1  I    9.8
                 I   9.8  I   9.1  I   5.6  I  10.2  I  10.3  I
                 I   5.6  I   0.8  I   0.1  I   2.6  I   0.7  I
                -I--------I--------I--------I--------I--------I
            0.  I   723  I   133  I    31  I   262  I    83  I   1232
NEITHER A OR D   I  58.7  I  10.8  I   2.5  I  21.3  I   6.7  I   17.2
                 I  17.7  I  21.3  I  21.7  I  14.3  I  17.1  I
                 I  10.1  I   1.9  I   0.4  I   3.7  I   1.2  I
                -I--------I--------I--------I--------I--------I
            1.  I  2308  I   382  I    86  I  1071  I   284  I   4131
AGREE            I  55.9  I   9.2  I   2.1  I  25.9  I   6.9  I   57.6
                 I  56.4  I  61.1  I  60.1  I  58.5  I  58.4  I
                 I  32.2  I   5.3  I   1.2  I  14.9  I   4.0  I
                -I--------I--------I--------I--------I--------I
            2.  I   550  I    42  I    15  I   264  I    52  I    923
STRONGLY AGREE   I  59.6  I   4.6  I   1.6  I  28.6  I   5.6  I   12.9
                 I  13.4  I   6.7  I  10.5  I  14.4  I  10.7  I
                 I   7.7  I   0.6  I   0.2  I   3.7  I   0.7  I
                -I--------I--------I--------I--------I--------I
         COLUMN     4090      625      143     1832      486     7176
         TOTAL      57.0      8.7      2.0     25.5      6.8    100.0
```

1 OUT OF   25 (4.0%) OF THE VALID CELLS HAVE EXPECTED CELL FREQUENCY LESS THAN 5.0.
MINIMUM EXPECTED CELL FREQUENCY =   3.746
CHI SQUARE =   51.83913 WITH 16 DEGREES OF FREEDOM   SIGNIFICANCE =   0.0000
PEARSON'S R = 0.00526 SIGNIFICANCE =   0.3280

NUMBER OF MISSING OBSERVATIONS =   918

```
                  LIBTYPE
         COUNT  I
         ROW PCT IA.R.L. L OTHER AC COMMUNIT PUBLIC   STATE AN   ROW
         COL PCT IIBS      ADEMIC   Y COLLEG          D FEDERA   TOTAL
         TOT PCT I    1.I      2.I      3.I      4.I      5.I
RQ35            --------I--------I--------I--------I--------I--------I
           -2.  I   599  I    75  I    25  I   271  I    70  I   1040
STRONGLY DISAGRE I  57.6  I   7.2  I   2.4  I  26.1  I   6.7  I   14.8
                 I  14.9  I  12.0  I  17.6  I  15.4  I  14.5  I
                 I   8.5  I   1.1  I   0.4  I   3.9  I   1.0  I
                -I--------I--------I--------I--------I--------I
           -1.  I  2075  I   321  I    84  I   924  I   282  I   3686
DISAGREE         I  56.3  I   8.7  I   2.3  I  25.1  I   7.7  I   52.5
                 I  51.8  I  51.4  I  59.2  I  52.5  I  58.4  I
                 I  29.6  I   4.6  I   1.2  I  13.2  I   4.0  I
                -I--------I--------I--------I--------I--------I
            0.  I   927  I   143  I    26  I   390  I   104  I   1590
NEITHER A OR D   I  58.3  I   9.0  I   1.6  I  24.5  I   6.5  I   22.7
                 I  23.1  I  22.9  I  18.3  I  22.2  I  21.5  I
                 I  13.2  I   2.0  I   0.4  I   5.6  I   1.5  I
                -I--------I--------I--------I--------I--------I
            1.  I   314  I    65  I     5  I   130  I    20  I    534
AGREE            I  58.8  I  12.2  I   0.9  I  24.3  I   3.7  I    7.6
                 I   7.8  I  10.4  I   3.5  I   7.4  I   4.1  I
                 I   4.5  I   0.9  I   0.1  I   1.9  I   0.3  I
                -I--------I--------I--------I--------I--------I
            2.  I    93  I    20  I     2  I    45  I     7  I    167
STRONGLY AGREE   I  55.7  I  12.0  I   1.2  I  26.9  I   4.2  I    2.4
                 I   2.3  I   3.2  I   1.4  I   2.6  I   1.4  I
                 I   1.3  I   0.3  I   0.0  I   0.6  I   0.1  I
                -I--------I--------I--------I--------I--------I
         COLUMN     4008      624      142     1760      483     7017
         TOTAL      57.1      8.9      2.0     25.1      6.9    100.0
```

1 OUT OF   25 (4.0%) OF THE VALID CELLS HAVE EXPECTED CELL FREQUENCY LESS THAN 5.0.
MINIMUM EXPECTED CELL FREQUENCY =   3.380
CHI SQUARE =   33.49246 WITH 16 DEGREES OF FREEDOM   SIGNIFICANCE =   0.0064
PEARSON'S R =-0.02560 SIGNIFICANCE =   0.0160

NUMBER OF MISSING OBSERVATIONS =   1077

```
                   LIBTYPE
            COUNT  I
            ROW PCT IA.R.L. L OTHER AC COMMUNIT PUBLIC    STATE AN   ROW
            COL PCT I IBS     ADEMIC   Y COLLEG           D FEDERA   TOTAL
            TOT PCT I     1.I      2.I      3.I      4.I      5.I
RQ36        --------I--------I--------I--------I--------I--------I
               -2.  I    414 I     38 I     25 I    192 I     45 I    714
STRONGLY DISAGRE I  58.0 I    5.3 I    3.5 I   26.9 I    6.3 I   10.3
                 I  10.6 I    6.3 I   17.4 I   10.7 I    9.6 I
                 I   6.0 I    0.5 I    0.4 I    2.8 I    0.6 I
            -I--------I--------I--------I--------I--------I
               -1.  I   1860 I    309 I     72 I    888 I    241 I   3370
DISAGREE         I  55.2 I    9.2 I    2.1 I   26.4 I    7.2 I   48.6
                 I  47.5 I   50.8 I   50.0 I   49.5 I   51.2 I
                 I  26.8 I    4.5 I    1.0 I   12.8 I    3.5 I
            -I--------I--------I--------I--------I--------I
                0.  I    912 I    120 I     30 I    323 I    104 I   1489
NEITHER A OR D   I  61.2 I    8.1 I    2.0 I   21.7 I    7.0 I   21.5
                 I  23.3 I   19.7 I   20.8 I   18.0 I   22.1 I
                 I  13.2 I    1.7 I    0.4 I    4.7 I    1.5 I
            -I--------I--------I--------I--------I--------I
                1.  I    603 I    107 I     15 I    290 I     65 I   1080
AGREE            I  55.8 I    9.9 I    1.4 I   26.9 I    6.0 I   15.6
                 I  15.4 I   17.6 I   10.4 I   16.2 I   13.8 I
                 I   8.7 I    1.5 I    0.2 I    4.2 I    0.9 I
            -I--------I--------I--------I--------I--------I
                2.  I    129 I     34 I      2 I    101 I     16 I    282
STRONGLY AGREE   I  45.7 I   12.1 I    0.7 I   35.8 I    5.7 I    4.1
                 I   3.3 I    5.6 I    1.4 I    5.6 I    3.4 I
                 I   1.9 I    0.5 I    0.0 I    1.5 I    0.2 I
            -I--------I--------I--------I--------I--------I
            COLUMN    3918     608     144    1794     471    6935
            TOTAL     56.5     8.8     2.1    25.9     6.8   100.0

CHI SQUARE =    65.64958 WITH  16 DEGREES OF FREEDOM   SIGNIFICANCE =   0.0000
PEARSON'S R = 0.00194  SIGNIFICANCE =  0.4359

NUMBER OF MISSING OBSERVATIONS =     1159
```

```
                   LIBTYPE
            COUNT  I
            ROW PCT IA.R.L. L OTHER AC COMMUNIT PUBLIC    STATE AN   ROW
            COL PCT I IBS     ADEMIC   Y COLLEG           D FEDERA   TOTAL
            TOT PCT I     1.I      2.I      3.I      4.I      5.I
RQ37        --------I--------I--------I--------I--------I--------I
               -2.  I    397 I     30 I     15 I    144 I     40 I    626
STRONGLY DISAGRE I  63.4 I    4.8 I    2.4 I   23.0 I    6.4 I    9.6
                 I  10.6 I    5.3 I   12.0 I    9.1 I    8.6 I
                 I   6.1 I    0.5 I    0.2 I    2.2 I    0.6 I
            -I--------I--------I--------I--------I--------I
               -1.  I   1554 I    252 I     59 I    597 I    233 I   2695
DISAGREE         I  57.7 I    9.4 I    2.2 I   22.2 I    8.6 I   41.5
                 I  41.3 I   44.5 I   47.2 I   37.7 I   50.0 I
                 I  23.9 I    3.9 I    0.9 I    9.2 I    3.6 I
            -I--------I--------I--------I--------I--------I
                0.  I    788 I    114 I     31 I    326 I     85 I   1344
NEITHER A OR D   I  58.6 I    8.5 I    2.3 I   24.3 I    6.3 I   20.7
                 I  21.0 I   20.1 I   24.8 I   20.6 I   18.2 I
                 I  12.1 I    1.8 I    0.5 I    5.0 I    1.3 I
            -I--------I--------I--------I--------I--------I
                1.  I    826 I    144 I     17 I    412 I     91 I   1490
AGREE            I  55.4 I    9.7 I    1.1 I   27.7 I    6.1 I   22.9
                 I  22.0 I   25.4 I   13.6 I   26.0 I   19.5 I
                 I  12.7 I    2.2 I    0.3 I    6.3 I    1.4 I
            -I--------I--------I--------I--------I--------I
                2.  I    196 I     26 I      3 I    103 I     17 I    345
STRONGLY AGREE   I  56.8 I    7.5 I    0.9 I   29.9 I    4.9 I    5.3
                 I   5.2 I    4.6 I    2.4 I    6.5 I    3.6 I
                 I   3.0 I    0.4 I    0.0 I    1.6 I    0.3 I
            -I--------I--------I--------I--------I--------I
            COLUMN    3761     566     125    1582     466    6500
            TOTAL     57.9     8.7     1.9    24.3     7.2   100.0

CHI SQUARE =    60.65688 WITH  16 DEGREES OF FREEDOM   SIGNIFICANCE =   0.0000
PEARSON'S R = 0.02092  SIGNIFICANCE =  0.0459

NUMBER OF MISSING OBSERVATIONS =     1594
```

```
                    LIBTYPE
            COUNT   I
            ROW PCT IA.R.L.  L OTHER AC COMMUNIT PUBLIC     STATE AN    ROW
            COL PCT IIBS       ADEMIC   Y COLLEG             D FEDERA   TOTAL
            TOT PCT I    1. I     2. I      3. I      4. I      5. I
RQ38        --------I--------I--------I--------I--------I--------I
            -2.   I    606  I     88  I     18  I    152  I     38  I    902
STRONGLY DISAGRE  I   67.2  I    9.8  I    2.0  I   16.9  I    4.2  I   12.6
                  I   14.7  I   14.1  I   12.7  I    8.4  I    7.8  I
                  I    8.4  I    1.2  I    0.3  I    2.1  I    0.5  I
            -I--------I--------I--------I--------I--------I
            -1.   I   1840  I    291  I     63  I    597  I    161  I   2952
DISAGREE          I   62.3  I    9.9  I    2.1  I   20.2  I    5.5  I   41.1
                  I   44.7  I   46.8  I   44.4  I   32.8  I   33.1  I
                  I   25.6  I    4.1  I    0.9  I    8.3  I    2.2  I
            -I--------I--------I--------I--------I--------I
            0.    I    686  I     88  I     33  I    294  I     91  I   1192
NEITHER A OR D    I   57.6  I    7.4  I    2.8  I   24.7  I    7.6  I   16.6
                  I   16.7  I   14.1  I   23.2  I   16.2  I   18.7  I
                  I    9.6  I    1.2  I    0.5  I    4.1  I    1.3  I
            -I--------I--------I--------I--------I--------I
            1.    I    689  I    113  I     24  I    481  I    135  I   1442
AGREE             I   47 8  I    7.8  I    1.7  I   33.4  I    9.4  I   20.1
                  I   16.7  I   18.2  I   16.9  I   26.5  I   27.8  I
                  I    9.6  I    1.6  I    0.3  I    6.7  I    1.9  I
            -I--------I--------I--------I--------I--------I
            2.    I    293  I     42  I      4  I    294  I     61  I    694
STRONGLY AGREE    I   42.2  I    6.1  I    0.6  I   42.4  I    8.8  I    9.7
                  I    7.1  I    6.8  I    2.8  I   16.2  I   12.6  I
                  I    4.1  I    0.6  I    0.1  I    4.1  I    0.8  I
            -I--------I--------I--------I--------I--------I
            COLUMN     4114      622      142     1818      486     7182
            TOTAL      57.3      8.7      2.0     25.3      6.8    100.0
```

CHI SQUARE =   314.07861 WITH 16 DEGREES OF FREEDOM   SIGNIFICANCE =   0.0
PEARSON'S R = 0.18947 SIGNIFICANCE = 0.0000

NUMBER OF MISSING OBSERVATIONS =   912

```
                    LIBTYPE
            COUNT   I
            ROW PCT IA.R.L.  L OTHER AC COMMUNIT PUBLIC     STATE AN    ROW
            COL PCT IIBS       ADEMIC   Y COLLEG             D FEDERA   TOTAL
            TOT PCT I    1. I     2. I      3. I      4. I      5. I
RQ39        --------I--------I--------I--------I--------I--------I
            -2.   I    219  I     22  I      3  I    132  I     17  I    393
STRONGLY DISAGRE  I   55.7  I    5.6  I    0.8  I   33.6  I    4.3  I    5.7
                  I    5.5  I    3.7  I    2.2  I    7.8  I    3.6  I
                  I    3.2  I    0.3  I    0.0  I    1.9  I    0.2  I
            -I--------I--------I--------I--------I--------I
            -1.   I    606  I     88  I     17  I    293  I     73  I   1077
DISAGREE          I   56.3  I    8.2  I    1.6  I   27.2  I    6.8  I   15.7
                  I   15.3  I   14.8  I   12.6  I   17.3  I   15.4  I
                  I    8.8  I    1.3  I    0.2  I    4.3  I    1.1  I
            -I--------I--------I--------I--------I--------I
            0.    I    593  I     84  I     32  I    331  I     58  I   1098
NEITHER A OR D    I   54.0  I    7.7  I    2.9  I   30.1  I    5.3  I   16.0
                  I   15.0  I   14.1  I   23.7  I   19.5  I   12.3  I
                  I    8.7  I    1.2  I    0.5  I    4.8  I    0.8  I
            -I--------I--------I--------I--------I--------I
            1.    I   2082  I    338  I     65  I    802  I    281  I   3568
AGREE             I   58.4  I    9.5  I    1.8  I   22.5  I    7.9  I   52.1
                  I   52.7  I   56.8  I   48.1  I   47.3  I   59.4  I
                  I   30.4  I    4.9  I    0.9  I   11.7  I    4.1  I
            -I--------I--------I--------I--------I--------I
            2.    I    453  I     63  I     18  I    136  I     44  I    714
STRONGLY AGREE    I   63.4  I    8.8  I    2.5  I   19.0  I    6.2  I   10.4
                  I   11.5  I   10.6  I   13.3  I    8.0  I    9.3  I
                  I    6.6  I    0.9  I    0.3  I    2.0  I    0.6  I
            -I--------I--------I--------I--------I--------I
            COLUMN     3953      595      135     1694      473     6850
            TOTAL      57.7      8.7      2.0     24.7      6.9    100.0
```

CHI SQUARE =   84.59540 WITH 16 DEGREES OF FREEDOM   SIGNIFICANCE =   0.0000
PEARSON'S R =-0.04658 SIGNIFICANCE = 0.0001

NUMBER OF MISSING OBSERVATIONS =   1244

```
                   LIBTYPE
           COUNT   I
           ROW PCT IA.R.L. L OTHER AC COMMUNIT PUBLIC   STATE AN   ROW
           COL PCT IIBS      ADEMIC   Y COLLEG          D FEDERA   TOTAL
           TOT PCT I    1.I     2.I      3.I     4.I      5.I
RQ40       --------I--------I--------I--------I--------I--------I
              -2.  I   791  I    95  I    24  I   248  I    86  I   1244
STRONGLY DISAGRE I  63.6  I   7.6  I   1.9  I  19.9  I   6.9  I   18.6
                 I  20.4  I  16.4  I  17.6  I  15.2  I  18.7  I
                 I  11.8  I   1.4  I   0.4  I   3.7  I   1.3  I
           -I--------I--------I--------I--------I--------I
              -1.  I  1892  I   319  I    62  I   732  I   235  I   3240
DISAGREE         I  58.4  I   9.8  I   1.9  I  22.6  I   7.3  I   48.5
                 I  48.8  I  55.2  I  45.6  I  44.7  I  51.0  I
                 I  28.3  I   4.8  I   0.9  I  10.9  I   3.5  I
           -I--------I--------I--------I--------I--------I
               0.  I   710  I    92  I    32  I   367  I    72  I   1273
NEITHER A OR D   I  55.8  I   7.2  I   2.5  I  28.8  I   5.7  I   19.0
                 I  18.3  I  15.9  I  23.5  I  22.4  I  15.6  I
                 I  10.6  I   1.4  I   0.5  I   5.5  I   1.1  I
           -I--------I--------I--------I--------I--------I
               1.  I   349  I    63  I    15  I   213  I    51  I    691
AGREE            I  50.5  I   9.1  I   2.2  I  30.8  I   7.4· I   10.3
                 I   9.0  I  10.9  I  11.0  I  13.0  I  11.1  I
                 I   5.2  I   0.9  I   0.2  I   3.2  I   0.8  I
           -I--------I--------I--------I--------I--------I
               2.  I   134  I     9  I     3  I    76  I    17  I    239
STRONGLY AGREE   I  56.1  I   3.8  I   1.3  I  31.8  I   7.1  I    3.6
                 I   3.5  I   1.6  I   2.2  I   4.6  I   3.7  I
                 I   2.0  I   0.1  I   0.0  I   1.1  I   0.3  I
           -I--------I--------I--------I--------I--------I
           COLUMN     3876      578      136     1636      461     6687
           TOTAL      58.0      8.6      2.0     24.5      6.9    100.0
```

1 OUT OF   25 (4.0%) OF THE VALID CELLS HAVE EXPECTED CELL FREQUENCY LESS THAN 5.0.
MINIMUM EXPECTED CELL FREQUENCY =   4.861
CHI SQUARE =   79.17741 WITH 16 DEGREES OF FREEDOM   SIGNIFICANCE = 0.0000
PEARSON'S R = 0.07052 SIGNIFICANCE =   0.0000

NUMBER OF MISSING OBSERVATIONS =   1407

```
                   LIBTYPE
           COUNT   I
           ROW PCT IA.R.L. L OTHER AC COMMUNIT PUBLIC   STATE AN   ROW
           COL PCT IIBS      ADEMIC   Y COLLEG          D FEDERA   TOTAL
           TOT PCT I    1.I     2.I      3.I     4.I      5.I
RQ41       --------I--------I--------I--------I--------I--------I
              -2.  I   720  I   169  I    38  I   540  I   204  I   1671
STRONGLY DISAGRE I  43.1  I  10.1  I   2.3  I  32.3  I  12.2  I   28.3
                 I  22.5  I  30.7  I  28.4  I  34.4  I  45.6  I
                 I  12.2  I   2.9  I   0.6  I   9.2  I   3.5  I
           -I--------I--------I--------I--------I--------I
              -1.  I  1290  I   251  I    61  I   672  I   172  I   2446
DISAGREE         I  52.7  I  10.3  I   2.5  I  27.5  I   7.0  I   41.5
                 I  40.4  I  45.6  I  45.5  I  42.7  I  38.5  I
                 I  21.9  I   4.3  I   1.0  I  11.4  I   2.9  I
           -I--------I--------I--------I--------I--------I
               0.  I   785  I    71  I    21  I   239  I    45  I   1161
NEITHER A OR D   I  67.6  I   6.1  I   1.8  I  20.6  I   3.9  I   19.7
                 I  24.6  I  12.9  I  15.7  I  15.2  I  10.1  I
                 I  13.3  I   1.2  I   0.4  I   4.1  I   0.8  I
           -I--------I--------I--------I--------I--------I
               1.  I   276  I    52  I    11  I    81  I    17  I    437
AGREE            I  63.2  I  11.9  I   2.5  I  18.5  I   3.9  I    7.4
                 I   8.6  I   9.4  I   8.2  I   5.2  I   3.8  I
                 I   4.7  I   0.9  I   0.2  I   1.4  I   0.3  I
           -I--------I--------I--------I--------I--------I
               2.  I   122  I     8  I     3  I    40  I     9  I    182
STRONGLY AGREE   I  67.0  I   4.4  I   1.6  I  22.0  I   4.9  I    3.1
                 I   3.8  I   1.5  I   2.2  I   2.5  I   2.0  I
                 I   2.1  I   0.1  I   0.1  I   0.7  I   0.2  I
           -I--------I--------I--------I--------I--------I
           COLUMN     3193      551      134     1572      447     5897
           TOTAL      54.1      9.3      2.3     26.7      7.6    100.0
```

1 OUT OF   25 (4.0%) OF THE VALID CELLS HAVE EXPECTED CELL FREQUENCY LESS THAN 5.0.
MINIMUM EXPECTED CELL FREQUENCY =   4.136
CHI SQUARE =   243.52049 WITH 16 DEGREES OF FREEDOM   SIGNIFICANCE = 0.0
PEARSON'S R =-0.16923 SIGNIFICANCE =   0.0000

NUMBER OF MISSING OBSERVATIONS =   2197

```
                       LIBTYPE
              COUNT  I
              ROW PCT IA.R.L. L OTHER AC COMMUNIT PUBLIC     STATE AN    ROW
              COL PCT IIBS      ADEMIC   Y COLLEG            D FEDERA    TOTAL
              TOT PCT I     1.I      2.I      3.I      4.I      5. I
RQ42          --------I--------I--------I--------I--------I--------I
              -2.  I    557  I     64  I     12  I    176  I     61  I    870
STRONGLY DISAGRE I   64.0  I    7.4  I    1.4  I   20.2  I    7.0  I   12.4
                 I   13.9  I   10.7  I    8.5  I    9.9  I   12.7  I
                 I    8.0  I    0.9  I    0.2  I    2.5  I    0.9  I
              -I--------I--------I--------I--------I--------I
              -1.  I   1670  I    288  I     50  I    618  I    234  I   2860
DISAGREE         I   58.4  I   10.1  I    1.7  I   21.6  I    8.2  I   40.9
                 I   41.8  I   48.2  I   35.5  I   34.9  I   48.9  I
                 I   23.9  I    4.1  I    0.7  I    8.8  I    3.3  I
              -I--------I--------I--------I--------I--------I
              0.  I    701  I    128  I     35  I    343  I    101  I   1308
NEITHER A OR D   I   53.6  I    9.8  I    2.7  I   26.2  I    7.7  I   18.7
                 I   17.5  I   21.4  I   24.8  I   19.3  I   21.1  I
                 I   10.0  I    1.8  I    0.5  I    4.9  I    1.4  I
              -I--------I--------I--------I--------I--------I
              1.  I    725  I    102  I     35  I    406  I     61  I   1329
AGREE            I   54.6  I    7.7  I    2.6  I   30.5  I    4.6  I   19.0
                 I   18.1  I   17.1  I   24.8  I   22.9  I   12.7  I
                 I   10.4  I    1.5  I    0.5  I    5.8  I    0.9  I
              -I--------I--------I--------I--------I--------I
              2.  I    344  I     16  I      9  I    230  I     22  I    621
STRONGLY AGREE   I   55.4  I    2.6  I    1.4  I   37.0  I    3.5  I    8.9
                 I    8.6  I    2.7  I    6.4  I   13.0  I    4.6  I
                 I    4.9  I    0.2  I    0.1  I    3.3  I    0.3  I
              -I--------I--------I--------I--------I--------I
          COLUMN    3997      598      141     1773      479      6988
          TOTAL     57.2      8.6      2.0     25.4      6.9    100.0
```

CHI SQUARE =   161.87123 WITH 16 DEGREES OF FREEDOM   SIGNIFICANCE =   0.0
PEARSON'S R = 0.05909 SIGNIFICANCE =   0.0000

NUMBER OF MISSING OBSERVATIONS =   1106

```
                    LIBTYPE

              COUNT  IA.R.L. L OTHER AC COMMUNIT PUBLIC    STATE AN
              ROW PCT IIBS     ADEMIC   Y COLLEG           D FEDERA    ROW
              COL PCT I                    E                 L        TOTAL
                     I     1  I      2  I      3  I      4  I      5  I
RQUEST43      --------I--------I--------I--------I--------I--------I
           RQ43A     I    391  I     77  I     14  I    239  I     63  I    784
KEYBOARD CONFUSING   I   49.9  I    9.8  I    1.8  I   30.5  I    8.0  I   11.0
                     I    9.8  I   12.2  I    9.9  I   12.8  I   12.8  I
                     I--------I--------I--------I--------I--------I
           RQ43B     I    334  I     36  I      6  I    131  I     50  I    557
GLARE ON SCREEN      I   60.0  I    6.5  I    1.1  I   23.5  I    9.0  I    7.8
                     I    8.4  I    5.7  I    4.2  I    7.0  I   10.1  I
                     I--------I--------I--------I--------I--------I
           RQ43C     I   3527  I    582  I    135  I   1741  I    452  I   6437
LETTERS EASY TO READ I   54.8  I    9.0  I    2.1  I   27.0  I    7.0  I   90.3
                     I   88.5  I   91.9  I   95.1  I   93.1  I   91.5  I
                     I--------I--------I--------I--------I--------I
           RQ43D     I    362  I     43  I     11  I    119  I     37  I    572
LIGHTING TOO BRIGHT  I   63.3  I    7.5  I    1.9  I   20.8  I    6.5  I    8.0
                     I    9.1  I    6.8  I    7.7  I    6.4  I    7.5  I
                     I--------I--------I--------I--------I--------I
           RQ43E     I   2599  I    445  I     81  I   1271  I    269  I   4665
WRITING SPACE OK     I   55.7  I    9.5  I    1.7  I   27.2  I    5.8  I   65.5
                     I   65.2  I   70.3  I   57.0  I   67.9  I   54.5  I
                     I--------I--------I--------I--------I--------I
           RQ43F     I    465  I     94  I     21  I    179  I     45  I    804
NOISE DISTRACTING    I   57.8  I   11.7  I    2.6  I   22.3  I    5.6  I   11.3
                     I   11.7  I   14.8  I   14.8  I    9.6  I    9.1  I
                     I--------I--------I--------I--------I--------I
           RQ43G     I    343  I     52  I     16  I    162  I     24  I    597
TABLE HEIGHT RIGHT   I   57.5  I    8.7  I    2.7  I   27.1  I    4.0  I    8.4
                     I    8.6  I    8.2  I   11.3  I    8.7  I    4.9  I
                     I--------I--------I--------I--------I--------I
           RQ43H     I    728  I     28  I     97  I    189  I    420  I   1462
PRINTER EASY TO USE  I   49.8  I    1.9  I    6.6  I   12.9  I   28.7  I   20.5
                     I   18.3  I    4.4  I   68.3  I   10.1  I   85.0  I
                     I--------I--------I--------I--------I--------I
           COLUMN       3987      633      142     1871      494     7127
           TOTAL        55.9      8.9      2.0     26.3      6.9    100.0
```

PERCENTS AND TOTALS BASED ON RESPONDENTS

   7127 VALID CASES   967 MISSING CASES

LIBTYPE

COUNT ROW PCT COL PCT	A.R.L. L IBS 1	OTHER AC ADEMIC 2	COMMUNIT Y COLLEG E 3	PUBLIC 4	STATE AN D FEDERA L 5	ROW TOTAL
RQUEST44						
RQ44A STEP BY STEP INSTRUC	725 42.4 17.6	186 10.9 28.8	20 1.2 13.6	637 37.3 33.9	142 8.3 29.9	1710 23.6
RQ44B SEARCH BY TITLE WORD	646 50.3 15.7	141 11.0 21.9	28 2.2 19.0	469 36.5 25.0	0 0.0 0.0	1284 17.7
RQ44C SUBJECT WORD SEARCH	960 54.5 23.4	183 10.4 28.4	41 2.3 27.9	576 32.7 30.7	1 0.1 0.2	1761 24.3
RQ44D LIMIT BY DATE OF PUB	537 66.3 13.1	75 9.3 11.6	13 1.6 8.8	185 22.8 9.8	0 0.0 0.0	810 11.2
RQ44E LIMIT BY LANGUAGE	572 85.1 13.9	30 4.5 4.7	3 0.4 2.0	66 9.8 3.5	1 0.1 0.2	672 9.3
RQ44F JOURNAL TITLE ABBRV	1016 71.8 24.7	126 8.9 19.5	17 1.2 11.6	183 12.9 9.7	73 5.2 15.4	1415 19.5
RQ44G CHANGE DISPLAY ORDER	450 53.7 10.9	73 8.7 11.3	15 1.8 10.2	241 28.8 12.8	59 7.0 12.4	838 11.5
RQ44H VIEW RELATED WORDS	1960 60.7 47.7	265 8.2 41.1	69 2.1 46.9	737 22.8 39.2	199 6.2 41.9	3230 44.5
COLUMN TOTAL	4110 56.6	645 8.9	147 2.0	1879 25.9	475 6.5	7256 100.0

PERCENTS AND TOTALS BASED ON RESPONDENTS

(CONTINUED)

LIBTYPE

COUNT ROW PCT COL PCT	A.R.L. L IBS 1	OTHER AC ADEMIC 2	COMMUNIT Y COLLEG E 3	PUBLIC 4	STATE AN D FEDERA L 5	ROW TOTAL
RQUEST44						
RQ44I SRCH FOR ILLUS & BIB	767 60.9 18.7	102 8.1 15.8	26 2.1 17.7	279 22.1 14.8	86 6.8 18.1	1260 17.4
RQ44J SRCH BY CALL NUMBER	428 70.2 10.4	64 10.5 9.9	8 1.3 5.4	67 11.0 3.6	43 7.0 9.1	610 8.4
RQ44K PRINT SEARCH RESULTS	1088 60.1 26.5	168 9.3 26.0	41 2.3 27.9	512 28.3 27.2	1 0.1 0.2	1810 24.9
RQ44L SRCH CONTENTS-INDEX	1814 59.7 44.1	282 9.3 43.7	57 1.9 38.8	663 21.8 35.3	222 7.3 46.7	3038 41.9
RQ44M IF BOOK CHECKED OUT	1019 53.5 24.8	301 15.8 46.7	27 1.4 18.4	349 18.3 18.6	210 11.0 44.2	1906 26.3
RQ44N LIB LOCATION OF BOOK	530 48.3 12.9	152 13.8 23.6	17 1.5 11.6	260 23.7 13.8	139 12.7 29.3	1098 15.1
RQ44O NONE	200 57.0 4.9	19 5.4 2.9	30 8.5 20.4	85 24.2 4.5	17 4.8 3.6	351 4.8
COLUMN TOTAL	4110 56.6	645 8.9	147 2.0	1879 25.9	475 6.5	7256 100.0

PERCENTS AND TOTALS BASED ON RESPONDENTS

7256 VALID CASES   838 MISSING CASES

LIBTYPE

	COUNT ROW PCT COL PCT	A.R.L. L IBS 1	OTHER AC ADEMIC 2	COMMUNIT Y COLLEG E 3	PUBLIC 4	STATE AN D FEDERA L 5	ROW TOTAL
RQUEST45							
RQ45A MORE TERMINALS		2022 54.8 48.9	323 8.8 50.4	81 2.2 55.9	1019 27.6 54.8	245 6.6 51.4	3690 50.8
RQ45B TERMS IN OTHER LOCAT		1547 67.9 37.4	140 6.1 21.8	38 1.7 26.2	423 18.6 22.7	132 5.8 27.7	2280 31.4
RQ45C TERMS OUTSIDE LIBR		1712 67.6 41.4	258 10.2 40.2	39 1.5 26.9	374 14.8 20.1	150 5.9 31.4	2533 34.9
RQ45D COMMAND CHART POSTED		1161 55.0 28.1	172 8.2 26.8	26 1.2 17.9	616 29.2 33.1	135 6.4 28.3	2110 29.1
RQ45E MANUAL AT TERMINAL		776 53.0 18.8	121 8.3 18.9	15 1.0 10.3	551 37.7 29.6	0 0.0 0.0	1463 20.1
RQ45F MANUAL FOR PURCHASE		307 50.5 7.4	53 8.7 8.3	8 1.3 5.5	155 25.5 8.3	85 14.0 17.8	608 8.4
RQ45G TRAINING SESSIONS		474 47.2 11.5	112 11.1 17.5	17 1.7 11.7	277 27.6 14.9	125 12.4 26.2	1005 13.8
RQ45H A-V TRAINING PROGR		392 48.6 9.5	77 9.6 12.0	17 2.1 11.7	247 30.6 13.3	73 9.1 15.3	806 11.1
COLUMN TOTAL		4138 57.0	641 8.8	145 2.0	1860 · 25.6	477 6.6	7261 100.0

PERCENTS AND TOTALS BASED ON RESPONDENTS

(CONTINUED)

LIBTYPE

	COUNT ROW PCT COL PCT	A.R.L. L IBS 1	OTHER AC ADEMIC 2	COMMUNIT Y COLLEG E 3	PUBLIC 4	STATE AN D FEDERA L 5	ROW TOTAL
RQUEST45							
RQ45I NONE		620 53.4 15.0	113 9.7 17.6	32 2.8 22.1	320 27.5 17.2	77 6.6 16.1	1162 16.0
COLUMN TOTAL		4138 57.0	641 8.8	145 2.0	1860 25.6	477 6.6	7261 100.0

PERCENTS AND TOTALS BASED ON RESPONDENTS

7261 VALID CASES   833 MISSING CASES

LIBTYPE

		A.R.L. LIBS	OTHER ACADEMIC	COMMUNITY COLLEGE	PUBLIC	STATE AND FEDERAL	ROW TOTAL
	COUNT ROW PCT COL PCT	1	2	3	4	5	
RQUEST46							
RQ46A DISSERTATIONS		869 67.6 23.1	66 5.1 15.4	10 0.8 6.9	134 10.4 10.1	207 16.1 46.0	1286 21.0
RQ46B MOTION PICTURE FILMS		530 60.5 14.1	98 11.2 22.9	35 4.0 24.3	137 15.6 10.3	76 8.7 16.9	876 14.3
RQ46C GOV PUBLICATIONS		1290 74.6 34.2	96 5.6 22.4	28 1.6 19.4	315 18.2 23.8	0 0.0 0.0	1729 28.3
RQ46D JOURNAL TITLES		634 45.5 16.8	232 16.7 54.2	73 5.2 50.7	453 32.5 34.2	0 0.0 0.0	1392 22.8
RQ46E MAPS		503 58.2 13.3	63 7.3 14.7	18 2.1 12.5	281 32.5 21.2	0 0.0 0.0	865 14.1
RQ46F MANUSCRIPTS		335 64.1 8.9	19 3.6 4.4	10 1.9 6.9	96 18.4 7.2	63 12.0 14.0	523 8.5
RQ46G MUSIC SCORES		309 64.5 8.2	41 8.6 9.6	24 5.0 16.7	83 17.3 6.3	22 4.6 4.9	479 7.8
RQ46H NEWSPAPERS		1182 65.6 31.4	142 7.9 33.2	43 2.4 29.9	260 14.4 19.6	175 9.7 38.9	1802 29.5
COLUMN TOTAL		3769 61.6	428 7.0	144 2.4	1326 21.7	450 7.4	6117 100.0

PERCENTS AND TOTALS BASED ON RESPONDENTS

(CONTINUED)

LIBTYPE

		A.R.L. LIBS	OTHER ACADEMIC	COMMUNITY COLLEGE	PUBLIC	STATE AND FEDERAL	ROW TOTAL
	COUNT ROW PCT COL PCT	1	2	3	4	5	
RQUEST46							
RQ46I RECORDS OR TAPES		716 57.4 19.0	55 4.4 12.9	32 2.6 22.2	411 33.0 31.0	33 2.6 7.3	1247 20.4
RQ46J TECHNICAL REPORTS		727 65.9 19.3	64 5.8 15.0	26 2.4 18.1	190 17.2 14.3	96 8.7 21.3	1103 18.0
RQ46K MORE OLDER BOOKS		1220 77.9 32.4	89 5.7 20.8	24 1.5 16.7	54 3.4 4.1	180 11.5 40.0	1567 25.6
RQ46L NONE		360 53.6 9.6	58 8.6 13.6	19 2.8 13.2	203 30.2 15.3	32 4.8 7.1	672 11.0
RQ46M OTHER		114 49.1 3.0	12 5.2 2.8	6 2.6 4.2	81 34.9 6.1	19 8.2 4.2	232 3.8
COLUMN TOTAL		3769 61.6	428 7.0	144 2.4	1326 21.7	450 7.4	6117 100.0

PERCENTS AND TOTALS BASED ON RESPONDENTS

6117 VALID CASES   1977 MISSING CASES

```
                    LIBTYPE
            COUNT   I
            ROW PCT IA.R.L. L OTHER AC COMMUNIT PUBLIC   STATE AN   ROW
            COL PCT IIBS      ADEMIC   Y COLLEG          D FEDERA  TOTAL
            TOT PCT I    1. I     2. I     3. I     4. I     5. I
RQ48        --------I--------I--------I--------I--------I--------I
               1.   I  1542  I   199  I    44  I    82  I    54  I  1921
DAILY              I  80.3  I  10.4  I   2.3  I   4.3  I   2.8  I  25.8
                   I  36.6  I  30.6  I  29.9  I   4.2  I  10.8  I
                   I  20.7  I   2.7  I   0.6  I   1.1  I   0.7  I
               -I--------I--------I--------I--------I--------I
               2.   I  1810  I   341  I    69  I   804  I   139  I  3163
WEEKLY             I  57.2  I  10.8  I   2.2  I  25.4  I   4.4  I  42.4
                   I  42.9  I  52.5  I  46.9  I  41.5  I  27.7  I
                   I  24.3  I   4.6  I   0.9  I  10.8  I   1.9  I
               -I--------I--------I--------I--------I--------I
               3.   I   515  I    69  I    27  I   652  I   111  I  1374
MONTHLY            I  37.5  I   5.0  I   2.0  I  47.5  I   8.1  I  18.4
                   I  12.2  I  10.6  I  18.4  I  33.6  I  22.2  I
                   I   6.9  I   0.9  I   0.4  I   8.7  I   1.5  I
               -I--------I--------I--------I--------I--------I
               4.   I   202  I    29  I     5  I   231  I    83  I   550
4 TIMES YEAR       I  36.7  I   5.3  I   0.9  I  42.0  I  15.1  I   7.4
                   I   4.8  I   4.5  I   3.4  I  11.9  I  16.6  I
                   I   2.7  I   0.4  I   0.1  I   3.1  I   1.1  I
               -I--------I--------I--------I--------I--------I
               5.   I    51  I     3  I     0  I    33  I    36  I   123
ONCE A  YEAR       I  41.5  I   2.4  I   0.0  I  26.8  I  29.3  I   1.7
                   I   1.2  I   0.5  I   0.0  I   1.7  I   7.2  I
                   I   0.7  I   0.0  I   0.0  I   0.4  I   0.5  I
               -I--------I--------I--------I--------I--------I
               6.   I    96  I     9  I     2  I   136  I    78  I   321
NOT BEFORE TODAY   I  29.9  I   2.8  I   0.6  I  42.4  I  24.3  I   4.3
                   I   2.3  I   1.4  I   1.4  I   7.0  I  15.6  I
                   I   1.3  I   0.1  I   0.0  I   1.8  I   1.0  I
               -I--------I--------I--------I--------I--------I
            COLUMN    4216      650      147     1938      501     7452
            TOTAL     56.6       8.7      2.0     26.0      6.7    100.0
```

1 OUT OF   30 (3.3%) OF THE VALID CELLS HAVE EXPECTED CELL FREQUENCY LESS THAN 5.0.
MINIMUM EXPECTED CELL FREQUENCY = 2.426
CHI SQUARE = 1492.45752 WITH 20 DEGREES OF FREEDOM   SIGNIFICANCE = 0.0
PEARSON'S R = 0.36929 SIGNIFICANCE = 0.0000

NUMBER OF MISSING OBSERVATIONS =   642

```
                    LIBTYPE
            COUNT   I
            ROW PCT IA.R.L. L OTHER AC COMMUNIT PUBLIC   STATE AN   ROW
            COL PCT IIBS      ADEMIC   Y COLLEG          D FEDERA  TOTAL
            TOT PCT I    1. I     2. I     3. I     4. I     5. I
RQ49        --------I--------I--------I--------I--------I--------I
               1.   I   719  I    72  I    26  I   619  I   137  I  1573
EVERY   VISIT      I  45.7  I   4.6  I   1.7  I  39.4  I   8.7  I  21.1
                   I  17.0  I  11.1  I  17.7  I  31.9  I  27.3  I
                   I   9.6  I   1.0  I   0.3  I   8.3  I   1.8  I
               -I--------I--------I--------I--------I--------I
               2.   I  1691  I   233  I    52  I   621  I   156  I  2753
MOST    VISITS     I  61.4  I   8.5  I   1.9  I  22.6  I   5.7  I  36.9
                   I  40.0  I  35.8  I  35.4  I  32.0  I  31.1  I
                   I  22.6  I   3.1  I   0.7  I   8.3  I   2.1  I
               -I--------I--------I--------I--------I--------I
               3.   I  1303  I   236  I    59  I   332  I    68  I  1998
OCCASIONALLY       I  65.2  I  11.8  I   3.0  I  16.6  I   3.4  I  26.8
                   I  30.8  I  36.3  I  40.1  I  17.1  I  13.5  I
                   I  17.5  I   3.2  I   0.8  I   4.4  I   0.9  I
               -I--------I--------I--------I--------I--------I
               4.   I   253  I    48  I     2  I    80  I    25  I   408
RARELY             I  62.0  I  11.8  I   0.5  I  19.6  I   6.1  I   5.5
                   I   6.0  I   7.4  I   1.4  I   4.1  I   5.0  I
                   I   3.4  I   0.6  I   0.0  I   1.1  I   0.3  I
               -I--------I--------I--------I--------I--------I
               5.   I   260  I    61  I     8  I   290  I   116  I   735
NOT BEFORE TODAY   I  35.4  I   8.3  I   1.1  I  39.5  I  15.8  I   9.8
                   I   6.2  I   9.4  I   5.4  I  14.9  I  23.1  I
                   I   3.5  I   0.8  I   0.1  I   3.9  I   1.6  I
               -I--------I--------I--------I--------I--------I
            COLUMN    4226      650      147     1942      502     7467
            TOTAL     56.6       8.7      2.0     26.0      6.7    100.0
```

CHI SQUARE =   588.98218 WITH 16 DEGREES OF FREEDOM   SIGNIFICANCE = 0.0
PEARSON'S R = 0.00455 SIGNIFICANCE = 0.3471

NUMBER OF MISSING OBSERVATIONS =   627

```
                LIBTYPE
         COUNT  I
         ROW PCT IA.R.L. L OTHER AC COMMUNIT PUBLIC   STATE AN   ROW
         COL PCT IIBS      ADEMIC   Y COLLEG           D FEDERA   TOTAL
         TOT PCT I    1.I      2.I      3.I      4.I      5.I
RQ50     --------I--------I--------I--------I--------I--------I
            1.   I   442   I    55   I     5   I   243   I   125   I   870
EVERY  VISIT     I  50.8   I   6.3   I   0.6   I  27.9   I  14.4   I  12.4
                 I  10.5   I   8.5   I   3.4   I  15.8   I  25.5   I
                 I   6.3   I   0.8   I   0.1   I   3.5   I   1.8   I
                 -I--------I--------I--------I--------I--------I
            2.   I   872   I   123   I    11   I   366   I   120   I  1492
MOST   VISITS    I  58.4   I   8.2   I   0.7   I  24.5   I   8.0   I  21.2
                 I  20.7   I  19.0   I   7.5   I  23.9   I  24.4   I
                 I  12.4   I   1.8   I   0.2   I   5.2   I   1.7   I
                 -I--------I--------I--------I--------I--------I
            3.   I  1575   I   243   I    49   I   449   I   102   I  2418
OCCASIONALLY     I  65.1   I  10.0   I   2.0   I  18.6   I   4.2   I  34.4
                 I  37.5   I  37.5   I  33.3   I  29.3   I  20.8   I
                 I  22.4   I   3.5   I   0.7   I   6.4   I   1.5   I
                 -I--------I--------I--------I--------I--------I
            4.   I   937   I   173   I    42   I   272   I    71   I  1495
RARELY           I  62.7   I  11.6   I   2.8   I  18.2   I   4.7   I  21.3
                 I  22.3   I  26.7   I  28.6   I  17.7   I  14.5   I
                 I  13.3   I   2.5   I   0.6   I   3.9   I   1.0   I
                 -I--------I--------I--------I--------I--------I
            5.   I   379   I    54   I    40   I   204   I    73   I   750
NOT BEFORE TODAY I  50.5   I   7.2   I   5.3   I  27.2   I   9.7   I  10.7
                 I   9.0   I   8.3   I  27.2   I  13.3   I  14.9   I
                 I   5.4   I   0.8   I   0.6   I   2.9   I   1.0   I
                 -I--------I--------I--------I--------I--------I
         COLUMN     4205      648      147     1534      491      7025
         TOTAL      59.9      9.2      2.1     21.8      7.0     100.0

CHI SQUARE =  290.19116 WITH  16 DEGREES OF FREEDOM   SIGNIFICANCE =  0.0
PEARSON'S R =-0.05267  SIGNIFICANCE =  0.0000

NUMBER OF MISSING OBSERVATIONS =    1069
```

```
                LIBTYPE
         COUNT  I
         ROW PCT IA.R.L. L OTHER AC COMMUNIT PUBLIC   STATE AN   ROW
         COL PCT IIBS      ADEMIC   Y COLLEG           D FEDERA   TOTAL
         TOT PCT I    1.I      2.I      3.I      4.I      5.I
RQ51     --------I--------I--------I--------I--------I--------I
            1.   I   496   I    56   I    25   I   326   I    62   I   965
DAILY            I  51.4   I   5.8   I   2.6   I  33.8   I   6.4   I  13.0
                 I  11.8   I   8.6   I  17.0   I  17.0   I  12.4   I
                 I   6.7   I   0.8   I   0.3   I   4.4   I   0.8   I
                 -I--------I--------I--------I--------I--------I
            2.   I   784   I    99   I    21   I   258   I    78   I  1240
WEEKLY           I  63.2   I   8.0   I   1.7   I  20.8   I   6.3   I  16.7
                 I  18.7   I  15.3   I  14.3   I  13.5   I  15.6   I
                 I  10.6   I   1.3   I   0.3   I   3.5   I   1.1   I
                 -I--------I--------I--------I--------I--------I
            3.   I   580   I    80   I    19   I   224   I    61   I   964
MONTHLY          I  60.2   I   8.3   I   2.0   I  23.2   I   6.3   I  13.0
                 I  13.8   I  12.3   I  12.9   I  11.7   I  12.2   I
                 I   7.8   I   1.1   I   0.3   I   3.0   I   0.8   I
                 -I--------I--------I--------I--------I--------I
            4.   I   537   I    79   I     8   I   187   I    69   I   880
4 TIMES A YEAR   I  61.0   I   9.0   I   0.9   I  21.3   I   7.8   I  11.9
                 I  12.8   I  12.2   I   5.4   I   9.8   I  13.8   I
                 I   7.2   I   1.1   I   0.1   I   2.5   I   0.9   I
                 -I--------I--------I--------I--------I--------I
            5.   I   386   I    73   I     6   I   157   I    49   I   671
ONCE A  YEAR     I  57.5   I  10.9   I   0.9   I  23.4   I   7.3   I   9.1
                 I   9.2   I  11.3   I   4.1   I   8.2   I   9.8   I
                 I   5.2   I   1.0   I   0.1   I   2.1   I   0.7   I
                 -I--------I--------I--------I--------I--------I
            6.   I  1416   I   261   I    68   I   765   I   180   I  2690
NEVER            I  52.6   I   9.7   I   2.5   I  28.4   I   6.7   I  36.3
                 I  33.7   I  40.3   I  46.3   I  39.9   I  36.1   I
                 I  19.1   I   3.5   I   0.9   I  10.3   I   2.4   I
                 -I--------I--------I--------I--------I--------I
         COLUMN     4199      648      147     1917      499      7410
         TOTAL      56.7      8.7      2.0     25.9      6.7     100.0

CHI SQUARE =  115.98837 WITH  20 DEGREES OF FREEDOM   SIGNIFICANCE =  0.0000
PEARSON'S R = 0.02087  SIGNIFICANCE =  0.0362

NUMBER OF MISSING OBSERVATIONS =     684
```

```
                          LIBTYPE
                COUNT   I
                ROW PCT IA.R.L. L OTHER AC COMMUNIT PUBLIC    STATE AN   ROW
                COL PCT IIBS      ADEMIC   Y COLLEG           D FEDERA  TOTAL
                TOT PCT I    1.I     2.I      3.I      4.I       5.I
RQ52            --------I--------I--------I--------I--------I--------I
                    1.  I   2756 I    279 I     91 I   1329 I    236 I   4691
NOTICED TERM IN     I   58.8 I    5.9 I    1.9 I   28.3 I    5.0 I   63.6
                    I   66.0 I   43.5 I   62.3 I   69.5 I   47.0 I
                    I   37.4 I    3.8 I    1.2 I   18.0 I    3.2 I
                  -I--------I--------I--------I--------I--------I
                    2.  I    524 I    112 I     19 I     62 I     33 I    750
LIBRARY TOUR        I   69.9 I   14.9 I    2.5 I    8.3 I    4.4 I   10.2
                    I   12.6 I   17.5 I   13.0 I    3.2 I    6.6 I
                    I    7.1 I    1.5 I    0.3 I    0.8 I    0.4 I
                  -I--------I--------I--------I--------I--------I
                    3.  I    114 I     14 I      3 I    133 I     12 I    276
ARTICLE-ANNOUNCE    I   41.3 I    5.1 I    1.1 I   48.2 I    4.3 I    3.7
                    I    2.7 I    2.2 I    2.1 I    7.0 I    2.4 I
                    I    1.5 I    0.2 I    0.0 I    1.8 I    0.2 I
                  -I--------I--------I--------I--------I--------I
                    4.  I    192 I     61 I     13 I     18 I     23 I    307
INSTRUCTOR          I   62.5 I   19.9 I    4.2 I    5.9 I    7.5 I    4.2
                    I    4.6 I    9.5 I    8.9 I    0.9 I    4.6 I
                    I    2.6 I    0.8 I    0.2 I    0.2 I    0.3 I
                  -I--------I--------I--------I--------I--------I
                    5.  I    324 I     65 I     11 I    178 I    110 I    688
FRIEND - FAMILY     I   47.1 I    9.4 I    1.6 I   25.9 I   16.0 I    9.3
                    I    7.8 I   10.1 I    7.5 I    9.3 I   21.9 I
                    I    4.4 I    0.9 I    0.1 I    2.4 I    1.5 I
                  -I--------I--------I--------I--------I--------I
                    6.  I    265 I    110 I      9 I    193 I     88 I    665
LIBRARY STAFF       I   39.8 I   16.5 I    1.4 I   29.0 I   13.2 I    9.0
                    I    6.3 I   17.2 I    6.2 I   10.1 I   17.5 I
                    I    3.6 I    1.5 I    0.1 I    2.6 I    1.2 I
                  -I--------I--------I--------I--------I--------I
                COLUMN    4175      641      146     1913      502     7377
                 TOTAL    56.6      8.7      2.0     25.9      6.8    100.0

CHI SQUARE =   626.54492 WITH  20 DEGREES OF FREEDOM   SIGNIFICANCE =  0.0
PEARSON'S R = 0.09709  SIGNIFICANCE =  0.0000

NUMBER OF MISSING OBSERVATIONS =      717
```

```
                          LIBTYPE
                COUNT   IA.R.L. L OTHER AC COMMUNIT PUBLIC    STATE AN
                ROW PCT IIBS      ADEMIC   Y COLLEG           D FEDERA   ROW
                COL PCT I                  E                  L         TOTAL
                        I    1  I    2  I    3  I    4  I    5  I
RQUEST53        --------I--------I--------I--------I--------I--------I
                RQ53A   I    631 I    119 I     20 I    313 I     68 I   1151
FROM A FRIEND           I   54.8 I   10.3 I    1.7 I   27.2 I    5.9 I   15.5
                        I   15.0 I   18.4 I   13.6 I   16.4 I   13.5 I
                        I--------I--------I--------I--------I--------I
                RQ53B   I   2341 I    307 I     68 I    884 I    355 I   3955
BY PRINTED INSTR        I   59.2 I    7.8 I    1.7 I   22.4 I    9.0 I   53.3
                        I   55.7 I   47.6 I   46.3 I   46.2 I   70.6 I
                        I--------I--------I--------I--------I--------I
                RQ53C   I   1352 I    192 I     65 I    426 I    112 I   2147
BY INSTR ON TERMINAL    I   63.0 I    8.9 I    3.0 I   19.8 I    5.2 I   29.0
                        I   32.2 I   29.8 I   44.2 I   22.3 I   22.3 I
                        I--------I--------I--------I--------I--------I
                RQ53D   I    858 I    275 I     59 I    733 I    268 I   2193
FROM LIBRARY STAFF      I   39.1 I   12.5 I    2.7 I   33.4 I   12.2 I   29.6
                        I   20.4 I   42.6 I   40.1 I   38.3 I   53.3 I
                        I--------I--------I--------I--------I--------I
                RQ53E   I    302 I     95 I     24 I     17 I     20 I    458
FROM LIBRARY COURSE     I   65.9 I   20.7 I    5.2 I    3.7 I    4.4 I    6.2
                        I    7.2 I   14.7 I   16.3 I    0.9 I    4.0 I
                        I--------I--------I--------I--------I--------I
                RQ53F   I      0 I      6 I      7 I      1 I      1 I     15
AUDIO-VISUAL PROG       I    0.0 I   40.0 I   46.7 I    6.7 I    6.7 I    0.2
                        I    0.0 I    0.9 I    4.8 I    0.1 I    0.2 I
                        I--------I--------I--------I--------I--------I
                RQ53G   I    876 I     99 I     33 I    399 I     59 I   1466
BY MYSELF               I   59.8 I    6.8 I    2.3 I   27.2 I    4.0 I   19.8
                        I   20.8 I   15.3 I   22.4 I   20.8 I   11.7 I
                        I--------I--------I--------I--------I--------I
                COLUMN    4205      645      147     1914      503     7414
                 TOTAL    56.7      8.7      2.0     25.8      6.8    100.0

PERCENTS AND TOTALS BASED ON RESPONDENTS

   7414 VALID CASES           680 MISSING CASES
```

```
                   LIBTYPE
          COUNT  I
          ROW PCT IA.R.L. L OTHER AC COMMUNIT PUBLIC    STATE AN  ROW
          COL PCT IIBS      ADEMIC   Y COLLEG           D FEDERA  TOTAL
          TOT PCT I    1.I      2.I      3.I      4.I      5.I
RQ54      --------I--------I--------I--------I--------I--------I
              1.  I     27  I      1  I      1  I    102  I      3  I    134
14 AND  UNDER     I   20.1  I    0.7  I    0.7  I   76.1  I    2.2  I    1.8
                  I    0.6  I    0.2  I    0.7  I    5.3  I    0.6  I
                  I    0.4  I    0.0  I    0.0  I    1.4  I    0.0  I
                 -I--------I--------I--------I--------I--------I
              2.  I    832  I    120  I     48  I    424  I     34  I   1458
15 - 19 YEARS     I   57.1  I    8.2  I    3.3  I   29.1  I    2.3  I   19.6
                  I   19.7  I   18.5  I   32.7  I   22.0  I    6.7  I
                  I   11.2  I    1.6  I    0.6  I    5.7  I    0.5  I
                 -I--------I--------I--------I--------I--------I
              3.  I   1886  I    339  I     66  I    360  I    162  I   2813
20 - 24 YEARS     I   67.0  I   12.1  I    2.3  I   12.8  I    5.8  I   37.8
                  I   44.7  I   52.2  I   44.9  I   18.7  I   32.1  I
                  I   25.3  I    4.6  I    0.9  I    4.8  I    2.2  I
                 -I--------I--------I--------I--------I--------I
              4.  I   1057  I    126  I     23  I    576  I    196  I   1978
25 - 34 YEARS     I   53.4  I    6.4  I    1.2  I   29.1  I    9.9  I   26.6
                  I   25.1  I   19.4  I   15.6  I   29.9  I   38.8  I
                  I   14.2  I    1.7  I    0.3  I    7.7  I    2.6  I
                 -I--------I--------I--------I--------I--------I
              5.  I    284  I     38  I      6  I    281  I     72  I    681
35 - 44 YEARS     I   41.7  I    5.6  I    0.9  I   41.3  I   10.6  I    9.1
                  I    6.7  I    5.8  I    4.1  I   14.6  I   14.3  I
                  I    3.8  I    0.5  I    0.1  I    3.8  I    1.0  I
                 -I--------I--------I--------I--------I--------I
              6.  I     77  I     23  I      2  I     97  I     23  I    222
45 - 54 YEARS     I   34.7  I   10.4  I    0.9  I   43.7  I   10.4  I    3.0
                  I    1.8  I    3.5  I    1.4  I    5.0  I    4.6  I
                  I    1.0  I    0.3  I    0.0  I    1.3  I    0.3  I
                 -I--------I--------I--------I--------I--------I
              7.  I     32  I      3  I      1  I     51  I     11  I     98
55 - 64 YEARS     I   32.7  I    3.1  I    1.0  I   52.0  I   11.2  I    1.3
                  I    0.8  I    0.5  I    0.7  I    2.6  I    2.2  I
                  I    0.4  I    0.0  I    0.0  I    0.7  I    0.1  I
                 -I--------I--------I--------I--------I--------I
          COLUMN     4217      650      147     1928      505      7447
           TOTAL     56.6      8.7      2.0     25.9      6.8    100.0
(CONTINUED)
```

```
                   LIBTYPE
          COUNT  I
          ROW PCT IA.R.L. L OTHER AC COMMUNIT PUBLIC    STATE AN  ROW
          COL PCT IIBS      ADEMIC   Y COLLEG           D FEDERA  TOTAL
          TOT PCT I    1.I      2.I      3.I      4.I      5.I
RQ54      --------I--------I--------I--------I--------I--------I
              8.  I     22  I      0  I      0  I     37  I      4  I     63
65 AND  OVER      I   34.9  I    0.0  I    0.0  I   58.7  I    6.3  I    0.8
                  I    0.5  I    0.0  I    0.0  I    1.9  I    0.8  I
                  I    0.3  I    0.0  I    0.0  I    0.5  I    0.1  I
                 -I--------I--------I--------I--------I--------I
          COLUMN     4217      650      147     1928      505      7447
           TOTAL     56.6      8.7      2.0     25.9      6.8    100.0
```

```
    5 OUT OF     40 ( 12.5%) OF THE VALID CELLS HAVE EXPECTED CELL FREQUENCY LESS THAN 5.0.
MINIMUM EXPECTED CELL FREQUENCY =   1.244
CHI SQUARE =    828.31055 WITH  28 DEGREES OF FREEDOM   SIGNIFICANCE =   0.0
PEARSON'S R = 0.14722  SIGNIFICANCE =   0.0000

NUMBER OF MISSING OBSERVATIONS = 647
```

```
                    LIBTYPE
            COUNT  I
            ROW PCT IA.R.L.  L OTHER AC COMMUNIT PUBLIC    STATE AN   ROW
            COL PCT IIBS       ADEMIC   Y COLLEG           D FEDERA   TOTAL
            TOT PCT I     1.I       2.I       3.I      4.I       5.I
RQ55        --------I--------I--------I--------I--------I--------I
            1.  I  1631  I   276  I    49  I   821  I   176  I    2953
  FEMALE        I  55.2  I   9.3  I   1.7  I  27.8  I   6.0  I    40.1
               I  39.1  I  42.8  I  33.6  I  43.1  I  35.2  I
               I  22.1  I   3.7  I   0.7  I  11.1  I   2.4  I
            -I--------I--------I--------I--------I--------I
            2.  I  2540  I   369  I    97  I  1084  I   324  I    4414
  MALE          I  57.5  I   8.4  I   2.2  I  24.6  I   7.3  I    59.9
               I  60.9  I  57.2  I  66.4  I  56.9  I  64.8  I
               I  34.5  I   5.0  I   1.3  I  14.7  I   4.4  I
            -I--------I--------I--------I--------I--------I
        COLUMN     4171      645      146     1905      500     7367
        TOTAL      56.6      8.8      2.0     25.9      6.8    100.0
```

CHI SQUARE =   18.39124 WITH   4 DEGREES OF FREEDOM   SIGNIFICANCE =   0.0010
PEARSON'S R =-0.01361   SIGNIFICANCE =   0.1213

NUMBER OF MISSING OBSERVATIONS =   727

```
                    LIBTYPE
            COUNT  I
            ROW PCT IA.R.L.  L OTHER AC COMMUNIT PUBLIC    STATE AN   ROW
            COL PCT IIBS       ADEMIC   Y COLLEG           D FEDERA   TOTAL
            TOT PCT I     1.I       2.I       3.I      4.I       5.I
RQ56        --------I--------I--------I--------I--------I--------I
            1.  I    33  I     2  I     0  I    37  I     2  I      74
  GRADE SCHOOL    I  44.6  I   2.7  I   0.0  I  50.0  I   2.7  I     1.0
               I   0.8  I   0.3  I   0.0  I   1.9  I   0.4  I
               I   0.4  I   0.0  I   0.0  I   0.5  I   0.0  I
            -I--------I--------I--------I--------I--------I
            2.  I   116  I     7  I    24  I   499  I    22  I     668
  HIGH  SCHOOL    I  17.4  I   1.0  I   3.6  I  74.7  I   3.3  I     9.0
               I   2.8  I   1.1  I  16.6  I  25.9  I   4.4  I
               I   1.6  I   0.1  I   0.3  I   6.7  I   0.3  I
            -I--------I--------I--------I--------I--------I
            3.  I  2221  I   438  I   112  I   547  I   113  I    3431
  SOME  COLLEGE   I  64.7  I  12.8  I   3.3  I  15.9  I   3.3  I    46.2
               I  52.9  I  67.5  I  77.2  I  28.4  I  22.4  I
               I  29.9  I   5.9  I   1.5  I   7.4  I   1.5  I
            -I--------I--------I--------I--------I--------I
            4.  I  1832  I   202  I     9  I   840  I   368  I    3251
 COLLEGE GRADUATE I  56.4  I   6.2  I   0.3  I  25.8  I  11.3  I    43.8
               I  43.6  I  31.1  I   6.2  I  43.7  I  72.9  I
               I  24.7  I   2.7  I   0.1  I  11.3  I   5.0  I
            -I--------I--------I--------I--------I--------I
        COLUMN     4202      649      145     1923      505     7424
        TOTAL      56.6      8.7      2.0     25.9      6.8    100.0
```

   1 OUT OF   20 (5.0%) OF THE VALID CELLS HAVE EXPECTED CELL FREQUENCY LESS THAN 5.0.
MINIMUM EXPECTED CELL FREQUENCY =   1.445
CHI SQUARE =   1382.59277 WITH 12 DEGREES OF FREEDOM   SIGNIFICANCE =   0.0
PEARSON'S R =-0.07126   SIGNIFICANCE =   0.0000

NUMBER OF MISSING OBSERVATIONS =   670

```
                      LIBTYPE
           COUNT   I
           ROW PCT IA.R.L. L OTHER AC COMMUNIT  ROW
           COL PCT IIBS      ADEMIC   Y COLLEG  TOTAL
           TOT PCT I    1.I       2.I      3.I
RQ57       --------I--------I--------I--------I
       1.  I   1123 I    127 I     16 I  1266
ART AND HUMANITI I   88.7 I   10.0 I    1.3 I  26.1
                 I   27.5 I   20.1 I   11.3 I
                 I   23.1 I    2.6 I    0.3 I
          -I--------I--------I--------I
       2.  I    481 I     74 I      9 I   564
PHYS-BIO SCIENCE I   85.3 I   13.1 I    1.6 I  11.6
                 I   11.8 I   11.7 I    6.3 I
                 I    9.9 I    1.5 I    0.2 I
          -I--------I--------I--------I
       3.  I    753 I     96 I      5 I   854
SOCIAL   SCIENCES I   88.2 I   11.2 I    0.6 I  17.6
                  I   18.4 I   15.2 I    3.5 I
                  I   15.5 I    2.0 I    0.1 I
          -I--------I--------I--------I
       4.  I    482 I    126 I     37 I   645
BUSINESS-MANAGEM I   74.7 I   19.5 I    5.7 I  13.3
                 I   11.8 I   20.0 I   26.1 I
                 I    9.9 I    2.6 I    0.8 I
          -I--------I--------I--------I
       5.  I    189 I     74 I      4 I   267
EDUCATION        I   70.8 I   27.7 I    1.5 I   5.5
                 I    4.6 I   11.7 I    2.8 I
                 I    3.9 I    1.5 I    0.1 I
          -I--------I--------I--------I
       6.  I    495 I     54 I     29 I   578
ENGINEERING      I   85.6 I    9.3 I    5.0 I  11.9
                 I   12.1 I    8.6 I   20.4 I
                 I   10.2 I    1.1 I    0.6 I
          -I--------I--------I--------I
       7.  I    233 I     28 I      9 I   270
MEDICAL-HEALTH S I   86.3 I   10.4 I    3.3 I   5.6
                 I    5.7 I    4.4 I    6.3 I
                 I    4.8 I    0.6 I    0.2 I
          -I--------I--------I--------I
           COLUMN     4083      631      142   4856
           TOTAL      84.1     13.0      2.9  100.0
(CONTINUED)
```

```
                      LIBTYPE
           COUNT   I
           ROW PCT IA.R.L. L OTHER AC COMMUNIT  ROW
           COL PCT IIBS      ADEMIC   Y COLLEG  TOTAL
           TOT PCT I    1.I       2.I      3.I
RQ57       --------I--------I--------I--------I
       8.  I     83 I      6 I      6 I    95
LAW              I   87.4 I    6.3 I    6.3 I   2.0
                 I    2.0 I    1.0 I    4.2 I
                 I    1.7 I    0.1 I    0.1 I
          -I--------I--------I--------I
       9.  I    114 I     28 I     25 I   167
MAJOR UNDECLARED I   68.3 I   16.8 I   15.0 I   3.4
                 I    2.8 I    4.4 I   17.6 I
                 I    2.3 I    0.6 I    0.5 I
          -I--------I--------I--------I
      10.  I    130 I     18 I      2 I   150
INTERDISCIPLINAR I   86.7 I   12.0 I    1.3 I   3.1
                 I    3.2 I    2.9 I    1.4 I
                 I    2.7 I    0.4 I    0.0 I
          -I--------I--------I--------I
           COLUMN     4083      631      142   4856
           TOTAL      84.1     13.0      2.9  100.0
```

    3 OUT OF   30 (10.0%) OF THE VALID CELLS HAVE EXPECTED CELL FREQUENCY LESS THAN 5.0.
MINIMUM EXPECTED CELL FREQUENCY =   2.778
CHI SQUARE =   259.11157 WITH 18 DEGREES OF FREEDOM   SIGNIFICANCE =   0.0
PEARSON'S R = 0.09715   SIGNIFICANCE =   0.0000

NUMBER OF MISSING OBSERVATIONS =   3238

```
                        LIBTYPE
              COUNT   IA.R.L. L OTHER AC COMMUNIT
              ROW PCT IIBS      ADEMIC   Y COLLEG   ROW
              COL PCT I                   E        TOTAL
                      I     1  I    2   I    3   I
RQUEST58        ------I-------I--------I--------I
              RQ58A   I  2966  I   469  I   130  I   3565
  COURSE WORK          I  83.2  I  13.2  I   3.6  I   74.4
                      I  73.8  I  75.3  I  88.4  I
                      I-------I--------I--------I
              RQ58B   I   388  I    64  I     4  I    456
  TEACHING             I  85.1  I  14.0  I   0.9  I    9.5
                      I   9.7  I  10.3  I   2.7  I
                      I-------I--------I--------I
              RQ58C   I  1534  I   235  I    38  I   1807
  RESEARCH             I  84.9  I  13.0  I   2.1  I   37.7
                      I  38.2  I  37.7  I  25.9  I
                      I-------I--------I--------I
              COLUMN    4019      623      147      4789
              TOTAL     83.9     13.0      3.1     100.0
```

PERCENTS AND TOTALS BASED ON RESPONDENTS

   4789 VALID CASES   3305 MISSING CASES

```
                      LIBTYPE
              COUNT   I
              ROW PCT IA.R.L. L OTHER AC COMMUNIT   ROW
              COL PCT IIBS      ADEMIC   Y COLLEG   TOTAL
              TOT PCT I    1.  I   2.  I    3.  I
RQ59            ------I-------I--------I--------I
                 1.   I   904  I   198  I   121  I   1223
  FRESHMAN-SOPHOMO    I  73.9  I  16.2  I   9.9  I   25.7
                      I  22.7  I  31.9  I  82.9  I
                      I  19.0  I   4.2  I   2.5  I
                  -I--------I--------I--------I
                 2.   I  1352  I   256  I    10  I   1618
  JUNIOR--SENIOR      I  83.6  I  15.8  I   0.6  I   34.1
                      I  33.9  I  41.2  I   6.8  I
                      I  28.5  I   5.4  I   0.2  I
                  -I--------I--------I--------I
                 3.   I   542  I    94  I     1  I    637
  GRADUATE-MASTERS    I  85.1  I  14.8  I   0.2  I   13.4
                      I  13.6  I  15.1  I   0.7  I
                      I  11.4  I   2.0  I   0.0  I
                  -I--------I--------I--------I
                 4.   I   442  I    19  I     0  I    461
  GRADUATE-DOCTORA    I  95.9  I   4.1  I   0.0  I    9.7
                      I  11.1  I   3.1  I   0.0  I
                      I   9.3  I   0.4  I   0.0  I
                  -I--------I--------I--------I
                 5.   I   108  I     1  I     1  I    110
  GRADUATE-PROFESS    I  98.2  I   0.9  I   0.9  I    2.3
                      I   2.7  I   0.2  I   0.7  I
                      I   2.3  I   0.0  I   0.0  I
                  -I--------I--------I--------I
                 6.   I   158  I    31  I     0  I    189
  FACULTY             I  83.6  I  16.4  I   0.0  I    4.0
                      I   4.0  I   5.0  I   0.0  I
                      I   3.3  I   0.7  I   0.0  I
                  -I--------I--------I--------I
                 7.   I   132  I     1  I     0  I    133
  STAFF               I  99.2  I   0.8  I   0.0  I    2.8
                      I   3.3  I   0.2  I   0.0  I
                      I   2.8  I   0.0  I   0.0  I
                  -I--------I--------I--------I
              COLUMN    3984      621      146      4751
              TOTAL     83.9     13.1      3.1     100.0
(CONTINUED)
```

```
                    LIBTYPE
            COUNT   I
            ROW PCT IA.R.L. L OTHER AC COMMUNIT   ROW
            COL PCT IIBS      ADEMIC   Y COLLEG  TOTAL
            TOT PCT I     1.I      2.I      3.I
RQ59        --------I--------I--------I--------I
               8.   I   346  I    21  I    13  I   380
   OTHER   STATUS   I  91.1  I   5.5  I   3.4  I   8.0
                    I   8.7  I   3.4  I   8.9  I
                    I   7.3  I   0.4  I   0.3  I
                   -I--------I--------I--------I
            COLUMN     3984      621      146     4751
            TOTAL      83.9     13.1      3.1    100.0

    2 OUT OF   24 (  8.3%) OF THE VALID CELLS HAVE EXPECTED CELL FREQUENCY LESS THAN 5.0.
MINIMUM EXPECTED CELL FREQUENCY =   3.380
CHI SQUARE =    385.81934 WITH  14 DEGREES OF FREEDOM    SIGNIFICANCE =   0.0
PEARSON'S R =-0.15706  SIGNIFICANCE =  0.0000

NUMBER OF MISSING OBSERVATIONS =    3343
```

APPENDIX 5

*Responses by
Type of Library
for the
Non-User Questionnaire*

LIBTYPE

COUNT ROW PCT COL PCT	ARL LIBS 1	OTHER AC ADEMIC 2	COMMUNIT Y COLLEG E 3	PUBLIC 4	STATE AN D FEDERA L 5	ROW TOTAL
RQUEST1						
RQ1A DO NOT LIKE TO USE C	150 44.4 10.1	42 12.4 5.6	27 8.0 11.9	95 28.1 9.0	24 7.1 6.4	338 8.7
RQ1B DID NOT KNOW THERE W	422 36.0 28.3	222 18.9 29.4	37 3.2 16.3	355 30.3 33.6	137 11.7 36.4	1173 30.0
RQ1C DO NOT KNOW WHERE IT	289 40.5 19.4	156 21.8 20.7	20 2.8 8.8	163 22.8 15.4	86 12.0 22.9	714 18.3
RQ1D NO TIME TO LEARN HOW	617 38.5 41.4	319 19.9 42.3	71 4.4 31.3	462 28.9 43.8	132 8.2 35.1	1601 41.0
RQ1E HAVE NOT TAKEN TRAIN	671 38.4 45.0	395 22.6 52.4	87 5.0 38.3	443 25.4 42.0	150 8.6 39.9	1746 44.7
RQ1F NO STAFF ASSISTANCE	117 37.6 7.8	81 26.0 10.7	15 4.8 6.6	83 26.7 7.9	15 4.8 4.0	311 8.0
RQ1G TERMINALS ALL IN USE	32 23.9 2.1	26 19.4 3.4	21 15.7 9.3	47 35.1 4.5	8 6.0 2.1	134 3.4
RQ1H NO NEED TO USE ANY L	624 40.1 41.8	323 20.8 42.8	140 9.0 61.7	376 24.2 35.6	92 5.9 24.5	1555 39.8
COLUMN TOTAL	1492 38.2	754 19.3	227 5.8	1056 27.0	376 9.6	3905 100.0

PERCENTS AND TOTALS BASED ON RESPONDENTS

(CONTINUED)

LIBTYPE

COUNT ROW PCT COL PCT	ARL LIBS 1	OTHER AC ADEMIC 2	COMMUNIT Y COLLEG E 3	PUBLIC 4	STATE AN D FEDERA L 5	ROW TOTAL
RQUEST1						
RQ1I CARD CATALOG EASIER	256 41.6 17.2	125 20.3 16.6	25 4.1 11.0	180 29.3 17.0	29 4.7 7.7	615 15.7
RQ1J CARD CATALOG CONTAIN	57 34.1 3.8	28 16.8 3.7	21 12.6 9.3	47 28.1 4.5	14 8.4 3.7	167 4.3
RQ1K VISITOR-INFREQUENT U	355 31.9 23.8	150 13.5 19.9	31 2.8 13.7	385 34.6 36.5	193 17.3 51.3	1114 28.5
COLUMN TOTAL	1492 38.2	754 19.3	227 5.8	1056 27.0	376 9.6	3905 100.0

PERCENTS AND TOTALS BASED ON RESPONDENTS

3905 VALID CASES   76 MISSING CASES

```
                   LIBTYPE
          COUNT  I
          ROW PCT IARL LIBS OTHER AC COMMUNIT PUBLIC    STATE AN    ROW
          COL PCT I         ADEMIC   Y COLLEG           D FEDERA   TOTAL
          TOT PCT I     1.I      2.I      3.I      4.I      5.I
QST2      --------I--------I--------I--------I--------I--------I
          1.  I     33 I     40 I     11 I     49 I     15 I     148
DAY OR  MORE  I   22.3 I   27.0 I    7.4 I   33.1 I   10.1 I     3.8
              I    2.2 I    5.3 I    4.9 I    4.7 I    4.0 I
              I    0.9 I    1.0 I    0.3 I    1.3 I    0.4 I
          -I--------I--------I--------I--------I--------I
          2.  I     48 I     37 I      6 I     32 I     32 I     155
HALF DAY - A DAY I  31.0 I   23.9 I    3.9 I   20.6 I   20.6 I     4.0
              I    3.2 I    4.9 I    2.7 I    3.1 I    8.6 I
              I    1.2 I    1.0 I    0.2 I    0.8 I    0.8 I
          -I--------I--------I--------I--------I--------I
          3.  I    126 I     80 I     15 I     52 I     38 I     311
1 HOUR- HALF DAY I  40.5 I   25.7 I    4.8 I   16.7 I   12.2 I     8.0
              I    8.5 I   10.6 I    6.7 I    5.0 I   10.2 I
              I    3.3 I    2.1 I    0.4 I    1.3 I    1.0 I
          -I--------I--------I--------I--------I--------I
          4.  I    318 I    188 I     44 I    164 I     76 I     790
30 MIN - 1 HOUR  I  40.3 I   23.8 I    5.6 I   20.8 I    9.6 I    20.4
              I   21.4 I   25.0 I   19.6 I   15.8 I   20.3 I
              I    8.2 I    4.9 I    1.1 I    4.2 I    2.0 I
          -I--------I--------I--------I--------I--------I
          5.  I    402 I    200 I     76 I    234 I     92 I    1004
15 - 30 MINUTES  I  40.0 I   19.9 I    7.6 I   23.3 I    9.2 I    25.9
              I   27.0 I   26.6 I   33.9 I   22.6 I   24.6 I
              I   10.4 I    5.2 I    2.0 I    6.0 I    2.4 I
          -I--------I--------I--------I--------I--------I
          6.  I    562 I    207 I     72 I    504 I    121 I    1466
0 - 15  MINUTES  I  38.3 I   14.1 I    4.9 I   34.4 I    8.3 I    37.8
              I   37.7 I   27.5 I   32.1 I   48.7 I   32.4 I
              I   14.5 I    5.3 I    1.9 I   13.0 I    3.1 I
          -I--------I--------I--------I--------I--------I
          COLUMN   1489     752      224     1035     374     3874
          TOTAL    38.4     19.4      5.8     26.7      9.7    100.0

CHI SQUARE =   153.08191 WITH  20 DEGREES OF FREEDOM   SIGNIFICANCE =  0.0
PEARSON'S R = 0.00604  SIGNIFICANCE =  0.3536

NUMBER OF MISSING OBSERVATIONS =     107
```

```
                   LIBTYPE
          COUNT  I
          ROW PCT IARL LIBS OTHER AC COMMUNIT PUBLIC    STATE AN    ROW
          COL PCT I         ADEMIC   Y COLLEG           D FEDERA   TOTAL
          TOT PCT I     1.I      2.I      3.I      4.I      5.I
QST3      --------I--------I--------I--------I--------I--------I
          1.  I      9 I     15 I     16 I     17 I      3 I      60
VERY    DIFFICUL I  15.0 I   25.0 I   26.7 I   28.3 I    5.0 I     1.5
              I    0.6 I    2.0 I    7.1 I    1.6 I    0.8 I
              I    0.2 I    0.4 I    0.4 I    0.4 I    0.1 I
          -I--------I--------I--------I--------I--------I
          2.  I    219 I    151 I     41 I    158 I     57 I     626
SOMEWHAT DIFFICU I  35.0 I   24.1 I    6.5 I   25.2 I    9.1 I    16.0
              I   14.5 I   19.9 I   18.2 I   15.1 I   15.0 I
              I    5.6 I    3.9 I    1.0 I    4.0 I    1.5 I
          -I--------I--------I--------I--------I--------I
          3.  I    700 I    386 I    100 I    429 I    196 I    1811
SOMEWHAT EASY    I  38.7 I   21.3 I    5.5 I   23.7 I   10.8 I    46.2
              I   46.5 I   50.9 I   44.4 I   40.9 I   51.7 I
              I   17.9 I    9.9 I    2.6 I   11.0 I    5.0 I
          -I--------I--------I--------I--------I--------I
          4.  I    578 I    206 I     68 I    444 I    123 I    1419
VERY    EASY  I   40.7 I   14.5 I    4.8 I   31.3 I    8.7 I    36.2
              I   38.4 I   27.2 I   30.2 I   42.4 I   32.5 I
              I   14.8 I    5.3 I    1.7 I   11.3 I    3.1 I
          -I--------I--------I--------I--------I--------I
          COLUMN   1506     758      225     1048     379     3916
          TOTAL    38.5     19.4      5.7     26.8      9.7    100.0

    1 OUT OF    20 ( 5.0%) OF THE VALID CELLS HAVE EXPECTED CELL FREQUENCY LESS THAN 5.0.
MINIMUM EXPECTED CELL FREQUENCY =   3.447
CHI SQUARE =   113.74948 WITH  12 DEGREES OF FREEDOM   SIGNIFICANCE =  0.0000
PEARSON'S R = 0.00060  SIGNIFICANCE =  0.4851

NUMBER OF MISSING OBSERVATIONS =     65
```

```
                    LIBTYPE
             COUNT  I
             ROW PCT IARL LIBS OTHER AC COMMUNIT PUBLIC   STATE AN  ROW
             COL PCT I         ADEMIC   Y COLLEG           D FEDERA  TOTAL
             TOT PCT I     1. I     2. I     3. I     4. I     5. I
QST4         --------I--------I--------I--------I--------I--------I
               1.    I   625  I   316  I   110  I   480  I   214  I   1745
VERY FAVORABLE       I  35.8  I  18.1  I   6.3  I  27.5  I  12.3  I   45.9
                     I  43.0  I  42.3  I  50.0  I  47.4  I  58.6  I
                     I  16.5  I   8.3  I   2.9  I  12.6  I   5.6  I
                    -I--------I--------I--------I--------I--------I
               2.    I   699  I   352  I    73  I   402  I   118  I   1644
SOMEWHAT FAVORAB     I  42.5  I  21.4  I   4.4  I  24.5  I   7.2  I   43.3
                     I  48.1  I  47.1  I  33.2  I  39.7  I  32.3  I
                     I  18.4  I   9.3  I   1.9  I  10.6  I   3.1  I
                    -I--------I--------I--------I--------I--------I
               3.    I   106  I    64  I    23  I    99  I    26  I    318
SOMEWHAT UNFAVOR     I  33.3  I  20.1  I   7.2  I  31.1  I   8.2  I    8.4
                     I   7.3  I   8.6  I  10.5  I   9.8  I   7.1  I
                     I   2.8  I   1.7  I   0.6  I   2.6  I   0.7  I
                    -I--------I--------I--------I--------I--------I
               4.    I    24  I    15  I    14  I    31  I     7  I     91
VERY    UNFAVORA     I  26.4  I  16.5  I  15.4  I  34.1  I   7.7  I    2.4
                     I   1.7  I   2.0  I   6.4  I   3.1  I   1.9  I
                     I   0.6  I   0.4  I   0.4  I   0.8  I   0.2  I
                    -I--------I--------I--------I--------I--------I
            COLUMN      1454     747      220     1012     365     3798
            TOTAL       38.3    19.7      5.8     26.6     9.6    100.0

CHI SQUARE =     74.32248 WITH  12 DEGREES OF FREEDOM   SIGNIFICANCE =   0.0000
PEARSON'S R =-0.03223  SIGNIFICANCE =   0.0235

NUMBER OF MISSING OBSERVATIONS =       183
```

```
                    LIBTYPE
             COUNT  I
             ROW PCT IARL LIBS OTHER AC COMMUNIT PUBLIC   STATE AN  ROW
             COL PCT I         ADEMIC   Y COLLEG           D FEDERA  TOTAL
             TOT PCT I     1. I     2. I     3. I     4. I     5. I
QST5         --------I--------I--------I--------I--------I--------I
               1.    I   430  I   244  I    61  I   409  I   175  I   1319
VERY    LIKELY       I  32.6  I  18.5  I   4.6  I  31.0  I  13.3  I   34.0
                     I  28.8  I  32.3  I  27.2  I  39.5  I  46.4  I
                     I  11.1  I   6.3  I   1.6  I  10.5  I   4.5  I
                    -I--------I--------I--------I--------I--------I
               2.    I   631  I   329  I   101  I   387  I   132  I   1580
SOMEWHAT LIKELY      I  39.9  I  20.8  I   6.4  I  24.5  I   8.4  I   40.7
                     I  42.3  I  43.5  I  45.1  I  37.4  I  35.0  I
                     I  16.2  I   8.5  I   2.6  I  10.0  I   3.4  I
                    -I--------I--------I--------I--------I--------I
               3.    I   278  I   123  I    43  I   143  I    46  I    633
SOMEWHAT UNLIKEL     I  43.9  I  19.4  I   6.8  I  22.6  I   7.3  I   16.3
                     I  18.6  I  16.3  I  19.2  I  13.8  I  12.2  I
                     I   7.2  I   3.2  I   1.1  I   3.7  I   1.2  I
                    -I--------I--------I--------I--------I--------I
               4.    I   153  I    60  I    19  I    97  I    24  I    353
VERY    UNLIKELY     I  43.3  I  17.0  I   5.4  I  27.5  I   6.8  I    9.1
                     I  10.3  I   7.9  I   8.5  I   9.4  I   6.4  I
                     I   3.9  I   1.5  I   0.5  I   2.5  I   0.6  I
                    -I--------I--------I--------I--------I--------I
            COLUMN      1492     756      224     1036     377     3885
            TOTAL       38.4    19.5      5.8     26.7     9.7    100.0

CHI SQUARE =     71.64859 WITH  12 DEGREES OF FREEDOM   SIGNIFICANCE =   0.0000
PEARSON'S R =-0.10055  SIGNIFICANCE =   0.0000

NUMBER OF MISSING OBSERVATIONS =        96
```

LIBTYPE

QST6

COUNT ROW PCT COL PCT TOT PCT	ARL LIBS 1.	OTHER AC ADEMIC 2.	COMMUNIT Y COLLEG 3.	PUBLIC 4.	STATE AN D FEDERA 5.	ROW TOTAL
1. BETTER	394 32.2 28.7 10.9	270 22.1 37.1 7.5	118 9.6 53.2 3.3	308 25.2 32.1 8.5	134 10.9 40.0 3.7	1224 33.8
2. EQUAL	224 38.5 16.3 6.2	136 23.4 18.7 3.8	45 7.7 20.3 1.2	153 26.3 16.0 4.2	24 4.1 7.2 0.7	582 16.1
3. WORSE	46 32.9 3.3 1.3	25 17.9 3.4 0.7	15 10.7 6.8 0.4	43 30.7 4.5 1.2	11 7.9 3.3 0.3	140 3.9
4. CAN'T DECIDE	711 42.5 51.7 19.7	296 17.7 40.7 8.2	44 2.6 19.8 1.2	455 27.2 47.4 12.6	166 9.9 49.6 4.6	1672 46.2
COLUMN TOTAL	1375 38.0	727 20.1	222 6.1	959 26.5	335 9.3	3618 100.0

CHI SQUARE =   120.15497 WITH 12 DEGREES OF FREEDOM   SIGNIFICANCE = 0.0000
PEARSON'S R =-0.03913 SIGNIFICANCE = 0.0093

NUMBER OF MISSING OBSERVATIONS =   363

LIBTYPE

QST7

COUNT ROW PCT COL PCT TOT PCT	ARL LIBS 1.	OTHER AC ADEMIC 2.	COMMUNIT Y COLLEG 3.	PUBLIC 4.	STATE AN D FEDERA 5.	ROW TOTAL
1. DAILY	575 55.5 38.3 14.7	293 28.3 38.6 7.5	103 9.9 45.8 2.6	43 4.2 4.1 1.1	22 2.1 5.8 0.6	1036 26.5
2. WEEKLY	540 42.6 36.0 13.8	289 22.8 38.1 7.4	90 7.1 40.0 2.3	304 24.0 29.1 7.8	45 3.5 11.8 1.2	1268 32.4
3. MONTHLY	181 27.4 12.1 4.6	85 12.9 11.2 2.2	18 2.7 8.0 0.5	314 47.5 30.1 8.0	63 9.5 16.5 1.6	661 16.9
4. 4 TIMES A YEAR	117 27.5 7.8 3.0	45 10.6 5.9 1.2	2 0.5 0.9 0.1	200 46.9 19.2 5.1	62 14.6 16.3 1.6	426 10.9
5. ONCE A YEAR	24 15.6 1.6 0.6	17 11.0 2.2 0.4	4 2.6 1.8 0.1	47 30.5 4.5 1.2	62 40.3 16.3 1.6	154 3.9
6. NOT BEFORE TODAY	65 17.8 4.3 1.7	30 8.2 4.0 0.8	8 2.2 3.6 0.2	135 37.0 12.9 3.5	127 34.8 33.3 3.2	365 9.3
COLUMN TOTAL	1502 38.4	759 19.4	225 5.8	1043 26.7	381 9.7	3910 100.0

CHI SQUARE = 1260.94434 WITH 20 DEGREES OF FREEDOM   SIGNIFICANCE = 0.0
PEARSON'S R = 0.44303 SIGNIFICANCE = 0.0000

NUMBER OF MISSING OBSERVATIONS =   71

```
                  LIBTYPE
          COUNT  I
          ROW PCT IARL LIBS OTHER AC COMMUNIT PUBLIC    STATE AN   ROW
          COL PCT I        ADEMIC   Y COLLEG           D FEDERA  TOTAL
          TOT PCT I    1. I     2. I     3. I     4. I     5. I
RQ8       --------I--------I--------I--------I--------I--------I
             1.  I   111  I    32  I     2  I   136  I    74  I    355
EVERY   VISIT   I  31.3  I   9.0  I   0.6  I  38.3  I  20.8  I    9.7
                I   7.4  I   4.2  I   0.9  I  15.1  I  25.3  I
                I   3.0  I   0.9  I   0.1  I   3.7  I   2.0  I
          -I--------I--------I--------I--------I--------I
             2.  I   233  I   121  I     2  I   164  I    37  I    557
MOST    VISITS  I  41.8  I  21.7  I   0.4  I  29.4  I   6.6  I   15.2
                I  15.6  I  16.0  I   0.9  I  18.2  I  12.6  I
                I   6.4  I   3.3  I   0.1  I   4.5  I   1.0  I
          -I--------I--------I--------I--------I--------I
             3.  I   513  I   303  I    29  I   274  I    36  I   1155
OCCASIONALLY    I  44.4  I  26.2  I   2.5  I  23.7  I   3.1  I   31.5
                I  34.4  I  40.0  I  12.9  I  30.5  I  12.3  I
                I  14.0  I   8.3  I   0.8  I   7.5  I   1.0  I
          -I--------I--------I--------I--------I--------I
             4.  I   454  I   215  I    81  I   153  I    25  I    928
RARELY          I  48.9  I  23.2  I   8.7  I  16.5  I   2.7  I   25.3
                I  30.4  I  28.4  I  36.2  I  17.0  I   8.5  I
                I  12.4  I   5.9  I   2.2  I   4.2  I   0.7  I
          -I--------I--------I--------I--------I--------I
             5.  I   181  I    86  I   110  I   172  I   121  I    670
NOT BEFORE TODAY I  27.0  I  12.8  I  16.4  I  25.7  I  18.1  I   18.3
                I  12.1  I  11.4  I  49.1  I  19.1  I  41.3  I
                I   4.9  I   2.3  I   3.0  I   4.7  I   3.3  I
          -I--------I--------I--------I--------I--------I
          COLUMN    1492     757     224     899     293     3665
          TOTAL     40.7    20.7     6.1    24.5     8.0   100.0
```

CHI SQUARE = 605.72461 WITH 16 DEGREES OF FREEDOM SIGNIFICANCE = 0.0
PEARSON'S R =-0.01320 SIGNIFICANCE = 0.2121

NUMBER OF MISSING OBSERVATIONS =   316

```
                  LIBTYPE
          COUNT  I
          ROW PCT IARL LIBS OTHER AC COMMUNIT PUBLIC    STATE AN   ROW
          COL PCT I        ADEMIC   Y COLLEG           D FEDERA  TOTAL
          TOT PCT I    1. I     2. I     3. I     4. I     5. I
QST9      --------I--------I--------I--------I--------I--------I
             1.  I   106  I    64  I    13  I   111  I    31  I    325
DAILY           I  32.6  I  19.7  I   4.0  I  34.2  I   9.5  I    8.4
                I   7.1  I   8.4  I   5.8  I  10.8  I   8.2  I
                I   2.7  I   1.7  I   0.3  I   2.9  I   0.8  I
          -I--------I--------I--------I--------I--------I
             2.  I   232  I    98  I    20  I    97  I    44  I    491
WEEKLY          I  47.3  I  20.0  I   4.1  I  19.8  I   9.0  I   12.7
                I  15.6  I  12.9  I   8.9  I   9.4  I  11.7  I
                I   6.0  I   2.5  I   0.5  I   2.5  I   1.1  I
          -I--------I--------I--------I--------I--------I
             3.  I   187  I    82  I     8  I    81  I    50  I    408
MONTHLY         I  45.8  I  20.1  I   2.0  I  19.9  I  12.3  I   10.5
                I  12.6  I  10.8  I   3.6  I   7.9  I  13.3  I
                I   4.8  I   2.1  I   0.2  I   2.1  I   1.3  I
          -I--------I--------I--------I--------I--------I
             4.  I   158  I    67  I    11  I    72  I    45  I    353
4 TIMES A YEAR  I  44.8  I  19.0  I   3.1  I  20.4  I  12.7  I    9.1
                I  10.6  I   8.8  I   4.9  I   7.0  I  12.0  I
                I   4.1  I   1.7  I   0.3  I   1.9  I   1.2  I
          -I--------I--------I--------I--------I--------I
             5.  I   165  I    72  I     2  I    74  I    32  I    345
ONCE A  YEAR    I  47.8  I  20.9  I   0.6  I  21.4  I   9.3  I    8.9
                I  11.1  I   9.5  I   0.9  I   7.2  I   8.5  I
                I   4.3  I   1.9  I   0.1  I   1.9  I   0.8  I
          -I--------I--------I--------I--------I--------I
             6.  I   638  I   376  I   170  I   595  I   174  I   1953
NEVER           I  32.7  I  19.3  I   8.7  I  30.5  I   8.9  I   50.4
                I  42.9  I  49.5  I  75.9  I  57.8  I  46.3  I
                I  16.5  I   9.7  I   4.4  I  15.4  I   4.5  I
          -I--------I--------I--------I--------I--------I
          COLUMN    1486     759     224    1030     376     3875
          TOTAL     38.3    19.6     5.8    26.6     9.7   100.0
```

CHI SQUARE = 161.55388 WITH 20 DEGREES OF FREEDOM SIGNIFICANCE = 0.0
PEARSON'S R = 0.05943 SIGNIFICANCE = 0.0001

NUMBER OF MISSING OBSERVATIONS =   106

```
                    LIBTYPE
           COUNT  I
           ROW PCT IARL LIBS OTHER AC COMMUNIT PUBLIC    STATE AN   ROW
           COL PCT I        ADEMIC   Y COLLEG          D FEDERA   TOTAL
           TOT PCT I    1.I     2.I      3.I      4.I      5.I
QST10      --------I--------I--------I--------I--------I--------I
              1.  I     2   I     2   I    0    I   15   I    1   I     20
  14 AND  UNDER  I  10.0   I  10.0   I   0.0   I  75.0   I   5.0   I    0.5
                 I   0.1   I   0.3   I   0.0   I   1.4   I   0.3   I
                 I   0.1   I   0.1   I   0.0   I   0.4   I   0.0   I
                -I--------I--------I--------I--------I--------I
              2.  I   339   I   163   I   48    I  111   I   27   I    688
  15 - 19 YEARS  I  49.3   I  23.7   I   7.0   I  16.1   I   3.9   I   17.5
                 I  22.5   I  21.3   I  21.3   I  10.6   I   7.1   I
                 I   8.6   I   4.1   I   1.2   I   2.8   I   0.7   I
                -I--------I--------I--------I--------I--------I
              3.  I   748   I   405   I  118    I  197   I  115   I   1583
  20 - 24 YEARS  I  47.3   I  25.6   I   7.5   I  12.4   I   7.3   I   40.3
                 I  49.6   I  53.0   I  52.4   I  18.7   I  30.1   I
                 I  19.0   I  10.3   I   3.0   I   5.0   I   2.9   I
                -I--------I--------I--------I--------I--------I
              4.  I   311   I   134   I   33    I  300   I  106   I    884
  25 - 34 YEARS  I  35.2   I  15.2   I   3.7   I  33.9   I  12.0   I   22.5
                 I  20.6   I  17.5   I  14.7   I  28.5   I  27.7   I
                 I   7.9   I   3.4   I   0.8   I   7.6   I   2.7   I
                -I--------I--------I--------I--------I--------I
              5.  I    59   I    38   I   14    I  169   I   67   I    347
  35 - 44 YEARS  I  17.0   I  11.0   I   4.0   I  48.7   I  19.3   I    8.8
                 I   3.9   I   5.0   I   6.2   I  16.1   I  17.5   I
                 I   1.5   I   1.0   I   0.4   I   4.3   I   1.7   I
                -I--------I--------I--------I--------I--------I
              6.  I    30   I    14   I    8   I   104   I   29   I    185
  45 - 54 YEARS  I  16.2   I   7.6   I   4.3   I  56.2   I  15.7   I    4.7
                 I   2.0   I   1.8   I   3.6   I   9.9   I   7.6   I
                 I   0.8   I   0.4   I   0.2   I   2.6   I   0.7   I
                -I--------I--------I--------I--------I--------I
              7.  I    12   I     3   I    3   I    82   I   27   I    127
  55 - 64 YEARS  I   9.4   I   2.4   I   2.4   I  64.6   I  21.3   I    3.2
                 I   0.8   I   0.4   I   1.3   I   7.8   I   7.1   I
                 I   0.3   I   0.1   I   0.1   I   2.1   I   0.7   I
                -I--------I--------I--------I--------I--------I
          COLUMN      1508      764      225     1052      382     3931
           TOTAL      38.4     19.4      5.7     26.8      9.7    100.0
(CONTINUED)
```

```
                    LIBTYPE
           COUNT  I
           ROW PCT IARL LIBS OTHER AC COMMUNIT PUBLIC    STATE AN   ROW
           COL PCT I        ADEMIC   Y COLLEG          D FEDERA   TOTAL
           TOT PCT I    1.I     2.I      3.I      4.I      5.I
QST10      --------I--------I--------I--------I--------I--------I
              8.  I     7   I     5   I    1   I    74   I   10   I     97
  65 AND  OVER   I   7.2   I   5.2   I   1.0   I  76.3   I  10.3   I    2.5
                 I   0.5   I   0.7   I   0.4   I   7.0   I   2.6   I
                 I   0.2   I   0.1   I   0.0   I   1.9   I   0.3   I
                -I--------I--------I--------I--------I--------I
          COLUMN      1508      764      225     1052      382     3931
           TOTAL      38.4     19.4      5.7     26.8      9.7    100.0
```

   3 OUT OF   40 (7.5%) OF THE VALID CELLS HAVE EXPECTED CELL FREQUENCY LESS THAN 5.0.
MINIMUM EXPECTED CELL FREQUENCY =   1.145
CHI SQUARE =   865.16064 WITH 28 DEGREES OF FREEDOM   SIGNIFICANCE =   0.0
PEARSON'S R = 0.37031   SIGNIFICANCE =   0.0000

NUMBER OF MISSING OBSERVATIONS =   50

```
               LIBTYPE
         COUNT  I
         ROW PCT IARL LIBS OTHER AC COMMUNIT PUBLIC   STATE AN   ROW
         COL PCT I        ADEMIC   Y COLLEG          D FEDERA   TOTAL
         TOT PCT I    1.I      2.I      3.I      4.I      5.I
QST11    --------I--------I--------I--------I--------I--------I
           1.    I    629  I    356  I    113  I    600  I    171  I  1869
FEMALE           I   33.7  I   19.0  I    6.0  I   32.1  I    9.1  I  47.9
                 I   42.0  I   46.8  I   50.4  I   57.8  I   45.1  I
                 I   16.1  I    9.1  I    2.9  I   15.4  I    4.4  I
                 -I--------I--------I--------I--------I--------I
           2.    I    869  I    405  I    111  I    438  I    208  I  2031
MALE             I   42.8  I   19.9  I    5.5  I   21.6  I   10.2  I  52.1
                 I   58.0  I   53.2  I   49.6  I   42.2  I   54.9  I
                 I   22.3  I   10.4  I    2.8  I   11.2  I    5.3  I
                 -I--------I--------I--------I--------I--------I
         COLUMN     1498      761      224     1038      379      3900
         TOTAL      38.4     19.5      5.7     26.6      9.7     100.0

CHI SQUARE =     63.90050 WITH  4 DEGREES OF FREEDOM   SIGNIFICANCE =   0.0000
PEARSON'S R =-0.09409  SIGNIFICANCE =   0.0000

NUMBER OF MISSING OBSERVATIONS =        81
```

```
               LIBTYPE
         COUNT  I
         ROW PCT IARL LIBS OTHER AC COMMUNIT PUBLIC   STATE AN   ROW
         COL PCT I        ADEMIC   Y COLLEG          D FEDERA   TOTAL
         TOT PCT I    1.I      2.I      3.I      4.I      5.I
QST12    --------I--------I--------I--------I--------I--------I
           1.    I      6  I      3  I      1  I     16  I      1  I    27
GRADE SCHOOL     I   22.2  I   11.1  I    3.7  I   59.3  I    3.7  I   0.7
                 I    0.4  I    0.4  I    0.4  I    1.5  I    0.3  I
                 I    0.2  I    0.1  I    0.0  I    0.4  I    0.0  I
                 -I--------I--------I--------I--------I--------I
           2.    I     48  I     30  I     15  I    190  I     36  I   319
HIGH  SCHOOL     I   15.0  I    9.4  I    4.7  I   59.6  I   11.3  I   8.1
                 I    3.2  I    3.9  I    6.7  I   18.1  I    9.5  I
                 I    1.2  I    0.8  I    0.4  I    4.8  I    0.9  I
                 -I--------I--------I--------I--------I--------I
           3.    I    892  I    533  I    184  I    372  I    115  I  2096
SOME  COLLEGE    I   42.6  I   25.4  I    8.8  I   17.7  I    5.5  I  53.4
                 I   59.2  I   69.9  I   81.8  I   35.5  I   30.3  I
                 I   22.7  I   13.6  I    4.7  I    9.5  I    2.9  I
                 -I--------I--------I--------I--------I--------I
           4.    I    562  I    197  I     25  I    470  I    227  I  1481
COLLEGE GRAD     I   37.9  I   13.3  I    1.7  I   31.7  I   15.3  I  37.8
                 I   37.3  I   25.8  I   11.1  I   44.8  I   59.9  I
                 I   14.3  I    5.0  I    0.6  I   12.0  I    5.8  I
                 -I--------I--------I--------I--------I--------I
         COLUMN     1508      763      225     1048      379      3923
         TOTAL      38.4     19.4      5.7     26.7      9.7     100.0

     2 OUT OF    20 ( 10.0%) OF THE VALID CELLS HAVE EXPECTED CELL FREQUENCY LESS THAN 5.0.
MINIMUM EXPECTED CELL FREQUENCY =  1.549
CHI SQUARE =    523.84155 WITH  12 DEGREES OF FREEDOM    SIGNIFICANCE =   0.0
PEARSON'S R = 0.00500  SIGNIFICANCE =   0.3772

NUMBER OF MISSING OBSERVATIONS =        58
```

```
                           LIBTYPE
                 COUNT   I
                 ROW PCT IARL LIBS OTHER AC COMMUNIT   ROW
                 COL PCT I          ADEMIC  Y COLLEG  TOTAL
                 TOT PCT I     1.I      2.I      3.I
RQ13             --------I--------I--------I--------I
                     1.  I    274  I     78  I     15  I    367
     ART & HUMANITIES  I   74.7  I   21.3  I    4.1  I   15.3
                       I   19.1  I   10.6  I    6.8  I
                       I   11.4  I    3.3  I    0.6  I
                     -I--------I--------I--------I
                     2.  I    164  I    106  I     13  I    283
     PHYS-BIO SCIENCE   I   58.0  I   37.5  I    4.6  I   11.8
                        I   11.4  I   14.4  I    5.9  I
                        I    6.9  I    4.4  I    0.5  I
                      -I--------I--------I--------I
                     3.  I    218  I     71  I     11  I    300
     SOCIAL   SCIENCES  I   72.7  I   23.7  I    3.7  I   12.5
                        I   15.2  I    9.7  I    5.0  I
                        I    9.1  I    3.0  I    0.5  I
                      -I--------I--------I--------I
                     4.  I    236  I    234  I     58  I    528
     BUSINESS-MANAGEM   I   44.7  I   44.3  I   11.0  I   22.1
                        I   16.4  I   31.8  I   26.1  I
                        I    9.9  I    9.8  I    2.4  I
                      -I--------I--------I--------I
                     5.  I     50  I     59  I     13  I    122
     EDUCATION          I   41.0  I   48.4  I   10.7  I    5.1
                        I    3.5  I    8.0  I    5.9  I
                        I    2.1  I    2.5  I    0.5  I
                      -I--------I--------I--------I
                     6.  I    233  I     80  I     52  I    365
     ENGINEERING        I   63.8  I   21.9  I   14.2  I   15.2
                        I   16.2  I   10.9  I   23.4  I
                        I    9.7  I    3.3  I    2.2  I
                      -I--------I--------I--------I
                     7.  I    125  I     45  I     26  I    196
     MEDICAL-HEALTH     I   63.8  I   23.0  I   13.3  I    8.2
                        I    8.7  I    6.1  I   11.7  I
                        I    5.2  I    1.9  I    1.1  I
                      -I--------I--------I--------I
                 COLUMN      1437      735      222     2394
                  TOTAL      60.0     30.7      9.3    100.0
(CONTINUED)
```

```
                           LIBTYPE
                 COUNT   I
                 ROW PCT IARL LIBS OTHER AC COMMUNIT   ROW
                 COL PCT I          ADEMIC  Y COLLEG  TOTAL
                 TOT PCT I     1.I      2.I      3.I
RQ13             --------I--------I--------I--------I
                     8.  I     46  I     10  I      1  I     57
     LAW                I   80.7  I   17.5  I    1.8  I    2.4
                        I    3.2  I    1.4  I    0.5  I
                        I    1.9  I    0.4  I    0.0  I
                      -I--------I--------I--------I
                     9.  I     51  I     40  I     33  I    124
     MAJOR UNDECLARED   I   41.1  I   32.3  I   26.6  I    5.2
                        I    3.5  I    5.4  I   14.9  I
                        I    2.1  I    1.7  I    1.4  I
                      -I--------I--------I--------I
                    10.  I     40  I     12  I      0  I     52
     INTERDISCIPLINAR   I   76.9  I   23.1  I    0.0  I    2.2
                        I    2.8  I    1.6  I    0.0  I
                        I    1.7  I    0.5  I    0.0  I
                      -I--------I--------I--------I
                 COLUMN      1437      735      222     2394
                  TOTAL      60.0     30.7      9.3    100.0
```

```
    1 OUT OF    30 (  3.3%) OF THE VALID CELLS HAVE EXPECTED CELL FREQUENCY LESS THAN 5.0.
MINIMUM EXPECTED CELL FREQUENCY = 4.822
CHI SQUARE =   236.87985 WITH  18 DEGREES OF FREEDOM   SIGNIFICANCE =  0.0
PEARSON'S R = 0.10581  SIGNIFICANCE =  0.0000

NUMBER OF MISSING OBSERVATIONS =    1587
```

```
                            LIBTYPE
                  COUNT   IARL LIBS OTHER AC COMMUNIT
                  ROW PCT I           ADEMIC   Y COLLEG      ROW
                  COL PCT I                     E          TOTAL
                          I     1   I    2    I    3    I
RQUEST14          --------I--------I--------I--------I
           RQ14A          I  1195   I   628   I   201   I    2024
  COURSE WORK             I  59.0   I  31.0   I   9.9   I    84.3
                          I  83.4   I  84.3   I  89.7   I
                          I--------I--------I--------I
           RQ14B          I    75   I    50   I     1   I     126
  TEACHING                I  59.5   I  39.7   I   0.8   I     5.2
                          I   5.2   I   6.7   I   0.4   I
                          I--------I--------I--------I
           RQ14C          I   325   I   154   I    44   I     523
  RESEARCH                I  62.1   I  29.4   I   8.4   I    21.8
                          I  22.7   I  20.7   I  19.6   I
                          I--------I--------I--------I
               COLUMN       1433       745       224         2402
               TOTAL        59.7      31.0       9.3        100.0

PERCENTS AND TOTALS BASED ON RESPONDENTS

   2402 VALID CASES          1579 MISSING CASES



                         LIBTYPE
                  COUNT   I
                  ROW PCT IARL LIBS OTHER AC COMMUNIT     ROW
                  COL PCT I           ADEMIC   Y COLLEG   TOTAL
                  TOT PCT I    1.  I    2.   I    3.  I
RQ15              --------I--------I--------I--------I
              1.  I   425   I   242   I   173   I     840
  FRESHMAN-SOPHOM    I  50.6   I  28.8   I  20.6   I    34.8
                     I  29.2   I  32.7   I  77.9   I
                     I  17.6   I  10.0   I   7.2   I
                   -I--------I--------I--------I
              2.  I   518   I   346   I    10   I     874
  JUNIOR--SENIOR     I  59.3   I  39.6   I   1.1   I    36.2
                     I  35.6   I  46.8   I   4.5   I
                     I  21.4   I  14.3   I   0.4   I
                   -I--------I--------I--------I
              3.  I   156   I    69   I     2   I     227
  GRADUATE-MASTERS   I  68.7   I  30.4   I   0.9   I     9.4
                     I  10.7   I   9.3   I   0.9   I
                     I   6.5   I   2.9   I   0.1   I
                   -I--------I--------I--------I
              4.  I   108   I    21   I     0   I     129
  GRADUATE-DOCTORA   I  83.7   I  16.3   I   0.0   I     5.3
                     I   7.4   I   2.8   I   0.0   I
                     I   4.5   I   0.9   I   0.0   I
                   -I--------I--------I--------I
              5.  I    60   I     5   I     4   I      69
  GRADUATE-PROFESS   I  87.0   I   7.2   I   5.8   I     2.9
                     I   4.1   I   0.7   I   1.8   I
                     I   2.5   I   0.2   I   0.2   I
                   -I--------I--------I--------I
              6.  I    29   I     8   I     0   I      37
  FACULTY            I  78.4   I  21.6   I   0.0   I     1.5
                     I   2.0   I   1.1   I   0.0   I
                     I   1.2   I   0.3   I   0.0   I
                   -I--------I--------I--------I
              7.  I    21   I     3   I     0   I      24
  STAFF              I  87.5   I  12.5   I   0.0   I     1.0
                     I   1.4   I   0.4   I   0.0   I
                     I   0.9   I   0.1   I   0.0   I
                   -I--------I--------I--------I
               COLUMN      1454       740       222         2416
               TOTAL       60.2      30.6       9.2        100.0
(CONTINUED)
```

```
                    LIBTYPE
              COUNT  I
              ROW PCT IARL LIBS OTHER AC COMMUNIT   ROW
              COL PCT I        ADEMIC   Y COLLEG  TOTAL
              TOT PCT I     1.I      2.I      3.I
RQ15          --------I--------I--------I--------I
               8.  I    137  I     46  I     33  I    216
    OTHER          I   63.4  I   21.3  I   15.3  I    8.9
                   I    9.4  I    6.2  I   14.9  I
                   I    5.7  I    1.9  I    1.4  I
              -I--------I--------I--------I
              COLUMN     1454      740      222     2416
              TOTAL      60.2     30.6      9.2    100.0
```

      2 OUT OF   24 (8.3%) OF THE VALID CELLS HAVE EXPECTED CELL FREQUENCY LESS THAN 5.0.
MINIMUM EXPECTED CELL FREQUENCY = 2.205
CHI SQUARE =   320.26929 WITH 14 DEGREES OF FREEDOM   SIGNIFICANCE =   0.0
PEARSON'S R =-0.12423 SIGNIFICANCE = 0.0000

NUMBER OF MISSING OBSERVATIONS =   1565

Subject Index